SKIP BAYLESS

SIMON & SCHUSTER

———

NEW YORK
LONDON
TORONTO
SYDNEY
TOKYO
SINGAPORE

THE BOYS

SIMON & SCHUSTER
Simon & Schuster Building
Rockefeller Center
1230 Avenue of the Americas
New York, New York 10020

SIMON & SCHUSTER and colophon are registered trademarks
of Simon & Schuster Inc.

Designed by Carla Weise / Levavi & Levavi
Manufactured in the United States of America

10 9 8 7 6 5 4 3 2 1

Library of Congress Cataloging-in-Publication Data
Bayless, Skip.
The boys / Skip Bayless.
p.   cm.
1. Dallas Cowboys (Football team)—History.   2. Super Bowl
(Football game).   I. Title.
GV956.D3B39   1993
796.332'64'097642812—dc20   93–20606
CIP

ISBN: 0-671-79359-4

TO MOM

Contents

Best Friends

THE ENTOURAGE PARADED OUT OF THE LOCKER-ROOM TUNNEL AS the third quarter ended at Texas Stadium. The group included Prince Bandar bin Sultan, Saudi Arabia's ambassador to the United States, one of the most powerful men in the Middle East, and one of the world's biggest Cowboy fans. Running interference for the prince were six of his bodyguards, who carried walkie-talkies and scanned the crowd.

But few if any among the rowdy crowd of 63,101 knew or cared who Prince Bandar was. At the head of this conspicuous contingent was Cowboy owner, president, and general manager Jerry Jones, who had become one of the most powerful men in Dallas and the National Football League. Many in the crowd gave Jones a standing roar.

What a moment this was for this man: just four years earlier, Jones had been the most hated man in Cowboydom—The Man Who Fired Tom Landry. But now Jones's Cowboys led the Bears, 27–0, in the regular-season finale. His 1992 Cowboys, already NFC

East champs, were about to win their thirteenth game. No Cowboy team ever had won thirteen, even under Landry.

For fans it was "Dallas in Wonderland" again. The Cowboys were back—back impossibly quickly from 1-15 in 1989. Just think: this team had been in position to win two of the games it had lost, to the Rams and Redskins. It could easily be 15-1. Crank up the new theme song at Texas Stadium, Thin Lizzy's "The Boys Are Back in Town."

Just four years earlier Jones had come from nowhere—well, Arkansas—to buy the Cowboys. He hired his "best friend" Jimmy Johnson, his University of Arkansas roommate and teammate, to replace the legendary Landry. Together, in 1989, Jones and Johnson led the NFL in ridicule received. Johnson came straight from the University of Miami with no NFL coaching experience. Johnson was dismissed as a "college coach" by Philadelphia Eagle coach Buddy Ryan. "No East Carolinas on an NFL schedule," Ryan said with a chuckle. Jones was nicknamed Jethro by fans and media critics, who considered this oilman the NFL equivalent of a Beverly Hillbilly. Jones and Johnson quickly traded their one superstar, Herschel Walker. They turned the Cowboys upside down. They didn't just disregard the NFL's how-to manual, they burned it.

Now this.

"This," Jones had said before leaving for the field, "is going to be the greatest story ever told. We're just on the second or third chapter of *Gone with the Wind* here. We are going to win Super Bowls." Plural.

Suddenly it seemed the Cowboys—the NFL's youngest team, according to the league office—had a chance to win the franchise's first NFL championship in fifteen years. Everything seemed to be coming up Rose Bowls, which was where Super Bowl XXVII would be played on January 31. Could it be? Emmitt Smith had just clinched his second straight NFL rushing title and had retired for the day, taking off his shoulder pads and putting on a ballcap. Quarterback Troy Aikman was safely done for the day, too. For the first time as a pro, Aikman had made it through a season without a serious injury. He would soon be named to the Pro Bowl, along with Smith and four other Cowboys on offense. This team was remarkably injury-free with two weeks to prepare for a home play-off game.

Had this team ever been blessed. Its offense was beginning to click and control the ball the way Joe Montana's San Francisco attack did in the early eighties. But it was the starless defense that had won over a city so easily star-struck. By holding the Bears to 92 total yards, the defense would clinch the NFL's No. 1 statistical ranking. "We check our egos at the door," said defensive coordinator Dave Wannstedt. "We've done it with blue-collar work ethic."

Yes, what a lovable bunch these 'Boys were. So young, innocent, unspoiled, and untroubled. So different from Landry's star-laden, made-for-Hollywood, private-party teams. America's Team was now Dallas's. Jones said, "Even prominent people in Dallas who experienced the great years of the past are telling me the excitement and feeling was never quite like this."

What a sight: Jerry Jones parading up the sideline toward the Cowboy bench, pumping both fists to the crowd. "Ca-boys!" he yelled again and again in his Arkansas twang. Jones was smiling so hard it looked as if his skin might split. Jones was almost always smiling—Steve McQueen in a fun-house mirror. Jerral Wayne Jones from Little Rock had become a chicken-fried piper to thousands of new-breed Cowboy fans. Jones, age fifty, had attracted about twenty thousand new season-ticket holders, with an average age of about thirty; when he bought the team, the average age of all season-ticket holders was about fifty-five. Jones had built a tented honky-tonk called the Corral outside Gate 8 in the parking lot, and he wasn't above sippin' a cold one and talkin' football with the Corral's clientele. Jones had shown folks it was okay to raise cain in what used to be Landry's house of worship. Now fans were raising the roof on the stadium without one. Johnson says, "It gets as loud as any domed stadium."

What a day this was to be a Cowboy fan at Texas Stadium.

This, however, was not a good day to be a Cowboy player or assistant coach.

Within minutes the locker-room roof would be raised by Johnson. He would chew out his team for the third straight week. Many players and assistants would worry that Johnson had finally slipped off the cliff's edge on which he coached. Johnson, a control freak, appeared to be out of control. The two assistants he called his "best friends," Wannstedt and offensive-line coach Tony Wise, both feared that Johnson had "lost it." So did many players, who found his behavior irrational, uncalled for, even meanspirited.

How could a coach find a reason to blow up over a blowout victory? A series of events, any of which would have kept Johnson on edge, combined to push him over it. One was a pair of fumbles lost by backup running back Curvin Richards, the second of which was returned 42 yards for a Bear touchdown that cut the Cowboy lead to 27–14 with 9:19 remaining. The blowout was becoming a football game again. The other was the arrival of Jones with Bandar and his men. While Johnson seethed, Jones and the prince were congratulating players in the bench area who appeared to be through for the day.

Bandar, forty-two, loves the Cowboys so much that if some international incident forces him back to "the Kingdom," as he calls Saudi Arabia, he has a tape of the Cowboy game flown via Concorde and military jets to Riyadh so he and his staff can view it the next day. At Texas Stadium, Prince Bandar blends into the luxury-box crowd, save for his distinctly Middle Eastern mustache. He wears a blazer, open-collared shirt, and sometimes even jeans. Jones and Prince Bandar have become big buddies—Jones just calls him Bandar. They share a passion for oil, gas, and football.

Jones is in awe of Bandar's wealth; he's said to be one of the world's richest men. Yet Jones treats Bandar royally for one other reason: the prince is regarded as perhaps Washington's most important contact in the Middle East. Before jetting to Dallas for the Bear game, Bandar spent Christmas with then-president Bush on a ranch outside Houston.

A Cowboy source says, "Jerry contributed heavily to [former Arkansas governor] Clinton's campaign, and obviously the Clinton administration wants to maintain a good relationship with Bandar."

Jones knows one of the quickest ways to please the prince is to take him down on the sideline during a game. And Jones figured that, at 27–0 after three quarters, the celebration had basically begun. But after Richards's second fumble, Bandar became just another groupie sheikh to Johnson. Asked the week before by CBS's Lesley Visser if he knew the U.S. had sent troops to Somalia, Johnson said, "Vaguely." She asked if Johnson could name five NBA players. "Who cares?" he said. His world begins and ends with football, and Jones had invaded it. Johnson couldn't stand to see Jones and his entourage basking prematurely in the glow of 13-3. Prince Bandar was the straw that broke the camel's back.

Johnson snapped.

"First team, get ready!" he yelled.

Smith and Aikman threw their pads and helmets back on. Aikman quickly began to warm up his arm. Line coach Wise said, "Everybody was wondering what the hell was going on." Did Johnson really want to risk sending Smith and Aikman back in against a 5-10 Bear team—back into a game that had no bearing on the Cowboys' play-off situation? The NFC East Champs had no hope of catching San Francisco for the best record in the conference. Johnson ordered some first-teamers back onto the field, but reason prevailed: Smith and Aikman remained on the sideline.

The Cowboys won, 27–14.

Before the media were allowed into the locker room, Johnson blasted the team for its sloppy play in the fourth quarter. Then he marched across the hall to an interview room with a podium set up for his postgame Q&A with the media. Usually after wins, these sessions last fifteen or twenty minutes. But for the third straight week, Johnson ended his interview quickly and heatedly. Even after the thirteenth win, Johnson appeared to be on the edge of a breakdown.

To the first five questions, he gave terse, defensive answers. When agitated in front of the media, Johnson's extraordinarily blue eyes dart from side to side as he weighs the consequences of a headline-making blowup. He smacks his lips as if he just tasted something sour. His face, rounded by nachos and Heinekens, grows danger-zone red.

Johnson, a neatness nut who, at age forty-nine, lives alone in a house with white carpet, said, "I was not happy with the sloppy play. I'm never happy with sloppy play. I'm never happy when we go out there and flop around." Eyes darting, lips smacking, face reddening. Next question: "Coach, are you glad to get your personal record up to .500?"

"No," Johnson said, and stormed off his platform, leaving reporters shaking their heads.

Ironically, Johnson had done a "Ditka," while down the hall Bear coach Mike Ditka was being as philosophical, quotable, and charming as Johnson can be. Ditka would soon be fired. Yet Ditka didn't live up to his Monster of the Midway image this day; graciously, he said, "We were a little overmatched. That's a very good football team, and I think they will prove that to a lot of people as they get into the play-offs."

That was news to the Cowboys. "This is a winning locker room?" guard John Gesek said after Johnson's tirade.

Another respected veteran, eighth-year punter Mike Saxon, was even more shaken. From the start in 1989, Saxon had been one of Johnson's biggest locker-room supporters. Saxon is a bright, perceptive Californian who helps run a real estate business. Saxon was in awe of Johnson's ability to evaluate talent and predict what would happen during games. But Johnson had rocked Saxon's faith.

"What is going on?" Saxon said. "He's always preached to us to stay positive. That was the first thing he said in '89: 'Stay positive.' This is positive? I mean, is he losing it? He even jumped on Tony Wise."

Wise had served under Johnson at Oklahoma State and the University of Miami. Wise had taken an offensive line considered one of the NFL's worst and turned it into one regarded by some experts as the best. Wise was about to spend a long, emotional month wondering what it really meant for Johnson to call him a close friend. For a while Johnson would quit speaking to Wise and even to Wannstedt, regarded by insiders as Johnson's closest friend.

As Wise left the coaches' dressing room following the Bear game, he was hoping Wannstedt would soon be offered a head-coaching job and would take Wise with him. Wise and Wannstedt are "like brothers," they say. Emotion rising in his voice, Wise said, "I'm going home and fix me a big, tall rum and tonic and try to figure out if we won or not. What's more fun, going seven and nine [as the Cowboys did in 1990] or thirteen and three? I mean, Curvin Richards just ended his career here."

Johnson had told assistants that Richards was history. He would be cut the following day, with Jones's approval.

Now Johnson steamed upstairs to Texas Stadium's Sam Houston Room, where he and his assistants always go to share beers and thoughts on the game. But Johnson didn't last long. He couldn't stand it. He took off for Jones's box. Johnson despises small talk and socializing with people he doesn't know. The last place he wants to go after games is Jones's box.

But this evening he was going to give Jones a piece of his bleepin' mind. Maybe he half-planned to quit. Assistants feared Johnson would cross the line with a profane insult and force Jones to fire him.

Moments later Larry Lacewell arrived at the coaches' gathering. Lacewell calls himself "one of Jimmy's two and a half friends around here—Wannstedt, Wise, and I'm the half because I'm not around as much as those two." In his first year as the Cowboys' college scouting director, Lacewell spent much of his time on the road sizing up potential draftees. But Lacewell, age fifty-six, has a deeper, more mature feel for Johnson than Wannstedt or Wise. Johnson coached defense under Lacewell at Wichita State, Iowa State, and Oklahoma. In May of 1992, Jones allowed Johnson to hire Lacewell.

"To tell you the truth," Lacewell says, "Jimmy mostly needed me to serve as a buffer between him and Jerry."

Johnson constantly complained to Lacewell about how Jones had cut scouting budgets and manpower until the Cowboys couldn't realistically compete with other NFL teams. Jones had fired pro personnel directors John Wooten and Bob Ackles and basically replaced them with himself. While Jones vowed to win a Super Bowl with a realistic budget, Johnson complained that his coaching staff was among the NFL's lowest paid, if not the lowest. Many assistants constantly complained about how tight Jones was with his money and compliments.

No doubt all this was boiling inside Johnson as he went to find Jones.

Lacewell was told at the coaches' gathering where Johnson had gone. "I said, 'Oh, shit, I better go find them.' When I walked in [Jones's suite], their noses were about three inches apart. I felt it was pretty heated, so I tried to make some jokes. I mean, Jimmy looked like he was about to blow. Then I said, 'Jimmy, you did win thirteen games. That's pretty damn good. Nobody around here has ever done that.' I think Jerry appreciated I was there. But all Jimmy would do was clench his teeth and say, 'Lace, I'll smile tomorrow.'

"The truth is, Jimmy was probably getting a little tight in the throat about Chicago getting it back to twenty-seven to fourteen. It's like he had been hexed by Jerry and the prince. I've been there

[Lacewell was three-time Southland Conference coach of the year at Arkansas State]. You're liable to lash out at anybody, even people close to you. I could really go off on people in my day, and I wasn't as bad as Jimmy is. Jimmy can go off and it might be *days*. With a Landry, you knew exactly what you were getting. But with Jimmy, you don't ever know for sure which dog's going to bite you. That's what can be hard about dealing with Jimmy.

"But think about it. You've got an owner with his own TV show, radio show, and newspaper column, and you've got a guy [Johnson] who believes he's the reason you're winning—nothing wrong with that—and it's inevitable you're going to have a clash. Jimmy gives one of his twenty-second press conferences and walks over and there's Jerry in the locker room with the prince, surrounded by writers. Jerry does give Jimmy plenty of reasons to have the red ass. Obviously, the way to handle it under the best of circumstances is to go in the next morning and sit down and say, 'I really have a problem with you having the prince on the sideline in the fourth quarter.' But that's not Jimmy Johnson."

Perhaps not. But the question many were asking themselves that night was: Just who is Jimmy Johnson?

Troy Aikman says many players were near-mutinous—and not just because of Johnson's strange behavior after the Bear game. Johnson had exploded after three straight games. He had let the players have it on the team plane returning home from a December 13 loss in Washington, saying they weren't taking it as hard as he was. It turned into an ugly scene that shook the franchise for a week and especially infuriated Aikman. His unusually emotional response came in the form of the most dominant performance of his career the following Monday night in Atlanta. He had finally taken over a game and taken over the team from a coach he had never quite trusted. For three seasons Johnson had doubted Aikman's delicate confidence and leadership ability, once going so far as to say privately, "Troy Aikman was a loser in college and he'll never be anything but a loser in the pros." Aikman had doubted Johnson's confidence in him after Johnson had drafted quarterback Steve Walsh in 1989 and had stuck with backup quarterback Steve Beuerlein when Aikman was ready to return from injury in 1991.

So Aikman felt he had to save the '92 season. He says, "Atlanta was a game that if we don't win, our season ends. Everything would have come completely apart." But thanks mostly to Aikman, the Cowboys blasted Atlanta, 41–17—yet Johnson blasted them again, during the fourth quarter and in the postgame locker room.

And now this franchise-record thirteenth win had triggered another tirade.

"My biggest concern at the time," Aikman says, "was that if we didn't win the Super Bowl, this football team would feel it hadn't accomplished anything because it was never given the opportunity to celebrate." Since the Washington loss, said Aikman, many players had been "extremely upset. There was so much discussion and bitterness by so many guys. Here we'd done everything we could for this guy. We had played our guts out. . . . It was like he had sold out on us."

Or had Johnson just flipped out? Why, minutes after the Bear game, did Johnson hint to assistants that he might quit? Was it just another of Johnson's inexplicable, unpredictable moods? Was this just another night in the life of "psycho Jimmy," as some insiders call him? Johnson's girlfriend, Rhonda Rookmaaker, told *The Dallas Morning News* that Johnson is "the moodiest man I know."

Johnson's worst moods are triggered by his rage to win. Johnson bases his entire existence on winning. To Johnson, nothing matters unless he wins. If he wins, he can basically do or say whatever he feels. He can rule his world. Johnson admits he neglected his ex-wife and two sons while rising through the coaching ranks. He proudly admits he has only a few friends—and those, he says, live with his moods or they find another friend.

Johnson heaps pressure on himself by vowing he will win. Johnson wills winning by making everyone around him believe he will win. He can be terribly cocky; he says he loves to gloat. But Johnson's dark side can turn him hopelessly negative and pessimistic. Sometimes, Johnson snaps under the pressure he inflicts on himself. A few days after the Bear game, Jerry Jones ended a long discussion of Johnson's Ahab-like obsession with winning by saying, "Of course, the one thing I would not want to see is for Jimmy to wind up in a mental institution."

But often, it is Jones who sets off Jimmy Johnson.

Jones is the one man in Johnson's world he cannot control. Like it or not, Johnson has a boss, and that boss insists on being

Johnson's general manager. By contract, one must approve any football move the other wants to make—but Jones breaks any ties. "The last word is mine," says Jones, who is actively involved in drafting, in trading, in everything but game-planning.

During the '92 season this often drove Johnson nuts. Johnson doesn't want to share the stage or overall credit with anyone, especially someone whose football knowledge he doesn't respect. A few days after the Bear game, Johnson indicated in an interview for this book that he was winning in spite of Jones. Meanwhile, Johnson's team believed it was winning in spite of its coach.

What a tumultuous time this was for a team on the edge of greatness.

What tormented Johnson was the image that he and Jones were "buddies from Arkansas." Drinking buddies. Football buddies. Partners. Johnson said, "I don't know where those [buddy] stories started. I didn't do anything to kill them. I don't know, maybe you don't want to hurt somebody's feelings. We never went out [socially at the University of Arkansas]. We were both offensive guards as sophomores. We did room together maybe twenty nights on the road, but that was because of our names [rooms were assigned by alphabetical order]. And we were cocaptains as seniors—*every* senior was a cocaptain."

Johnson rolled his eyes.

"I guess our wives got to know each other watching games together when we were on the road. And yes, Jerry and I did stay in touch because I was at Oklahoma State and he did a lot of business in Oklahoma City. But it was never this buddy-buddy thing. . . . Neither one of us ever talked about our futures. Jerry was going to make money and I was going to become an industrial psychologist."

Yet from the day Jones bought the team—the day of infamy for Landry lovers, February 25, 1989—the legend of Jimmy and Jerry had grown. Grown like Jones's nose? No, he never directly said he and Johnson had lain awake nights in their Arkansas dorm room discussing how, together, they would one day dominate the NFL. But Jones didn't say anything to discourage that myth, either. When he spoke of his coach—"Jimmeh" is the way the name rolls off Jones's Arkansas tongue—it always sounded as if they were close.

For sure it was a storybook angle for the media. It made for a convenient reference that fans could readily grasp—"Jimmy Johnson and Jerry Jones, roommates and cocaptains at the University of Arkansas . . ." So the "JJs" image spread—in Johnson's view—like a plague through America's sports sections.

Johnson was even irked that many Cowboy fans seemed to forget he's a native Texan, born and raised in Port Arthur down on the Gulf of Mexico.

Johnson was occasionally asked by interviewers about the advantages of having such a close relationship with an owner/GM who's his best friend. Johnson answered those questions carefully, vaguely, and tactfully. But privately Johnson fumed after reading quotes from Jones taking credit for playing key roles in making draft picks and trades and rebuilding the Cowboys so quickly. Johnson says Jones is "a frustrated football coach—everybody can see that." Johnson sometimes couldn't stand it that a guy who hadn't paid a nickel of coaching dues thought he could buy an NFL team for $150 million and immediately think he's one of the boys—one of the coaches and players. Johnson had spent a year as an assistant coach for a Picayune, Mississippi, high school team that went 0-10, then was an assistant at Louisiana Tech, Wichita State, Iowa State, Oklahoma, Arkansas, and Pitt. Johnson says, "I can X and O with anybody." Bitterly, he says, "The owner, president, *and* general manager of the Cowboys doesn't even watch any tape."

Johnson sometimes overheats at the thought of coaches he respects reading that he was ably assisted on a trade by Jones—by this guy who got rich quick and wants so badly to be cool and doesn't quite know how. Johnson is known for The Hair, his uniquely styled and sprayed coif. Some TV anchors would kill for Johnson's hair. Johnson is a Corvette lover, and his hair is designed something like a classic Corvette, metallic brown fiberglass curves with a prominent chrome bumper across the front. But Johnson's appearance doesn't stop with The Hair; he meticulously presents a best-dressed image in power suits and ties and privately makes fun of disheveled coaches he sees on TV.

Jones, on the other hand, still looks as if he pays $2.50 for his haircuts and always seems to be wearing slacks that are an inch short. Jones always wears a coat and tie—typically forgettable business attire—but in a roomful of downtown-Dallas businessmen you'd probably guess Jones was the one from Arkansas. He just has that look.

And this guy was now the hero of millions of Dallas Cowboy fans? "Puh-leeze," says Johnson, who shrugs and adds, "He needs this." Needs the constant media attention and banner-headline credit.

Through the season several assistant coaches tried cautiously to talk sense to Johnson about Jones. Their point: the coaching staff had so many more pressing problems. Why waste time and energy stewing over Jones's rampant ego? Again and again the assistants feared the team would tailspin—that it simply wasn't yet talented and experienced enough to avoid a losing streak. Yet Johnson kept letting Jones get to him.

Midway through the season, offensive coordinator Norv Turner said, "Sure, we hear all the stories about their clashes, and you don't know what to believe because you don't know which version to believe. But what's it matter, really? Why should Jimmy really care about what Jerry is telling his friends about how much he had to do with a trade? For that matter, why should Jimmy have to tell people he's involved in personnel decisions? We're all going to benefit from what's being built here because it's being built to last. This could really be something special if everyone accepts no one of us is any more important than anyone else and we just have patience."

It is difficult to know for sure how important a role Jones played in the two trades—for defensive end Charles Haley and safety Thomas Everett—that lifted the Cowboys into 13-3 Super Bowl contention. In interviews for this book Johnson and Jones gave conflicting interpretations. Yet Jones makes a solid case for himself. It sounds as if he played an essential role in both trades.

Since 1989 Jones has constantly asked for advice from other NFL owners—primarily the Raiders' Al Davis, one other owner who also serves as general manager. Jones spent hours learning from Davis, who taught Jones well. Though Johnson wouldn't admit it, Jones is now regarded in ownership circles as one of the NFL's shrewdest operators.

Is it the truth that haunts Johnson?

In a darkly sarcastic mood, Johnson once indicated his girlfriend knows about as much football as Jones. Johnson said, "Sometimes she'll say, 'Why do you let him get away with saying what he does [to the media about his trade involvement]?' . . . I don't know, I've gone from angry and hostile to trying to be a good company man to trying to tell the truth to 'I really don't care.' He owns the club. What can I do?"

Some days you brood or seethe quietly. Or you lose control and lash out at your boss, as Johnson had several times during the '92 season. "It doesn't take much to set me off," Johnson said. "It can be the littlest thing. Most people would say, 'What the shit?' But I let it distract me from my focus."

In the wake of the Bear game, that distraction could have become a full-blown battle for authority. That it didn't is a reflection of the man at whom the anger was directed. Through Johnson's three-week reign of terror, Jones was the one person in the organization who shrugged it off. The day after Johnson confronted him in his suite, Jones said he had seen Johnson at other times even more "puffed up" with anger. You had to wonder if Jones's relentless optimism made him oblivious to the depths of Johnson's bitterness. Was he being a little naive?

No, said Jones, "Jimmy's smart enough not to push me too far. Listen, Jimmy knows I can be volatile, too. I tried to explain to Jimmy that I respect the sanctity of the locker room and sidelines, but that there are certain things [such as entertaining Bandar and important sponsors] that just have to be done for the overall good of the club. Really, I have a better relationship with Jimmy than I've had with any partner I've ever had. Boy, I've had some that would shoot you between the eyes—that's an exaggeration, but if you've been out there in the real world dealing with people, this seems like a pleasure."

As the football-world pressure built on Johnson's Cowboys, Jones constantly provided that kind of bright-side balance and perspective.

He said, "Look, Jimmy hasn't changed one iota from the way he was in college. I knew exactly what I was getting into."

Yes, Johnson can turn quickly from enjoyable and generous to heartless and uncontrollably arrogant. Yet what Jones saw in Johnson was a rare eye for judging talent and a unique ability to prepare teams physically and emotionally for games big and little.

Jones was just cocky enough to think he could harness Johnson's explosive talent. Jones had helped create his "Jethro" image with a remark he made at a press conference the night he bought the team: "Jimmy Johnson will be worth five Heisman Trophy winners and five first-round draft choices." In retrospect, that was an understatement.

With a wink, Jones says, "Jimmy has given me that and more. He has dedicated his entire being to winning a Super Bowl for the Dallas Cowboys."

And, no matter how he feels about it, for his owner/GM.

So the day after the regular season ended, Jones said he was going to ride out Johnson's thunderstorm. Jones thought he could catch Johnson's lightning in a champagne bottle. He actually said Johnson's behavior could be good.

"My instincts tell me to let it run its course," Jones said. "Whatever, for lack of a better word, 'squirrelly' things Jimmy might do, these can be the kind of things that go into winning a Super Bowl. The team's saying, 'Jimmy did this, Jimmy did that,' and all of a sudden a lot of energy is building and you're working and pushing and pulling and you win it all."

Jones concluded he was 80 percent sure Johnson would make it through the play-offs without a major blowup or some sort of breakdown. And what if Johnson suddenly quit?

"The Dallas Cowboys will win Super Bowls without him," Jones said. Jones keeps a short mental list of head-coach replacements just in case "Jimmy got hit by a bus, God forbid." Yet Jones seriously doubted Johnson would resign: "He knows what a great situation he has here." In fact, the Bear-game clash ended in hugs, said Jones, grinning and shaking his head.

True, Jimmy? "Oh, I guess it will be okay for another couple of days," Johnson said. "But I honestly don't know if I'll last five or six more years here or five or six more days."

That's why what happened in the next five or six weeks was so amazing—more so than anyone outside the team knew.

Johnson and Jones would clash over Johnson's lack of community involvement, over a pep rally Jones staged at Texas Stadium, over budgets, over credit. As Wannstedt had grinned and said after so many games, "It was fuckin' nuts."

That sums up a season that ended out near Hollywood.

So how exactly did it all come and stay together? How did the 'Boys so quickly become men? Was youth their strength? Tenth-year defensive end Jim Jeffcoat kept saying, "This team is too young to know it isn't supposed to play its guts out every week." Of the players, only Aikman knew much about Johnson's clashes with Jones. Remember what former Cowboy guard Blaine Nye called rookie Clint Longley's touchdown pass that beat Washington on Thanksgiving Day of 1974? "The triumph of an uncluttered mind."

Was this? Who did deserve the most credit? The coach? The owner? The team, the quarterback, the assistant coaches? Is it possible that one man—Aikman—suddenly performed so unbeatably in late December and January that he made a pretty good team a great one in the play-offs and allowed Johnson and Jones to receive more credit than they deserve? Then again, where would Aikman have been without Norv Turner's system, play-calling, and emotional support? Would Johnson have quit or forced Jones to fire him if Dave Wannstedt hadn't been around to calm him, constructively criticize him, and mediate between Johnson and the players he alienated? Would the defense have played its guts out week after week for anyone but Wannstedt? Would the Cowboys have crumbled without cornerstones Turner and Wannstedt?

Very possibly.

How much of what happened simply had to do with a concept Johnson hates—luck? Was Jones, as several coaches figured, just a cockeyed optimist who stumbled into a championship? Or, as Al Davis taught him, did Jones subtly "coach the coach"? Was it Jones who saved Johnson from himself? Or did Johnson, who can be a convincing actor, script some of his eruptions and manipulate his team and staff into overachieving?

From a distance it appeared the Cowboys had started the latest NFL trend—the coach and owner/GM constantly communicating and teaming to handle holdouts, close key deals, and make the increasing number of quick, difficult decisions facing franchises as free agency escalates crazily. Yet few people outside the organization know how crazy the days often were inside the 1992 Cowboys, and how virtually impossible it would be for another team to copy what they somehow pulled off.

"One Huge Ego"

NFL DRAFT DAY, APRIL 26, 1992. IN THE COWBOYS' "WAR room" at Valley Ranch are Jimmy, Jerry, and a cast of what seemed like thousands, including an ESPN crew providing periodic live shots for its national audience. What a spare-no-expense brain trust this appeared to be—ten or twelve guys in coats and ties wedged around Jimmy Johnson and Jerry Jones, who sit elbow to elbow at a huge table covered with telephones and stacks of draft info.

This was the JJs' chance to wheel and deal and seal the lips of a new chorus of doubters among fans and media who had sprung up after the 12-5 Cowboys had lost an embarrassing second-round play-off game to the Detroit Lions, 38–6. The loss had felt like 1989 again.

The JJs had made ten trades to move up or down just before or during each of their first three drafts. They had especially commanded the NFL's attention during the 1991 draft, for which they had stockpiled ten picks in the first four rounds and eighteen for the total twelve rounds. This time they had two picks in each of the first three rounds. Critics said they would need them.

The JJs had gambled and lost two key performers to Plan B free agency. Middle linebacker Jack Del Rio and placekicker Ken Willis had not been among Dallas's thirty-seven protected players and had accepted offers from other teams, raising eyebrows and doubts. Del Rio and Willis said they called the JJs' bluff; both questioned the sincerity and integrity of Johnson and Jones. Both wondered loudly whether Jones would pay the price to sign nine potential starters whose contracts were up—the first time as an NFL owner Jones had faced such a financial firing line.

Willis had agreed to take a $25,000 advance against his salary to ignore any offers he might receive while left unprotected. Yet Willis said he was insulted by being pressured into taking such a token payoff "just so I wouldn't wind up in Jimmy's doghouse." When Tampa Bay offered to nearly double Willis's salary, to about $800,000 for two seasons, Willis took the money and ran. Many Dallas talk-show callers backed Willis, basically saying, "Willis beat the JJs at their own game. He stuck it to them before they stuck it to him."

Though won over by the team's turnaround, many fans still regarded the JJs as used-car dealers who would take advantage of their mothers. Johnson, with his sprayed hair, was seen as something of an anti-Landry. On newspaper pictures of Jones it's easy to draw horns and a pointed beard and make him look devilish.

Del Rio reinforced these suspicions. It was one thing for a second-year kicker to defect, another for a respected team leader and leading tackler to exit angrily. Del Rio was the team spokesman, the one player the PR department went to when it needed a pithy or profound quote for *Sports Illustrated* or a major newspaper. Del Rio figured he was left unprotected because the JJs were gambling he wouldn't leave a city that he and his family enjoyed and that provided so many endorsement opportunities for a handsome, white, well-spoken middle linebacker. Besides, how could Del Rio leave a defense designed to funnel ballcarriers to the middle linebacker?

After accepting Minnesota's offer, Del Rio said, "I believe you build a nucleus of players who stick with you through the years, and they're the ones who get the job done. . . . You build trust, then you can rise to the next level. It's an uneasy feeling for the veterans around here because it's clear that as soon as they find someone a hair quicker, you're gone. Jerry Jones is now a powerful man in this town, and he has thrown around his power without being concerned for the players or their feelings. Unfortunately, a lot of vets are coming up for contracts, guys like Michael Irvin, Mark Stepnoski, Jay Novacek, Tony Tolbert, Kenny Norton. If they go through what I did, I'm not sure they'll be able to come back in the right frame of mind."

Was Jones ready to try winning in the NFC East—which had produced the last two Super Bowl champs, New York and Washington—with a rookie middle linebacker? "You bet," Jones said, "if we get the one we want."

So the JJs again were again expected to send tremors through the draft. They had already made forty trades in three seasons. They had already considered adding to their dual picks in each of the first three rounds. "We could have had another first and another second," Jones said. Steve Beuerlein had replaced the injured Troy Aikman at quarterback and won six straight games before the debacle in Detroit. Beuerlein's value had soared. Jones had received "incredible" offers for him, he said, "but we're not going to trade him because we honestly believe we could win the whole thing this year. We may need Steve. We definitely need to make these picks count. They could put us over the top."

On ESPN, it appeared to many fans that the JJs had more scouts and personnel men on hand than picks. Yet many of those on camera weren't directly involved in the selection process. They represented a little one-upmanship between Johnson and Jones, a sort of nuclear-family buildup.

Jones had invited into the "war room" his son Stephen, twenty-seven, a former defensive back at Arkansas who was assistant general manager; son Jerry, Jr., who's in law school at Southern Methodist University in Dallas and plans to be an attorney for the club; and Mike McCoy, Jones's partner in the oil-and-gas business and the Cowboys' sole minority owner (5 percent). Jones also allows his treasurer, Jack Dixon, and marketing director, George Hayes, to wander in and out, along with big-dollar sponsors who advertise at Texas Stadium or on Cowboy broadcasts. Dixon and Hayes are part of the "Arkansas Mafia," the term used by others in the front office for staffers brought by Jones from his home state.

Johnson rolls his eyes over all the people Jones invites into the team's draft central. "But I can't control that," Johnson said. So Johnson invited his sons, Brent (a Dallas lawyer) and Chad (a

Dallas stockbroker), and his attorney and drinking buddy Nick Christin, who lives in Miami. It appeared Johnson was saying, "If Jerry's going to get all his people a shot on ESPN, I'll be represented, too."

The men who have the most draft input—the assistant coaches— were off camera.

The truth was that Johnson considered his scouting department one of the league's smallest, and more heads were about to roll. Personnel director John Wooten, who had served as Johnson's right-hand man during the three previous drafts, was fired by Jones after the '91 draft. Wooten, now a scout for the Philadelphia Eagles, said, "I was doing a lot of things Jerry wanted to do [such as making trade calls to other general managers]. I can understand why he let me go."

But Johnson could not understand the team's shrinking scouting budget. He said, "My assistant coaches are still willing to do a major part of the predraft scouting [studying college-game tapes and traveling to personally test and interview prospects, supplementing the reports of the four remaining scouts]. But my biggest concern is, how much longer will their total commitment last? At what point will I say, 'We've got to stay up here tonight and grind [Johnson's favorite word for hard work] on these tapes,' and they say, 'Sorry, you grind. I'm going home to have dinner with the family'? Other coaches I talk to just cannot believe the situation here."

Throughout the '92 season, most of Johnson's assistants would privately complain about how the NFL's hardest-working staff was probably the lowest paid. According to team sources, defensive coordinator Dave Wannstedt made around $120,000, while offensive coordinator Norv Turner who came from the Rams for the same salary he made as receivers coach, made slightly less than Wannstedt. Offensive-line coach Tony Wise, who had earned a reputation as one of the league's best, said he was embarrassed to tell peers what he was making and often heard that some line coaches made almost twice as much as he did. All the assistants who came with Johnson from the University of Miami began at $65,000 with the Cowboys; though Wise had been raised to $85,000 by 1992, that was still an entry-level wage by many teams' standards.

"But what can I do about the budget?" said Johnson, clearly steamed. "That's not my area."

No, it was Jones's.

A few days before the draft, Jones sat in his office—Tex Schramm's old office—and spoke emotionally about his goal and dream. Schramm, the president and general manager of the Landry Cowboys, commissioned the building of the team's Valley Ranch complex just as the bottom fell out of the Dallas economy in 1985. Valley Ranch is the name of an upper-middle-class subdivision not far from Dallas–Fort Worth Airport. This model community features apartments, condos, town houses, and houses—one occupied by Johnson just a mile or so from what Schramm originally called Cowboys Center and his critics called TexWorld. The headquarters and locker-room facilities occupy a one-story structure of Arizona sandstone that spreads for what seems like miles over eighty thousand square feet. Out back are two practice fields. Soon after Jones bought the team, he got lost in the maze of hallways and had to pick up the nearest phone and tell his secretary, "I'm at extension twenty-nine. Come find me." Cowboys Center symbolized Schramm's Cowboys: Texas-style garish and extravagant.

It did not suit Jones, who says he turns off the lights whenever he leaves a room. While playing at the University of Arkansas, Jones helped support himself by running carloads of fans to the Fayetteville airport right after games. They paid more because Jones could give them the lowdown on what really happened on the sideline and in the locker room.

Schramm built a national image of running "the finest organization in sports" by spending budgetless amounts of original owner Clint Murchison's money. But Murchison's financial empire collapsed, and second owner H. R. "Bum" Bright's was teetering when he sold the Cowboys and Texas Stadium to Jones for about $150 million. Jones kept Schramm around just long enough to guide him through the endless maze of expenses and payrolls.

"There was an awful lot of fat," said Jones, who began hacking away at it. Many employees hired by Schramm claimed that Jones initially told them their jobs were safe. "They misinterpreted," said Jones, who was scorched by the local media for being "deceitful" and "cold-blooded." In November of 1989, the *Dallas Times Herald* ran a story that said the Cowboys had fallen behind in paying routine bills and making mortgage payments, had held Troy Aikman's $1.5-million check until after banking hours, and were negotiating with a group of doctors interested in buying Cowboys Center.

Then, Jones explained, "Obviously, the Cowboys lost money last year [as Tom Landry's final team went 3-13]. That didn't discourage me, and I feel very strongly that it's a sound business. So when the Cowboys need any money for their cash flow, a part of what I do is provide that money."

Privately, Jones said he had enough money to "buy two football teams." He said he couldn't understand why he should apologize for cutting a few costs and corners, for making prudent long-range decisions, and for trying to turn the religious shrine known as the Dallas Cowboys into a profitable business. He decided to keep his headquarters at Cowboys Center, which became known simply as Valley Ranch. But he renegotiated the lease and cut staff and expenses by more than half, saving $6 million a year, Jones says. Jones remained in Schramm's spectacularly long office—maybe 30 yards from door to desk—but he never seemed to quite fit in it.

"Look," Jones said just before the draft, "I want people to know I'm not some rich kid who bought this thing and just throws money at it." He did not want to be an Eddie DeBartolo, Jr., whose San Francisco 49ers had won four Super Bowls with the NFL's highest player payroll and mounting red ink. Jones said, "I don't want this franchise ever to be owned by the banks."

In 1989, the Cowboys made $36.2 million in total revenue. In 1992, says Jones, the Cowboys made more than $65 million.

Jones is a chip off the old block of J. W. "Pat" Jones, who worked North Little Rock the way Jerry now works a Dallas crowd. Pat Jones knew everybody and, as an entrepreneur, would try just about anything. He scored in supermarkets and eventually in insurance, a business Jerry joined just out of college. But, said Jerry, his father gave him nothing: "I've been there when I didn't *have* any money. About twenty-five years ago, I flew into Love Field in Dallas and went to rent a car and had to watch them cut my credit card in two and say, 'Son, you're going to have to pay your bills.' I've been there making a deal when I was so scared my hand was shaking on the glass I was holding. I've been to war. Some in this league have and some haven't. . . . For me this is what I call 'mirror time.' Someday I want to look in the mirror—look inside my soul—and say, 'I did it right.' I won Super Bowls while operating a very sound business. That's what would mean most to me personally."

In contrast, Jimmy Johnson says money isn't that important to him. That's why, he says, he could make a great living at the blackjack tables, if he chose. "I have no fear of losing money," Johnson says. After the season, Johnson takes his assistants to the Bahamas, "and for the guys who don't make much money, I'll play for them and win them five thousand dollars or so." Just like that? Uncanny, assistants confirm. Johnson has losing nights, they say, but not often. Those who have watched him can't logically explain how he consistently beats a game rigged slightly to the house's advantage. Johnson, they say, almost seems to will himself into an unbeatable state. Johnson, with an IQ of 162, can immediately calculate odds at the gaming table just the way he does during football games. Even in college, says Johnson, he subsidized himself by cutting class to play bridge for money in the student center, often fleecing guys who "looked like Maynard G. Krebs." Still, associates of Jones note that the owner paid Johnson about $550,000 for 1992 and that he has a ten-year contract, which makes it a little easier for Johnson to say he doesn't care about money.

Jones puts a little different spin on Johnson's roulette-playing image. In college, Jones studied a principle called tolerance for ambiguity. (Jones earned a master's in business while finishing out his football eligibility.) "What this means," Jones said, "is that some people work better when they don't know what's going to happen, and some don't work well unless they know exactly what's going to happen. I've known Jimmy Johnson for a long, long time, and he's fine as long as he knows exactly what the rules are. You tell him he has sixty players or he has thirty players and that's it, he'll accept it and go on. You tell him it's fourth and a foot with the score ten to seven in the seventh ball game of the season, and he'll take a calculated risk and go for it. But he and I operate in different worlds. He has his thumb on everybody in his world. He completely controls it. I can't control my world. I make deals that often require a high tolerance for ambiguity, and I've been making them since I was sixteen years old.

"We've got all these [unsigned player] negotiations coming up, and sometimes the worst thing you can do is set a deadline. Jimmy's going to get upset and impatient, and lots of fans aren't going to understand. But this is my world. I look down that list and I don't see an Emmitt or a Troy. If, God forbid, Michael Irvin gets thrown in jail and is lost for the year, that wouldn't in any way make us think about calling off the season. I'm not going to say, 'Michael, I love you, how much do you want?' There probably will be a salary cap and that could cost us a key player or two down the road. Look what happened with [defensive tackle] Danny Noonan last camp. We let the coaches convince us they just absolutely couldn't live without Noonan and to give him what he wanted. Now we're hearing, 'You're paying a backup that much?' Now people won't trade for Noonan [who had lost his job to Russell Maryland] because of that salary."

Jones grinned. "Jimmy's in the right job, and so am I. If we switched, it wouldn't work."

On Draft Day, Jones tried to explain, their worlds orbit instead of colliding. Meaning that Jones balances Johnson's calculated risks by occasionally encouraging a gut-level plunge? A quick aside from college-scouting director Lacewell, who's known around football for his cocktail-hour storytelling: "Listen, I can bullshit with the best of 'em, and I find myself just sitting there, fascinated, listening to Jerry. He is completely unflappable. He can talk you into or out of anything. And it's amazing how right he can be about what's going to happen. It's amazing to watch his mind work—it's here, then here, then here"—Lacewell points to different spots on the ceiling. "Now, sometimes he'll start talking in circles and lose me. But I told him, 'They picked the wrong guy to be president.' I mean that. He is an amazing human being."

So who actually has the final say on Draft Day?

"Everybody misses a major point here," Jones said. "The decisions are being made jointly. Everybody jumped all over me about that 'jocks and socks' quote, but that's what happened." The night he bought the team, Jones told a news conference aired live on radio and TV that "my entire office and business will be at this complex. I intend to have an understanding of the complete situation, an understanding of the player situation, of the socks and jocks."

A jock-sniffer from Arkansas had just bought America's Team? "No," Jones said, "that wasn't it at all. People don't understand that the owners who cause problems are the ones who have very little idea what's really going on and storm in the locker room after the game and say, 'Why'd we run that play on fourth and one?' I know why we ran that play, and I'm quicker to say, 'Boy, that was a good idea that didn't work because so-and-so missed a block.' The more involved I am, the more likely I'll appreciate the way Jimmy wants to go in the draft. Jimmy has more input regarding the talent of the player, and I'm very careful not to constrain Jimmy's instinctive background. It's like, you have to let the players play, let their natural ability take over."

In other words, Jones would go along with Johnson on which cornerback to take. But Jones might rely on his own instincts on whether to trade dramatically up or down to take, say, a defensive lineman instead of a cornerback. This draft, Jones was also concerned about signability: Could he immediately make an oral agreement with a draftee's agent or would this rookie add another name to the dangerously long camp-holdout list?

"So I'll try to be very subtle in my influence," Jones said. "I'll give Jimmy this [a clinched fist] to encourage him if I like a trade that's been offered. Or maybe I'll give it this [a wince] if it doesn't quite make sense. I have the last word."

True, Johnson said before the draft. "But I can handle Jerry."

★ ★ ★

In Dallas, Johnson is a noted recluse. But the night before the draft Johnson and Nick Christin headed out to a hotel bar for beer— always Heineken over ice for Johnson—and nachos, Johnson's passion. "It was a feeding frenzy," said Johnson, who had been on a diet plan and dropped twenty-two pounds off his five-foot-ten frame, down to 197, in a competition with his assistants. As Johnson had walked out of a predraft press conference, he said, "Nobody asked me about my weight. That really pisses me off."

He sounded serious. Johnson reads nearly everything written about him and his team. In fact, Johnson's vacations never last more than a week at a time because reading his mail fascinates him and he doesn't want to get too far behind. Johnson is stung by "chubby" references or jokes about his hair. His hair he can control, but his weight is a roller-coaster ride. Through the season Johnson and several assistants would continue their think-tank jogs of about three miles several times a week, but his weight would rise steadily back to the 220 range. Stress will do that.

Yet, says Johnson, he always sleeps well before big games and Draft Days. "It's like in college when you know you're prepared for a test," Johnson says. "I'm completely prepared." While Landry relied almost solely on info provided by his scouts, Johnson rolls up his own sleeves. Not only does he read reports from assistants, doctors, trainers, strength coaches and all sorts of draft experts and bird dogs, as well as scouts, but by phone he "visits with" lots of college coaches he got to know coming up through the ranks. As a group, he and some of his assistants fly in Jones's jet to view firsthand the top prospects at schools that have several. Johnson's recall of information about every player on the board is mind-boggling. Johnson is a huge football fan. His life would probably be dominated by following football even if he weren't coaching. He is a draftnik with rare instincts—his own best scout.

Johnson says, "The biggest question you have to answer is simply, 'Can the guy play or not?' But I also think it's important for me personally to get a feel for the player himself: his style of play; how he would fit into the chemistry; his character; is he hungry to be the best he can be, or is he satisfied?"

Jones spent Saturday night before the draft at home, reading up on prospects, cramming. Though he's the life of constant parties and functions, Jones said, "I can't socialize the night before the draft. I would have been useless." He rarely sleeps much, maybe five hours a night. But before big games and the draft, Jones barely sleeps at all. He eats on the run, nibbling here and there. He rarely exercises. At five foot eleven he has no weight problems. But since the JJs took over the Cowboys, Jones has aged considerably quicker than Johnson.

Early Sunday, Draft Day, the JJs met to finalize their plan of attack. Then they shocked the world by not shocking it. A Redskin insider says, "Since we had won the Super Bowl and had two picks in the first round [Nos. 6 and 28], we figured Jimmy would shoot the moon trying to trade up ahead of us [Dallas had Nos. 13 and 24]. He surprised a lot of people when he didn't."

Johnson had identified Pitt defensive lineman Sean Gilbert as the best player in the draft. "He'll be a dominating player," Johnson said. Johnson assumed correctly that Indianapolis, with the draft's first two picks, would take Steve Emtman and Quentin Coryatt. So the Cowboys approached the Rams about trading up for the No. 3 pick—and Gilbert. "The price was just too steep," said Jones, who indicated he served as a governor on Johnson's emotions. The Rams indicated the No. 3 pick would cost the first of the Cowboys' first-rounders (No. 13) plus a starter, probably Michael Irvin, who had led the NFL in receiving yards and been MVP of the Pro Bowl. The JJs didn't pursue it.

Jones: "I said, 'If we sell the house for Gilbert, we're going to prevent ourselves from seeing what we have with all our good young linemen—Leon Lett, Tony Hill, Chad Hennings.' "

So Johnson refocused on need. "Sure, I liked Gilbert a lot," Johnson said. "But what good would he have done when Detroit was throwing five-yard outs up and down the field? [Lion quarterback Erik Kramer had completed 29 of 38 passes for 341 yards and 3 touchdowns in the play-off loss.] We needed people who can cover. The key to winning a Super Bowl will be how quickly our secondary solidifies itself."

Of the draft's cornerbacks, Johnson ranked Florida State's Terrell Buckley slightly above Texas A&M's Kevin Smith, and Smith slightly above Wisconsin's Troy Vincent. Gunning for Buckley, Johnson made a run at Cincinnati, which had the No. 4 pick. But Cincinnati chose instead to take Washington's second first-round pick (No. 28) to move down two spots, to No. 6. Washington took Heisman Trophy winner Desmond Howard at No. 4, and Green Bay snatched Buckley at 5. Vincent went seventh, to Miami. "I had told Terrell we'd take him if it fell right," said Johnson. Jones, in fact, had a Cowboy representative at Buckley's home ready to negotiate with him. "But the only long shot," Johnson said, "was for Terrell to fall to eight and us make a deal with Sam [New England GM Jankovich, who had been Johnson's athletic director at the University of Miami]."

Now Johnson, Jones, McCoy, and personnel man Bob Ackles were working the phones as if it were a telethon. "We've been criticized by some people for not better utilizing the Herschel Walker picks," said Jones. For getting too cute. For trading more to enhance their reputation than their team. Some of the Herschel haul (three first-rounders, three seconds, and two thirds from Minnesota) had been squandered in trades for Daniel Stubbs, Terrence Flagler, and Alonzo Highsmith, while others had produced Emmitt Smith, Russell Maryland, and were about to produce defensive backs Kevin Smith, Darren Woodson, and Clayton Holmes.

"But," said Jones, "people don't realize how much the Walker trade did for our reputation as people willing to deal, people with enough picks to gamble and maybe make some mistakes. People know we're always open for business."

Of the many offers flying back and forth, Jankovich tossed out the most intriguing. He wanted to move from 19 in the first round to 13, where the Cowboys sat, in exchange for the ninth pick in the second round. Jones loved it. Johnson wanted Kevin Smith but figured he'd still be available at 19.

Done deal. "That," said Jones, smiling hugely, "was when it got real dicey. This is where Jimmy likes a calculated risk, while I'm in the oil-and-gas business, which can be dangerous. Of course, we would have been sick if someone else had taken Kevin."

Johnson got that sinking feeling a moment after the Raiders took defensive lineman Chester McGlockten at 16. Next up: Atlanta. Then San Francisco, then Dallas. Johnson's information was that San Francisco wanted a defensive back, probably University of Washington safety Dana Hall. But what if the 49ers snatched Smith? Get Atlanta on the phone! The Falcons, who wanted running back Tony Smith, were willing to switch places, from 17 to 19, for a fourth-rounder. Johnson insisted the Falcons throw in their fifth-rounder. Done deal. Clock ticking. Dallas, from Atlanta, takes Kevin Smith.

ESPN live shot: high fives around the huge table at Valley Ranch.

"The gamble paid off," Jones said. "We got our extra second-round pick."

Yet didn't the gamble pay off literally, too? Did Jones want to take Smith four slots later so he could pay him No. 17 money and save around $500,000? Jones insists he offered Smith the same contract he would have had at No. 13—four years, $3.165 million. Still, at 13 New England took tackle Eugene Chung, who received a reported $3.9 million over four years.

At No. 24 the JJs took East Carolina middle linebacker Robert Jones. Dave Wannstedt had personally sized up the 236-pound Jones and felt strongly that he could start as a rookie. "Great work ethic and speed," Wannstedt said. "He'll make plays on the corners that Jack [Del Rio] just didn't have the speed to make."

In the second round, the Cowboys couldn't help but take Jackson State receiver Jimmy Smith. He wasn't a priority, but he had

slid out of the first round. "An Emmitt deal," said Johnson, refer-
ring to the franchise-making move he made in the '90 draft from 21
to 17 to pick off a falling Emmitt Smith. "People said he didn't have
NFL speed," Johnson said. "All I knew was that he always had
been and would be a producer."

But former Cowboy personnel director Wooten says he and other
NFL scouts tire of Cowboy gloating over the Smith pick. "Oh, I
can gloat with the best of 'em," says Johnson. Yet Wooten says,
"Jimmy had tried to move up to get defensive help. He had his
heart set on it, but nothing had clicked. But the week before the
draft, I had made a tentative deal with Pittsburgh to move up to
seventeen for a third [round pick]. When [it was Pittsburgh's turn],
Atlanta called Pittsburgh and offered a second-round pick to move
up, but the Steelers stuck by their word. If they hadn't, Emmitt
would be a Falcon. I think the world of Jimmy, but it amuses me
to hear about how Jimmy had all this foresight because [scout] Walt
Yowarsky was the one going nuts telling Jimmy to take Emmitt. I
was there. I saw it. And what if I hadn't made that call? Who's
going to make that call now?"

Jones? The owner/GM did make several more system-beating
calls on Draft Day. Over the phone, with the clock ticking, he
made tentative contractual agreements with the top five Cowboy
picks. The JJs had helped start this trend the draft before, when
they traded up for the first pick in the draft, then used it on Russell
Maryland, regarded as maybe the eighth or tenth best player. Yet
Maryland agreed to take a down-the-line salary and sign immediately. In 1990, Emmitt Smith had held out and missed all of training camp. Not Maryland. Not the top five '92 draftees.

"I told each one of them we were fully prepared to take someone
else if we couldn't agree," Jones said, then winked. "But I liked my
odds with [Kevin] Smith and [Robert] Jones because we knew they
both had grown up big Cowboy fans. So fundamentally," Jones
said, using one of his favorite words—one Johnson uses when doing
Jones impressions—"we had our top five signed and ready for
minicamps on Draft Day, which is basically unheard of. Do you
realize how much farther ahead our rookies will be?"

Yes, Jones had what he hoped would be the Cowboy equivalent
of the 49ers' 1981 draft, when rookies Ronnie Lott, Eric Wright,
and Carlton Williamson started in the secondary for the first 49er

Super Bowl champ. Could Smith replace hot-and-cold cornerback Ike Holt, the last of the five veterans who also came in the Walker trade? Could Jones quickly make critics forget Del Rio? And was that extra second-round pick worth the gamble of losing Smith? It was used on Arizona State linebacker-safety Darren Woodson.

Several rival scouts scoffed that Woodson was no better than a fourth- or fifth-rounder, a classic Cowboy reach, a guy with size (6-2, 218 pounds) and speed (on grass the Cowboys clocked him in 4.3 seconds for the 40-yard dash) who hadn't proven in college he could be a consistent contributor. Cowboy scouts disagreed vehemently on Woodson. Johnson followed his instincts—"on tapes he was just so physical, which is so important in the NFC East"—but didn't seem cocksure about Woodson.

Naturally, several teams called the league office to complain about Jones's signing tactics. Yet the NFL allows signability discussions before a player is drafted, as long as a specific offer isn't made. The NFL investigated; no action was taken. "We know the rules," said personnel director Ackles. "We're fine."

Jones was. Ackles soon wouldn't be.

★ ★ ★

Bobby Ackles was a Jimmy Johnson favorite, a quiet little man who works hard. Ackles was well known and well liked around the NFL and by the Dallas–Fort Worth media. Ackles worked the phones for Johnson, kept him apprised of NFL gossip (another Johnson passion), did groundwork contract negotiating, and took care of the endless administrative details with which Jones and son Stephen hadn't yet concerned themselves. Ackles had been hired by Schramm in 1986 to share duties with draft architect Gil Brandt and try to improve the Cowboys' trading relationship with the many teams that were sick of Cowboy gloating over "steals." Ackles came to Dallas from the Canadian Football League's B.C. Lions, where he had worked his way up from equipment manager to general manager.

But Ackles was doing a job that Jones and son eventually wanted to share, and he was making too much money ($128,000) for Jones's budget. Jones, in fact, told Ackles to casually begin looking for another job.

Yet Ackles says that when the CFL called in January of 1992 to interview him for its commissioner's vacancy, Jones said, "Check it out. Wouldn't it be a feather in our cap if you were offered the job and could turn it down to stay with the Cowboys?" Then, said Ackles, just before the draft Jones told him, "I'm going to fire Dick Mansperger [the director of college scouting, soon replaced by Lacewell]. I want you to take over college scouting."

The only tension between him and Jones, said Ackles, came after Ackles asked Jones for a play-off bonus in January. "We were the only team in the play-offs that didn't give its scouts a bonus," said Ackles. "But he said he'd give me one. Later, when I mentioned it to him again, he said something like, 'Knowing how I felt about play-off bonuses, you're holding me to it?' If he tells you you're going to get it, shouldn't you get it?"

Ackles received a $16,000 bonus. Then, the day Lacewell was hired, May 21, Jones called Ackles into his office to talk about Ackles's new duties. "At first," said Ackles, "he was talking about how much the Cowboys needed me. Then we got into reorganization of duties, he got very heated, and all of a sudden he said, 'You're out of here. You've got thirty days, and in fact, I want you out of your office by the end of the day.' I was stunned."

Ackles soon landed in Phoenix as college scouting director of the Cardinals.

An NFL insider in constant touch with GMs and coaches said Johnson privately was upset over the Ackles firing, though Johnson knew it was coming. The insider said, "People like Ackles, Mansperger, and Wooten had a lot to do with the rebuilding of the Cowboys, even if they weren't from Arkansas. Ackles and Jimmy had one of the best relationships of personnel guy and coach in the league. This is a move by Jerry to take a little more power from Jimmy. I hope Jerry's learned a lot from his lunches with Al Davis and his dinners with Don Shula because he's the only guy now."

Once more, Jones was barbecued by several columnists for the Ackles axing. In *USA Today*, pro football writer Gordon Forbes wrote, "Pro football always has been a cold, cruel business. But the Dallas Cowboys can claim the undisputed title of heavy-handed champions." Jones shifted quickly into damage control, calling several key media members to better explain his side of the story. Jones said, "Bob was in a 'looking for a job' mode and all of a sudden he wanted a bonus he said I'd promised and that I couldn't remember. As other people in the office said, Bob was the only one shocked by what happened. Now that I'm working directly with Stephen on contracts, it will be much more effective. After all, it's Stephen's money, too."

Before leaving town, on June 12, Ackles sat in the den of his Valley Ranch home and issued a warning: "I don't want this to sound like sour grapes. But what Jerry doesn't understand is that as GM he has to do everything in his power to make his coach successful. He's got a winner in Jimmy. But Jerry, because of his ego, thinks he can be Al Davis and he can't be. You can't buy forty years of experience. You sit down behind a projector and earn it. This is one business you can't just walk in and do all the things you think you can do. Jerry thinks that if Jimmy were gone tomorrow, he could actually step on the field and do it [coach], and he can't. Jimmy and his staff are very, very bright—very good teachers. Only one thing will stop them. One man. One huge ego."

Yet though many inside and outside the organization probably agreed with Ackles, Jones soon brought an honor to the Cowboys that only Hall of Famer Schramm before him had received. The *Dallas Morning News* story began, "The NFL may question the business tactics of Cowboys owner Jerry Jones, but it no longer questions his football qualifications." Commissioner Paul Tagliabue had named Jones to the prestigious competition committee, which recommends rules changes.

"It's a real compliment," Jones said in an interview for this book, "because I was told [by Tagliabue], 'You have a unique understanding of football. You have played it, you are a general manager, and you are a totally committed owner.' He said that's what the committee lost when it lost Paul Brown [the legendary coach and owner who died in 1990]. They needed an owner who played."

Yes, Jones was a starter at guard for a national championship team. "Oh, no, he wasn't a bad player," Johnson said. "About like me, an overachiever." Johnson obviously was a little better; he made some all-conference teams as a quick, wily defensive lineman nicknamed Jimmy Jumpup because he bounced up so quickly when knocked down. Jones, said Johnson, was "a small, quick guard who could run pretty well and tried hard."

Yet for all his ego, Jones rarely if ever mentions his playing days in interviews. He probably was as successful a player as any Cowboy assistant, not one of whom made it in pro football. Yet Cowboy coaches generally regarded Jones the way they would some overzealous fan who doesn't quite grasp what really goes on in football and can't quite speak locker-room lingo. Jones can't seem to shake the image of the rich rube. He still occasionally calls Wannstedt "Winestedt" and Michael Irvin "Irving." Front-office staffers still whisper about him as if they're Mr. Drysdales and Jane Hathaways and he's Jethro Jones, liable to get excited and do or say anything. When "Jerry strikes again," some staffers whistle "The Beverly Hillbillies" theme song.

While other GMs criticized Jones for not spending more time, as GM, around the players, fans would have ridiculed him if he had started hanging out in the locker room. After his opening "socks and jocks" speech, the fear among fans was that Jones had bought the Cowboys merely to rub egos with them. That didn't happen. Jones is friendly with players but keeps his distance. He has to maintain objectivity in negotiating contracts with them.

"I know what I'm doing," Jones said. Ackles believed Jones's ego dictates too many decisions. "I should have known I was doomed one day at the NFL meetings when I walked up and Jerry was talking to [NBC's] Will McDonough, who said [of Ackles to Jones], 'Well, here's the brains behind the Cowboys.'

"Listen, Jimmy's very volatile. I won't be surprised if he just gets up and walks out. The morale over there is awful—lots of people haven't had a raise since Jerry took over. Jimmy's very loyal to his coaches, but I don't think that would stop him from quitting if Jerry pushes him too far. They started clashing last training camp and it was uneasy all year. It will be interesting to see how long it lasts."

Twice Blessed

SOMETHING WAS GOING ON WITH TROY KENNETH AIKMAN, SOMEthing significant. It was early July in Dallas and he had plenty of reasons to overheat the ways cars and drivers did in Central Expressway traffic. His backup, Steve Beuerlein, had proven he could start for at least half the NFL's teams. While Aikman was hurt, Beuerlein's fan bandwagon had rolled through six straight wins in December and January. Jimmy Johnson proclaimed the job was again Aikman's to lose, but how quickly would he lose it if he started cold in September against Washington in the Monday-night opener and against the Giants six days later in the Meadowlands?

Assistant coaches were a little nervous about the potential season-wrecking quarterback controversy. Yet for the first time in his pro career, Aikman appeared almost serenely confident. "Troy is different," Johnson said. "Several people in the organization have mentioned that he seems more at peace than ever with everything." With camp just a week away, Johnson talked about "the

41

new Troy" every chance he got on TV, radio, and in the newspapers. Johnson seemed to be on a media campaign to convince everyone—especially Troy—that Aikman was different this year.

It was working.

"I feel much better about things than I ever have," Aikman said. "I'm now to the point where I'm comfortable with everyone in the entire organization, and that means a lot to me."

Just five months earlier, Aikman's faith in the JJs had been cracked again. Before the play-off games against the Bears and Lions, Aikman believed his injured knee was sufficiently healed to play. It was his job, his team, his city—and Dallas had gone crazy over the Cowboys' first play-off appearance since 1985. But Johnson told Aikman he didn't want to risk getting the knee hurt again. Aikman had little reason to trust that reasoning; Johnson had third-degree-burned him when he took quarterback Steve Walsh—*his* quarterback, from the University of Miami—in the '89 supplemental draft. Aikman suspected Johnson was sticking with Beuerlein for the same reasons he had an affinity for Walsh: dynamic leadership, ability to improvise, born winner. Beuerlein's hot hand also had something to do with Johnson's decision.

Whatever, Aikman was not happy with Johnson. "That really hurt," Aikman said. He moped on the sideline.

What happened next hurt Aikman as much as not playing. Aikman deeply values friendship, and assistant equipment man Jerry Fowler was a good buddy. Jones, through Johnson, fired Fowler, who had been with the organization for twelve years and made about $40,000 a year. A sensible budget cut? Not to Aikman. "Troy," says Fowler, "was furious."

The JJs can set off Aikman the way Jones can set off Johnson.

Aikman is an unusual mix of city and country. He spent the first twelve years of his life in the Los Angeles suburb of Cerritos. Then his family moved to a ranch near Henryetta, Oklahoma, a town of about six thousand where he eventually starred for the Henryetta Hens. Aikman began his college career at the University of Oklahoma, in Norman, but broke his leg against Johnson's Miami team, lost his job, and transferred to UCLA, where he was Hollywood-hyped for the Heisman. He's an unusual hybrid: a snuff-dipping quarterback who enjoys working on his home computer and reading, a twenty-six-year-old who cherishes pickups and privacy but is used to traffic and attention, a countrified city boy.

But Troy's father, Kenneth, definitely raised a throwback, a raw-boned boy with Jack Armstrong values. You work until your hands bleed, you show no pain, you keep your feelings to yourself, you treat people the way you want them to treat you, you do what you say you're going to, you do anything for a friend. "My father," says Troy, "is a guy you wouldn't want to mess with." Before retiring in 1991 to move to a four-hundred-acre ranch outside Dallas, Ken Aikman laid pipe for a living. He laid about nine miles of character in Troy. "A 'Men Don't Cry' upbringing," says former Cowboy quarterback Babe Laufenberg, one of Aikman's closest friends.

Yet Aikman does have an L.A. streak, that softer, sensitive side that sometimes leads to California-style introspection. One thing his father didn't give Troy was an "I love you." Ken Aikman told the *Fort Worth Star-Telegram*, "It's a situation where he doesn't have to ask to find out how I feel. He already knows. He doesn't need to be reassured." Jimmy Johnson's attitude precisely. Yet Johnson found that Troy needed to be reassured.

Troy spent much of his life trying to please his father. Just once, Troy wanted his dad to tell him how proud he was of Troy. Just once: for turning out to be a pretty decent guy or a fairly good quarterback. Aikman's first love had been baseball, but he went out for football in the eighth grade because he could tell his father wanted him to. Men play football.

In Henryetta, Aikman came to value trust above everything, even winning. Earn his trust and he'll do just about anything for you. In 1989 the JJs earned it and took advantage of it, in Aikman's bitter view at the time. They had the first pick in their first NFL draft. They flew Aikman in, entertained and toasted him at an airport hotel, told him he was the man around whom they wanted to rebuild. Aikman could have balked at playing for what would amount to an expansion team; he could have told the JJs he wasn't interested in having years knocked off his NFL life behind what appeared to be a thin blue line. Perhaps he could have forced a trade. But he didn't.

He was charmed by two of the most charming salesmen in Dallas, the JJs. Charmed by a couple of snakes, Aikman thought just two months after the draft, when the JJs gave up their 1990 first-round pick to take Steve Walsh in the supplemental draft. Aikman wouldn't have been quite so threatened if Walsh hadn't played and won for Johnson and many Cowboy assistants at Miami. Walsh was part of the Hurricane family, a bond that lasts long after players and coaches leave the school.

To his disbelief, Aikman soon found himself splitting training-camp snaps fifty-fifty with his alter ego. The knocks on Aikman in college: a little slow-minded, too unemotional to lead, couldn't lift his team in big games, not much feel for throwing deep, injury-prone because of a linebacker's macho mentality. And here was Walsh, "Jimmy's guy," the heady leader and international-finance major with a nice passing touch and a knack for winning and avoiding injury. Aikman was the six-foot-four, 230-pound prototype pro: big arm, big body. But when Aikman was injured, Walsh started and won the only game the Cowboys won in '89, at Washington. Walsh didn't have Aikman's rifle or his quick, compact release. But Walsh threw a lot of intangibles at you.

Now, Jones takes the blame for the Walsh pick: "I got a little carried away and influenced Jimmy. I just thought Steve would be a great asset, and as it turned out, he was."

Yes, in September of 1990 the JJs traded Walsh to New Orleans for a first-round pick, a second, and a third. After Walsh wound up on the Saint bench, it was easier for the JJs to wink and grin over the trade. But in the weeks after it was made, Johnson occasionally went a little haywire and agonized over whether he had kept the wrong quarterback. The job was now Aikman's, with no more Walsh threat or distraction. Yet as the Cowboys lost five of their next seven to fall to 3-7 in November 1990, Aikman regressed. He seemed more confused and unsure than he had been as a rookie. Johnson began to lose faith in Aikman because Aikman appeared to be losing faith in himself.

The Cowboys had lost two straight games without scoring a touchdown. To locker-room confidants and to media friends, Aikman was blaming it on offensive coordinator David Shula and on a lack of support from the head coach. Johnson had hit him with two more low blows, said Aikman: he had agreed to hire a friend of Aikman's as strength coach, then hired someone else (current strength-coach Mike Woicik); and he hadn't made any attempt to keep quarterback coach Jerry Rhome after he was offered a better salary by Phoenix. Aikman had trusted Rhome, and ten games into the season he was wondering if Johnson wanted him to fail.

Much of this got back to Johnson, who doesn't believe in stroking and babying the guy who was supposed to be the leader of his football team. While many fans viewed Aikman as a young John Wayne, coaches saw a tough guy with a crystal psyche.

The losses sent Johnson's mood careening into the danger zone. It was then that he told some media people off camera that Aikman "was a loser in college and he'll never be anything but a loser in the pros." Johnson's feelings got back to Aikman, who was beyond being surprised by anything Johnson said or did.

As the Cowboys prepared for their next game, against the Rams in Anaheim, California, a close friend of Aikman's said, "The situation has really gotten ugly. Troy is the first to admit he's got brainlock during games. He barely gets the play called in the huddle before guys are saying, 'Oh, shit, that'll never work!' So Troy's not the only one complaining. But Troy feels ostracized by the coaches. They haven't given him any support publicly or privately, and sometimes he just needs someone to put an arm around him and tell him everything's going to be okay. Remember, he's just in his second year, and just because a lot of people see him as a macho stud, he can be very sensitive.

"Don't underestimate how much Rhome meant to Troy. At least when Troy did something wrong, he had someone on the sideline to talk to—someone who had played quarterback. Johnson didn't. Neither did David Shula. Troy has no rapport with either of them, and Shula's up in the press box. Troy says he learned more at UCLA than he's learned from Shula. He says the guys on offense just shake their heads over the 'high school' game plans."

Shula, who had played receiver at Dartmouth, sometimes shook his head over Troy's inability to grasp an offense that Miami quarterback Dan Marino could speed-read. Yet David, working on father Don's staff, had repeatedly clashed with Marino, too. David was a nice young man who couldn't forget—or let you forget—that he was a Shula. Aikman isn't comfortable around people who take themselves too seriously. Other assistants were also having problems with Shula's superiority complex; Johnson, they said, had been overly impressed with David because of his last name. Assistant Tony Wise said, "Jimmy met David one day in Miami and he said, 'I met David Shula!' " In 1989 Johnson had agreed to give David a fresh start in Dallas, away from his father, who wanted David to make a name for himself, and in return

Don gave Johnson permission to hire Dave Wannstedt off the Dolphin staff.

Yes, things had gotten ugly.

Aikman was even deeply affected by critical newspaper columns I had written about him. I respected Johnson's instincts for whether a player could make it big or not, and perhaps I was too influenced at the time by Johnson's heat-of-the-moment uncertainty about his quarterback. Aikman's close friend told me, "What you write just eats him up." I said, "But that's just what concerns me about him. He should be stronger than that. Who cares what I write?"

"That," said the friend, "is exactly what I tell him."

But that Sunday in Anaheim, I was able to write something positive, and Johnson took the first small step toward repairing his relationship with Aikman. On the opening series, Aikman threw an interception that the Rams soon cashed into a 7–0 lead. Johnson, for the first time, walked to the end of the bench, put a hand on Aikman's shoulder pad, and told him not to worry about it. Aikman rebounded to throw for 303 yards and 3 touchdowns. The Cowboys won, 24–21.

Watching that day from the Ram side of the field was an assistant named Norval Turner. Turner believes in luck. Most coaches do. (Johnson, however, has a hard time even saying the word. "You make your own luck by hard work," Johnson insists.)

What soon happened had something to do with luck. Johnson was about to make a move that would be essential to what would happen in 1992, though it was hardly the result of careful design.

The Cowboys ended 1990 ranked twenty-eighth and last in offensive production, prompting Johnson to make a tough, gutsy decision. Johnson invited the wrath of Don Shula by demoting David, who soon left for an assistant's job in Cincinnati. Johnson even had the audacity to offer his coordinator's job to Gary Stevens, who had worked for Johnson at Miami and was coaching Don Shula's offense. At the Senior Bowl college all-star game in Mobile, Stevens basically accepted the job. Jones sent his jet for Stevens, and the Cowboys scheduled a press conference to introduce him.

About that time, Don Shula arrived in Mobile and put the fear of, well, Shula in Stevens. Stevens told Cowboy assistants that Shula told him if he took the job to replace David, he (Don) would make sure Stevens would never get a head-coaching job in the

NFL. Stevens remained with the Dolphins, and Johnson had to scramble.

With Wannstedt's input, Johnson threw together a list of potential replacements. He pursued San Diego coordinator Ted Tollner, but the Chargers wouldn't let him out of his contract. Same with Kansas City coordinator Joe Pendry. Johnson brought in Minnesota coordinator Bob Schnelker for an interview but decided he wasn't a good fit. Tampa Bay assistant Richard Williamson was discussed but didn't seem quite right. Johnson had interest in Ram quarterback coach Dick Coury, but Coury suddenly took a job with New England.

Well, said Wannstedt, there's always Norv Turner. Wannstedt and Turner had worked together on the Southern Cal staff. Turner had called hoping to get an interview when Johnson hired David Shula.

In the Ram offense Turner actually was third in command under coordinator Ernie Zampese, who had reached "guru" status, and Coury. Turner coached receivers. Turner, thirty-nine, had been a coordinator at Southern Cal, but not in the NFL. Would Johnson, whose expertise is defense, entrust his offense to a guy who hadn't run one in the pros? At first he considered hiring Turner as quarterback coach and finding a coordinator, but Johnson talked to former San Diego quarterback Dan Fouts, who was a year ahead of quarterback Turner at the University of Oregon. Fouts raved about Turner's humble, low-key personality and the West Coast passing game he could teach Aikman. Johnson asked Fouts to call Aikman and tell him the same thing.

Turner flew in for an interview. Turner met Aikman, who says, "I knew from the first moment we'd really get along." Johnson liked what he saw and heard. Bang, Johnson hired Turner and told him, "It's your baby." One thing about Johnson: he delegates.

Turner turned out to be the perfect man for the job. "Twenty years from now," Aikman says, "I'll be saying Norv Turner was the best thing that happened to me in my career." So what if Stevens, Tollner, or Pendry had taken the job? Did those three fall through and Turner fall into place because Johnson works harder than most coaches? No luck involved?

None, insists Johnson: "I was looking for somebody who had played quarterback. Norv was the right guy."

Former Cowboy personnel director John Wooten calls Turner "a half-assed college quarterback, just like Paul Brown and Bill Walsh were. They have great minds, they have a great grasp of the quarterback position, but they weren't so talented that it all came easily and naturally. They can teach it."

Turner is Aikman's kind of guy: a burgers-and-beers guy. A guy who cusses with you, not at you. Turner takes his job, but not himself, seriously. He can make Aikman laugh with a wry, sometimes silly sense of humor that doesn't translate in print. From a distance, Turner comes across as a pretty boring guy. "I guess if I weren't coaching, I'd be teaching social studies somewhere," he says. His straight brown hair doesn't always get combed. He's usually the first coach in the office, often by five A.M., and sometimes doesn't get around to shaving. He looks a lot more comfortable in coaching sweats than in the coat and tie he wears to road games.

Turner, who has little in common with Johnson, brought more coaching substance than style to Aikman's life. No hair spray or manicures for Turner, no peacock ego. To Aikman, an ounce of pretension is worth a pound of manure. Turner is a devoted husband and father of three, and Aikman became his kid brother and blood brother. As a senior starter at Oregon, Turner had taken the sort of beating Aikman sustained in his rookie NFL season. He could empathize with Troy's feelings and insecurities.

Aikman could trust Turner because he wasn't one of "them." Assistants Wannstedt, Wise, Hubbard Alexander, Joe Brodsky, Butch Davis, and Dave Campo had been part of Johnson's "family" at Miami. Wannstedt and Wise jogged and occasionally drank beer with Johnson. Turner did not. Turner got along well with the staff; unlike David Shula, Turner was open to suggestions. But he kept a little distance, in part for Aikman's sake. "Troy is very easy to deal with if you're on his side," Turner says. "If you aren't, you have a problem."

Turner dedicated himself to putting Aikman in an offense that played to Aikman's untapped strengths—his release, velocity, and accuracy. "Awesome" strengths, said Turner, who's usually given to understatement and pessimism. It was almost as if Turner arrived at the Clampett mansion and discovered they had hung their Rembrandt in the garage.

"Norv's a realist and I'm a realist," Aikman says. "I'm an optimist, too. But I know what it's going to take to win a certain game. With Norv, if I have some concerns, I can say something. Others on the staff had taken it like a sign of weakness."

Turner brought the West Coast influences of Walsh, Zampese, and former San Diego coach Don Coryell to the Dallas offense. He shortened Aikman's drops and many of the receivers' routes. Turner installed seam-splitting patterns thrown on timing before receivers break. But mainly, Turner simplified everything. He wanted Aikman and Emmitt Smith and the receivers to master a fairly small number of plays and be able to run them perfectly, repeatedly.

The Cowboy offense went from twenty-eighth and last to ninth in '91, Turner's first season.

As camp approached in July of '92, Aikman said, "I can't tell you how comfortable I am in this offense now. This is the first time I've said this, but I finally believe this team has what it takes to win a Super Bowl. First, Mr. Jones is going to have to sign a lot of important guys. But if he does, we have a chance to do something really big."

Jones says he had encouraged Johnson to work at repairing his relationship with Aikman and making the quarterback believe the coach finally believed in him. Johnson had made it a '92 priority. Aikman says Johnson did have a long, casual talk with him just before camp opened. It was a start, says the quarterback. "We just said, 'Hey, let's put everything behind us.' "

Jones says, "I never had any doubt Troy had the skills to be a great quarterback, but a lot of quarterbacks have the skills and fail. What you have to do is almost will your quarterback's success. You create an atmosphere that makes him feel like he *will* be successful."

That had been a secret of the JJs' success so far: create a hyperpositive force field. Keep saying, "We will win," and sooner or later people around you believe it's happening.

Still, despite the "new Troy," Turner remained uneasy. "That's all well and good," he said. "But what you worry about is what happens if Troy has a bad game or a bad half. You can't play the position if you know there's always a hook. With all the expectations for this team, with all the pressure . . . Jimmy wants to get it done now, and I've learned a lot from that way of thinking. But you have to have a certain amount of patience."

★ ★ ★

Patience isn't a Jimmy Johnson virtue. He had actually started training camp in Dallas in June and early July, before the team left for its Austin campsite. Johnson proudly mentioned he didn't know of another NFL team that had as many minicamps and quarterback schools as the Cowboys—"voluntary mandatory," Johnson called them. Under NFL rules, many of these workouts can't be mandatory even for players with contracts. No signed Cowboy missed one without permission. Only one of twelve *unsigned* Cowboys missed a session—starting linebacker Ken Norton, Jr.

"He will pay," Johnson told the media. Johnson told a team meeting, "I do care that you guys get what you deserve. But my job is to fuckin' win football games, and I believe there's enough talent in this room to win, no matter what happens to you unsigned guys."

Johnson's engine was running hot because the Cowboy schedule had been released. Off '91 won-lost records of opponents, it fell slightly behind the New York Giants' schedule as the league's most difficult. The Giants would play eleven teams with a .500 or better '91 record; the Cowboys would play ten. Extended training-camp holdouts, Johnson told the media, would be "disastrous."

Thank goodness, insiders were saying, that Johnson still had Dave around to calm him down.

"Dave" was Dave Wannstedt, who was even more the soul of the Cowboy defense than Turner was of the offense. If players didn't quite trust the JJs, they believed without question in their two coordinators. Wannstedt basically was the soul of the entire team, for he was the only man who could tell Johnson to relax or back off. "Jimmy and I," said defensive coordinator Wannstedt, "have had some very, very intense times together."

Those times had nearly ended in January, when Wannstedt appeared to be the leading candidate to replace Pittsburgh Steeler coach Chuck Noll. Wannstedt was made for the job. "I'm just a Pittsburgh guy," says David Raymond Wannstedt, who grew up the oldest of six children just outside Pittsburgh in Baldwin, where his dad worked twenty-three years in the J&L steel mill. At Pitt,

Wannstedt was an offensive lineman who blocked for future Cowboy star Tony Dorsett. Wannstedt was drafted in the fifteenth round by Green Bay and spent one year on injured reserve before returning to Pitt as an assistant coach. A couple of years later, he seriously considered going into some sort of FBI or police work.

But Pitt's defensive coordinator, Jimmy Johnson, talked Wannstedt out of it. Wannstedt followed Johnson to Oklahoma State, left for Southern Cal ('83–85), then rejoined Johnson at Miami. Johnson taught Wannstedt a lot about defense, which became Wannstedt's passion. Wannstedt, thirty-nine in January of 1992, all but worshiped Pittsburgh's Steel Curtain defense of the mid-to-late seventies. On his office bulletin board he keeps the game-by-game results of the '75 and '76 Steelers; highlighted in blue are games in which the Steelers allowed no touchdowns—five in '75 and eight in '76. "My daily inspiration," he says.

It appeared Wannstedt would be for the Steelers what ex-Bear Mike Ditka had been for Chicago—a roaring good fit. Wannstedt is a more balanced and perhaps more benevolent Ditka. He is a yeller and a hugger, emotional but never irrational. At six foot five and about 230 pounds, with a tough guy's mustache and dark, combed-back hair, Wannstedt's physical presence commands respect from players. Wannstedt could play "ruggedly handsome" in a football movie. "He has great presence," says Wise, Wannstedt's best friend.

Yet there is nothing Hollywood about Wannstedt, nothing phony or pretentious. Huge confidence, no huge ego. Like Turner, Wannstedt values family above all. He has been married to his wife, Jan, since he was in college. They have two daughters.

"The key to our defense," said veteran Jim Jeffcoat, "is that guys play so hard for Dave because they love him so much. He's straight with guys. He may not tell them what they want to hear, but you know he's at least being honest. He's a motivator, a communicator, very positive. A lot of times he'll come up with something and it'll work because he loves it so much that he gets you to love it. When he becomes a head coach, if he can get all forty-seven guys to play as hard every week as our defense does, it will be scary."

Wannstedt says, "A lot of coaches have come from around Pittsburgh. Ditka. Schottenheimer. Knox. Bugel. Joe Walton. It's that blue-collar personality. You treat people honestly, you work your ass off, and you're tough. Nothing comes easy. You grind it out. You try to convince your guys how much more successful they can be if they just give everything they have. I watch a lot of film. I see a lot of teams not playing as hard as they could. Forget the talent; if you don't play hard, you'll have problems. I have been very, very fortunate with the guys we have. I know they get paid to do this. But they give me everything, and you don't always see that. We were heavily criticized when we came from Miami. People said that college rah-rah bullshit wouldn't work in the pros. Well, we've done an awful lot with rah-rah."

Initially, Steeler director of football operations Tom Donahoe sounded as if he were leading cheers for Wannstedt. So why did Pittsburgh president Dan Rooney cool on Wannstedt? Sources say he came on too strong in interviews, detailing the budget and manpower he had to have to win. Obviously, Johnson had taught him well. Perhaps Rooney preferred a coach he could more easily mold and control. The Steelers surprised the NFL by opting for thirty-four-year-old Bill Cowher. The main reasons given: Cowher had seven years NFL experience (under Marty Schottenheimer at Cleveland and Kansas City) to Wannstedt's three, and Cowher knew Pittsburgh's division, the AFC Central, from his days as a player and coach in Cleveland.

Whatever, the Cowboys had again been blessed. Without Wannstedt, who would have taken offensive-line coach Wise with him, it would have been very difficult for the Cowboys to do what they did in '92–93.

God's will, Wannstedt called Pittsburgh's decision. As training camp approached, Wannstedt had rededicated himself to his faith. A Catholic, Wannstedt said, "I would hope I'd get another opportunity to be a head coach, and I want to prepare for it. You look at the great ones—Noll, Shula, Landry, Gibbs—and they're like this." He moves his hand along a straight, steady line. "No matter what happens—losing, criticism, whatever—you've got to have the balance that your faith provides. There is just so much out of your control. An injury or two and you go six and ten. And if you win, you can go the other way and turn into an egomaniac. Do you realize Chuck Noll has no memorabilia or awards on his office wall or at his home? You wouldn't even know he's a coach. With Shula, the meetings never start until he comes back from mass. So to me, how many games I eventually win won't mean a thing in the long run. What will count will be how much good I can do—how many lives I can touch for the better."

A fascinating contrast, Johnson and the man he called his best friend, Wannstedt. Insiders called Wannstedt Johnson's conscience.

Wannstedt said, "Friends of mine were really upset I didn't get the Pittsburgh job—it just seemed so right—but I went to church and prayed about it. I realized it just wasn't meant to be. Maybe this is meant to be."

This: one more year in Dallas with a defense longer on work ethic and emotion than first-round talent. No, Tom Landry's Flex didn't live here anymore. Though both are 4-3 alignments—four linemen, three linebackers—Wannstedt's defense is the flip of the Flex. No stars, no mystique. Says Dick Nolan, who helped Landry perfect the Flex, then coached defensive backs for Wannstedt in '89, "The Flex was step and read. This is read on the run." Shade and shoot gaps instead of controlling them. Speed. Quickness. Ends crashing upfield, linebackers gang-tackling, safeties playing like linebackers.

"What Dave is so good at," says Nolan, "is putting the right guy in the right place and making him understand exactly what has to be done to beat an opponent. They respond to Dave because they believe what he's telling them."

And Wannstedt had been telling his unsigned guys to hit the weight room. "It's truly amazing," Wannstedt said. "Signed, unsigned, they're all out here every day busting their ass in the weight room. You are not going to see anything like this in the NFL. They're getting the feeling they can be part of something great here."

Time out. A Jimmy Johnson team built on character and work ethic? Wasn't this the same casino king who coached the "Miami Vice" Hurricanes? As Johnson's 'Canes were introduced at the Orange Bowl, didn't they run through fake smoke? Didn't they wear army fatigues to an official function before the Fiesta Bowl? Didn't they invent trash-talking? Shouldn't their media-guide photos have been police mugshots?

Heaving a sigh, Johnson says, "People are going to see what they want to see. But the truth was, those Miami teams were built around very high character people. You don't think Russell Maryland is a quality person? Alfredo Roberts? Michael Irvin? No player on this team works harder than Michael Irvin. Think of the other players we had at Miami: Jerome Brown. Steve Walsh. On and on. Those were not 'renegade' teams. And this team—you haven't picked up the paper and read about one of our players being involved in an incident in the four years I've been here."

Jerry Jones on the fake smoke and fatigues: "If Jimmy had those to do over, I guarantee you he'd have taken the right fork instead of the left." Yes, images were formed that will haunt Johnson no matter what he accomplishes now. Johnson is an unpredictable mix of good and evil, vanity and humility, discipline and indulgence. Asked if he is religious, Johnson snaps, "I'm religious in my own way."

Johnson would need Wannstedt in '92.

What Wannstedt would need was a pass rusher.

He said of his defense that ranked twenty-sixth in sacks in '91, "We don't have that Charles Mann, Reggie White, Lawrence Taylor—that one guy who can get you the key sack when you need it. If you want to talk Super Bowl, you're going to have to find that guy during camp."

And if you don't?

"You pray," he said, and smiled.

Of Christians and Lionfish

St. Edward's University is hidden off I-35 in a wooded neighborhood just south of downtown Austin and the adjacent University of Texas campus. It's difficult to tell whether UT is in Austin or Austin is in UT; the campus seems that huge, its skyline that imposing. From nearby I-35, Memorial Stadium looks as if it would seat one hundred thousand on one side alone. The Erwin Center, also known as the Super Drum, looks more like a domed stadium than a basketball arena. The LBJ Library looks as if it could hold all the books Stephen King ever sold. "The University," as Texas Exes call it, seems to be a Stephen King world in which students could get lost and never be found.

Locals say that until three years ago, many Austinites didn't know St. Edward's existed. If they did, they weren't sure of its location. For what it's worth, it sits atop the highest point in Austin and has a Main Building, erected in 1888, that is a Texas historical landmark. But it took Jerry Jones of Little Rock, Arkansas, to put St. Ed's on the national map.

After one summer in Thousand Oaks, California, where the Cowboys had trained since 1963, Jones made a deal with the fathers of St. Edward's and the city fathers of Austin to move camp to the capital of Texas and its fourth-largest city. Made a heck of a deal, Jones did, cutting a half million bucks off what the old Cowboys had spent to spend a month or so in the paradise found around California Lutheran University. Though St. Ed's has a quaint little liberal arts campus, its location is anything but paradise.

South Austin is known somewhat derisively as Bubbaville; St. Ed's is surrounded by Ortegon Auto Body Repair, Cowtown Boots, El Gallo restaurant, and several motels that players wouldn't choose, unless maybe it was for an hour. Mostly, though, St. Ed's is surrounded in July and August by heat and humidity. That, for Jones and Jimmy Johnson, was a primary feature. Johnson especially believes in putting his teams in a 100-degree oven for a month.

Jones was more interested in the fact that about 70 percent of the state's population is located within 200 miles of Austin. Dallas is 200 miles to the north, Houston about 150 east southeast, and San Antonio just 75 miles to the southwest. Though Johnson balked at first, Jones put out the word that any and all Cowboy fans were welcome to watch camp practices, free of charge.

They overrun St. Ed's each morning and afternoon, sometimes five thousand strong, pressing up against waist-high chain-link fences covered with ads sold by the Cowboys, and fighting for the few seats in the bleachers on one side of the two practice fields. Players drive cars or golf carts the quarter mile from the locker room to the Spartan dorms and chow hall, mostly to avoid shrieking swarms of autograph seekers. Before and after workouts, Cowboy crazies mass along the fences of Autograph Alley, the walkway from the field to the locker room. Above the frantic hero worship looms the Main Building, a humbling Gothic-revival edifice of buffed white turrets and spires, but nobody ever seems to notice.

All but looming above the Main Building is Jerry Jones, whose presence often dominates camp. He's everywhere, wearing Cowboy ballcap, Cowboy shirt, and Cowboy shorts, blowing and going in his golf cart, conferring with Johnson along the sideline, negotiating with player agents via portable phone, signing autographs and doing interviews by the thousand, it seems. "Moving camp to

Austin was absolutely brilliant," says PR director Rich Dalrymple. As camp officially got rolling with the annual Blue-White intrasquad scrimmage on Sunday, July 19, 130 media people had already swarmed and about 350 would cover camp over the next month.

Dallas–Fort Worth was represented by four television stations, five radio stations, and eleven newspaper reporters. Those numbers would swell. Three Austin TV stations were on the scene, as well as three from San Antonio and one each from Wichita Falls, Waco, Abilene, Tyler, Lufkin, Nacogdoches, Tulsa (Okla.), and of course Little Rock. Just about every little town in Texas with a newspaper had sent or would send a reporter, and Jones would attempt to accommodate them all. The NFL's unwritten rule was that owners should be seen—on Sundays, from a distance—but not heard. But Jones had made himself as accessible to the media on a daily basis as perhaps any owner, GM, coach, or player in sports.

"If any of you couldn't be with us in California, that's why we're here," Jones told an opening media conference. Privately, he said, "Some people say I have an ego, and to an extent I do, but this is all a part of building equity in the club I paid all that money for. Do you realize the magnitude of the people you can reach every day from this one building?" He pointed to the media building, from which four sports talk shows a night would originate. "I hear, 'He never met an interview he didn't like.' But believe me, Tex Schramm never met one he didn't like, either. It's what this business is all about." It's free advertising. It's selling tickets and Cowboy merchandise and commercials in Cowboy TV and radio programming by creating a Cowboy consciousness. It's bombarding people's senses with Cowboys, Cowboys, Cowboys, until they cannot wait to attend or watch the first of five Cowboy exhibition games.

At least, that's how Jones was redefining the position of NFL owner/GM. In sarcastic asides to writers, Johnson occasionally compared the ad-covered fences with those of a minor-league baseball park. Still, "Jerry didn't get rich being dumb," Johnson said.

Jones said, "We want to do even better in this area [PR] than Tex did, and he was the master. We want our players exposed to this kind of media coverage so they'll be thoroughly prepared for playoff games and Super Bowls. We want to build so much excitement among our fans that it helps lift the players to another level. Don't you think you'd practice just a little harder if five thousand people are watching you every day?"

Jones excused himself to do a firing line of TV interviews along the edge of the field. It seemed almost surreal: The Man Who Fired Tom Landry had returned a conquering hero to the scene of the crime.

★ ★ ★

In the late afternoon of February 25, 1989, at the urging of Schramm, new owner Jones flew with Schramm to Austin to explain everything to Landry. Landry had starred at the University of Texas and has a home on a golf course just outside town. Those who have studied the events leading up to February 25 know that Jones did not bungle the firing of Landry; former Cowboy owner H. R. "Bum" Bright purposely let Landry twist in the winds of change. Bright said Landry "never gave me the time of day." Bright was disenchanted with Landry's last three records—7-9, 7-8, 3-13. Bright said he told Schramm to fire Landry in '87, but that Schramm quietly gave Landry a three-year contract, the last season worth $1 million. One reason Bright was intrigued by Jones—one of a dozen or so potential buyers—was that Jones made it clear from the start that he didn't want to risk such an enormous investment unless he could start fresh with Jimmy Johnson as his coach. Most other buyers wanted to go forward with Landry and Schramm.

Ironically, Johnson had been Schramm's top choice as a replacement for Landry—if Schramm could ever have worked up the courage to retire his business partner and image-gilding icon of twenty-nine years. Instead, Schramm talked Jones, who didn't know public relations from Puerto Rico, into accompanying him to the golf course where Landry was playing that Saturday. Only that morning had the deal been finalized. Only then was the team Jones's responsibility. But a "done deal" story had been aired three nights earlier by KXAS-TV, and Jones and Johnson had been photographed the night before at a Mexican restaurant in Dallas that they later learned was a Landry favorite. Johnson had flown in only to assure prospective minority investor Ed Smith that he would indeed coach the Cowboys if Jones and Smith closed the deal. But that picture, which appeared in the next day's *Dallas Morning News,* was worth a thousand curse words: it appeared to thousands of Landry fans that Jones and Johnson were celebrating Landry's impending demise at his favorite restaurant.

Jones, who had seldom dealt with reporters, stumbled headlong into a PR disaster. After closing the deal, if he had gone home to Little Rock and let emotions cool for a week or so, maybe the onus of firing Landry would have fallen more on Schramm and Bright. But Jones says he was following his Do-Right Rule: "I thought the right thing to do was go with Tex and tell Coach Landry how much I admired him and exactly why I wanted to go forward with Jimmy." Jones had also agreed to pick up the $1 million Landry's contract called for in '89.

Landry didn't appear to appreciate the gesture. To this day, he wants nothing to do with Jones. That night at Jones's introductory news conference in Dallas, few people seemed to be listening when Bright said, "What we have here is a new generation, someone with the competence and intelligence to help make the Cowboys what they once were."

What fans saw and heard, in a news conference that Schramm turned into a wake for Landry, was a typically exuberant Jones say Johnson would prove to be worth five Heisman Trophy winners and five first-round choices. Of that prediction, Randy Galloway of *The Dallas Morning News* wrote, "Jerry, you have so, so much to learn."

He did, though not about Johnson's value. Jethro Jones continued to put his foot in his mouth. He soon praised the Cowboy Cheerleaders—the safe-sex goddesses—by calling them the "pick of the litter." Right idea; wrong phrase. He said Troy Aikman wasn't just one of those rawboned quarterbacks who "looks good in the shower." That's an old coach's expression meaning, "The guy has the talent to match his physique." But Jones was now the owner of the Dallas Cowboys, and Cowboys owners weren't supposed to use such colorful or off-color phrases. The more Jones spoke in public, the more messes he made.

His team didn't fare any better. From Thousand Oaks to a thousand 1-15 jokes. A sample: Jerry Jones recently went to a black-tie function with only one shoe on. Someone said, "Jerry, you lost a shoe." Jerry said, "No, I found one." Or: Jerry Jones removed all the No Shirts, No Shoes, No Service signs at Texas Stadium so his relatives from Arkansas could come to games. Or: Jerry Jones is buying Southland Corp. and is changing the names of its convenience stores to 0-and-Eleven.

On the darker side, Jones received what he interpreted as a death threat from a group of religious zealots and Landry worshipers. A Dallas psychiatrist said a number of his patients were having nightmares about Jones. There were even a few sick Lee Jerry Oswald jokes. Jones had rocked Dallas to its foundation. He hadn't just replaced one football coach with another; Landry had become so much more than one of history's most successful football coaches. To millions of fans he was godlike. He was the ultimate role model: a Christian war-hero father figure who spoke all over the world for the Billy Graham Crusade. For years Dallas had hung its hat, image-wise, on the Man in the Hat.

And now Jones had come along, without apparent remorse or reverence, and tossed God's Coach out with the trash. He had torn down the religious institution known as America's Team. In its place was a 1-15 eyesore that might as well have been spray-painted Arkansas red and white.

The '89 season ended with a home loss on December 24 to Green Bay during which the stadium toilets froze.

But Jones wouldn't quit telling anyone who would listen that the Cowboys would soon be back on top where they belong. He wouldn't quit shaking hands, doing interviews, admitting when he was wrong, promising to do it right, turning the other cheek. Later, one of his harshest critics, Frank Luksa of *The Dallas Morning News,* wrote, "Pummeled in print—especially in my space—Jones never reacted with heat. Just the opposite. The worse I wrote of him, the kinder his response."

In '89, Jones hired a PR coach, a woman who was eventually hired to help players and coaches with other NFL teams. He was going to learn to win the interview game of think-fast. He relished subjecting himself to the most difficult interrogations, the live-TV questions asked by sportscasters who viewed him as The Jethro Who Fired Tom Landry. Within a year Jones could handle himself with the best of 'em, including Schramm. If he chose, he could be outspoken without being outrageous. Or he could turn tough questions into evangelical messages about how everything was being done in the best interest of "our fans."

PR became Jones's strength.

"Dad has a lot more upstairs than most people think," says son Stephen. "Or than he wants them to think. But what people don't understand about him is that if you say, 'I don't like Jerry Jones,' that's a dagger in him. He was taught that you don't want enemies. When you say you don't like him, that's very hard for him to understand. His dad used to go to restaurants by himself, just to meet new friends. He'd come home and say, 'I met four new friends.'

"It was amazing to watch Dad get up morning after morning that first year and go right back out there and try a little harder. We knew he was really hurting, but he didn't let on."

Like Johnson, Jones chose to read most of the criticism. But Jones didn't lash back or vow to make people eat their words. Here was a typical letter to the editor in a Dallas paper: "The Cowboy organization has become a circus with Jones the head clown. Johnson is a college coach with basically a college staff . . . and he's decimating the team. The time will come when Jones and Johnson will tuck their corkscrew tails between their legs and head back to Arkansas."

So, on July 19, 1992, in the shimmering heat along the St. Ed's sideline, a mirage appeared. Could that really be God's Quarterback, Roger Staubach, attending his first Blue-White scrimmage in Austin?

It was. Staubach, the Hall of Famer who played for Landry from 1969 to 1979, owns a Dallas real estate firm. Surrounded by reporters, Staubach delivered a powerful message—one he had already personally delivered to Landry: "I've told Coach Landry it would be very wise to put the past behind him and move forward."

The reference was to two official invitations, in '90 and '91, sent by Jones to Landry, offering to induct Landry into the Cowboy Ring of Honor. Landry, said Jones, ignored both. In large white letters the names of the seven players who have been inducted—including Staubach's—ring the inner wall of Texas Stadium. Landry, said Jones, had ignored several other attempts through intermediaries to make him aware of a standing invitation.

"You can politic this thing to death," Staubach said. "A lot more players belong in there and Coach Landry right in the middle of them. . . . When you start burning bridges, this life doesn't work. Tom Landry will always be recognized as something special. But the future is part of the past, just as the past is part of the future. I didn't know anything about Jones and Johnson, but the more I've watched, the more I've become a fan of the team. They've built it the right way, with talent and character. This team is fun to watch and fun to root for. The teams with finger-pointers and clubhouse lawyers won't last. Once people start putting themselves or money above winning, the team is in trouble. Championships are all that last. This team could win several Super Bowls. It's amazing how quickly this team came back."

Forgive and forget, Staubach was asking his old coach—for the good of old and new fans and Cowboy tradition. Heck, for the good of the economy. Staubach interrupted his blessing of the JJs to say, "Of course, I'm still in the real estate business in Dallas, and it does help business for the Cowboys to win. It helps everybody's business."

Yes, the JJs appeared to be having a profound effect on a rebounding Dallas economy. Yet Landry's cold shoulder has had a profound effect on Jones. This was the great Christian whom Jones had long revered? Did he consider Jones beneath him? Did he suspect Jones was trying to use him for instant credibility? Or was he using Jones to maintain his new role as a martyr?

Jones's emotions ranged from being disillusioned to offended to, "How can I ever expect the man I 'wronged' to let me induct him into the Ring of Honor?" Privately, Jones said, "Maybe he just didn't want to be associated with us at one and fifteen. But I've been surprised he hasn't responded, given what he believes. You'd hope to induct him on equal footing. You have that Super Bowl trophy in one hand and you shake his hand with the other and say, 'Coach, you built the tradition that made this possible.' "

★ ★ ★

Despite the thousands of converts Jones had won, his business practices continued to enrage many fans. Even as Staubach spoke in Austin, Jones was embroiled in yet another controversy among fans in Dallas.

The year before, customers had protested loudly when Jones stopped allowing them to bring alcoholic beverages into Texas Stadium so he could sell more himself—and increase annual revenue $1.2 million, he says. Jones had also alienated many longtime season-ticket holders with a plan called Pro Seat that forced them to pay extra just for the option to buy their seats for a certain number of years. Now Jones had set off another vocal minority with newspaper ads for a Special Team Package that hadn't quite made it clear that when single-game tickets went on sale, a like number would have to be purchased for an exhibition game. So the first morning, many people waited in line up to three hours to buy, say, four tickets to the Redskin game, only to be told they had to buy four to an exhibition game, too. Jones was again vilified as a "con artist" on talk shows and in letters to the editor.

Jones said, "We have to do a better job of communicating."

Yet the Cowboys soon sold out all three home exhibition games for the first time in team history, staffers said. If you win, fans will forgive almost any sin.

★ ★ ★

During a 1983 Cowboy-Raider game at Texas Stadium, Tex Schramm shot the finger at Raider managing general partner Al Davis. Schramm was a league man; some say former NFL commissioner Pete Rozelle was not only Schramm's dear friend but his puppet. Schramm despised Davis because Davis had broken the owners' fraternal bond in moving his Raiders from Oakland to Los Angeles. Davis despised Schramm's sway in the league office and what Davis considered the old Cowboys' hypocritical holier-than-thou image. Davis, who dresses himself and his team in black, often won with renegades, misfits, and castoffs whose battle cry was, "Just win, baby."

So it was that another miragelike sight appeared on the St. Ed's sideline the following Tuesday morning. Could that be Al Davis laughing and talking with the owner of the Cowboys? Yes, Davis and Jones sat side by side in a golf cart. Brooklyn meets Little Rock.

Jones says Davis often called him during the '89 season "just to tell me to keep my chin up. I sense some kinship there. He had been through some tough times, and we were going through some tough times."

What does Davis say about Jones? Davis rarely gives interviews; no kinship there. But Davis had accepted a Jones invitation: the Raiders had come to Austin to practice with and against the Cowboys six times in three days. The Cowboys' coaches were apprehensive. During camp in '89, the Raiders had manhandled the Cowboys—"men and boys," Dave Wannstedt remembered.

It didn't help their mood that during Sunday's intrasquad scrimmage, the 'Boys had beaten up each other. Rookie second-rounder Jimmy Smith had fractured his fibula after making an early catch. Rookie first-rounder Kevin Smith had nagging hamstring and ankle injuries and was unable to challenge starting cornerback Ike Holt, as coaches hoped. And now rookie first-rounder Robert Jones, already the starter at middle linebacker, had a groin pull.

Said scout Walter Juliff, "None of those three had a history of injury in high school or college. And now this. Is it going to be that kind of year?"

Jones was more concerned about his one-on-one sessions with Davis. In his plain dorm office down the hall from Johnson's room, Jones said, "No one—no one—has the total picture the way Al Davis does. He has been a football coach, a GM, an owner, and a commissioner. He is completely focused on all the right things, in my view. He appreciates how our game has to be exciting and appealing to the fans. He has moved a club to make it more viable. I know that's a sensitive area, but I sense great respect for Al among the other owners. There's obviously some resentment for some frailties he has. We all have those. But for Al to go through what he has, has taken great mental toughness.

"But understand, he's the one everybody listens to in our [owners'] meetings when it's time to look ahead and problem-solve. He's very imaginative. He's a go-for-it guy. He wants to make the big play. I love that."

Jones was humbling himself. He was playing just a little dumb, it appeared. He was asking the master every question he could squeeze in. "You have to be confident enough in yourself that you don't worry about saying the wrong thing around a man like Al. You can't worry about looking naive and maybe having him say, 'What a dumb son of a bitch.' I don't worry if he says something I don't understand and I ask, 'What's that?' I have my pride—I'm not the idiot who keeps saying, 'Hey [with a goofy grin], slap me again,' and you slap him again. But what's stronger than my ego is my greed for winning. No one in the world wants to win a Super Bowl more than I do."

From Davis, Jones was learning about coaching the coach. "He addresses the coaches the way coaches address the players," Jones said. From Davis, he was learning to coach coaches through extended player holdouts. Davis's theory as Jones understood it: Let the key veteran holdouts sit safely at home. Force the coaches to play backups and rookies and develop depth. Keep holdout starters from getting to camp too early and getting hurt or burned out in the heat. Let them get anxious to play. Let them start to soften their contractual demands. Give the stars a fair deal a week or so before the regular season starts.

Johnson's eye-rolling response: "Yeah, Jerry listens to whoever he wants to listen to. It's usually the last guy he talked to. If he just talked to [Philadelphia owner] Norm Braman, then he's talking about Norm's way. The fallacy to [the Davis holdout theory] is that Al has always had older teams. I promise you, if we don't get these guys in until the regular season, we will not be as good a football team as we could have been."

In the afternoon heat, the Cowboy-Raider practices often degenerated into fights—well, more like facemask-yanking rolls in the grass. The best one, ironically, featured the JJs' role-model Cowboy, defensive tackle Maryland, known for his heart and work ethic, versus Raider guard Steve Wisniewski, a Bible study leader. No blood, but lots of flailing. Do unto others? Cowboy coaches viewed the battles as a veteran team trying to maintain its physical and mental dominance over a young team it would play in a game that counted on October 25.

After the fourth practice, Wannstedt and Wise came off the field looking as if they might high-five. Stifling a grin, Wannstedt asked his buddy, "How'd your guys do?"

Wise said of his offensive line, "We kicked the shit out of 'em.

Wannstedt said, "Man, it was different than '89 when we had guys getting blown off the ball and I thought, 'Shit, we're in trouble.' These guys were not any more physical than we are."

That was a significant development for a staff that still doubted whether its team could play with the big boys.

Yet Wannstedt was frustrated by one drill in which his two second-year linebackers, Dixon Edwards and Godfrey Myles, had been run over repeatedly. Wannstedt was frustrated by Jerry Jones. On defense, Wannstedt was missing four unsigned starters:

linebacker Ken Norton, end Tony Tolbert, linebacker Vinson Smith, and safety James Washington. "I'm pumping up guys like Dixon Edwards [to the media]," Wannstedt said, "but we got to have Norton and we got to have Tolbert. Norton and Vinson Smith, would still be out there fighting those guys right now. We cannot think about lining up against the Redskins [in the September 7 opener] without those guys."

Jones's response: "We had a new coach last year, Ron Meeks [who left to work for new Cincinnati head coach David Shula], and Ron looked at all our film and said, 'That number fifty-one [Norton], he never makes any plays.' And now the coaches can't live without him?"

No, Jones was listening to Davis. His coaches might be frustrated, but soon the players would be, too, and then they'd sign for a salary Jones could live with. They would all have to work on their tolerance for ambiguity for a while.

★ ★ ★

The offensive star of the six Raider practices was a star-crossed receiver who some days wasn't sure he even wanted to play football. Alexander Wright had been blessed with everything but the stomach and savvy for this violent game. Wright was fresh off winning the NFL's Fastest Man competition in Palm Springs. For his size—six foot, 190—he could lift as much weight as any Cowboy. But he just didn't have what Norv Turner called "naturalness." Wright is a shy, gentle soul. Sometimes, Wright is bewildered by his physical gifts and how to apply them in life.

In a lengthy 1991 camp interview, Wright told of his childhood poverty in Columbus, Georgia, of how the father he idolized sometimes got into the liquor and forced Alexander into fistfights. Running into people on a football field never really appealed to him. After reading the quotes, Turner said, "Man, after you acknowledge that publicly, it is really tough to play this game."

Wright became a born-again Christian in 1990 and wasn't quite sure if the Lord wanted him to make money by playing pro football. But Johnson, who hoped to have some say in the matter, had spent the twenty-eighth pick in the draft on Wright. Johnson is a speed freak, and Wright had provided two breathtaking kickoff returns for touchdowns. But he remained jittery under punts, and he had caught just 21 passes in two seasons, none for TDs. Aikman didn't quite trust his hands or his nerve, and the coaches often argued into the night about Wright. Should he or sixth-year man Kelvin Martin be the third receiver (with Michael Irvin and Alvin Harper) or the kick returner?

Martin, at just 162 pounds, was a little too small. Coming off knee surgery in 1991, he was also too slow. Sometimes he frustrated Turner, who said, "How can Jimmy and Jerry be talking about winning a Super Bowl if you're going to go with Kelvin?" Yet Martin, nicknamed K Mart, did make more "money" catches than Wright, nicknamed Ace. Martin had stomach and savvy, said Turner.

But in passing drills against the Raiders, Alexander Wright was uncoverable. His planets were momentarily aligned. Little did he know he had played his way right out of Dallas.

★ ★ ★

One afternoon that week, practice stopped cold. For the good-humored Jones, it was suspended animation. For the assistants, who go running into the pile after every play, chiding or clapping, it was frozen silence. Emmitt was hurt.

Emmitt Smith, The Franchise.

The season teetered.

Smith, slowed by minor injuries at the University of Florida, hadn't missed a Cowboy game because of injury in his two pro seasons, '90 and '91. In '91, he said, he had felt intense pain only twice in the 414 times he ran with or caught the ball. In the opener at Cleveland, two Browns flew at him on the goal line and sandwiched his helmet between theirs. He scored, but was momentarily knocked unconscious. "I just remember Michael Irvin standing over me laughing that I didn't know where I was," Smith says.

The other time wasn't so funny. As he broke into the secondary against Phoenix, the ball slipped out of his hands and up into the air. As he reached for it, he lost sight of tacklers. A Cardinal plunged his helmet into Smith's testicles. "Now that was excruciating pain," Smith says.

Yet Smith is rarely vulnerable with a football in his grip. "He is so quick in a confined space," says Turner, "that people just can't get a good shot on him." Do you compare him with Barry Sanders? Thurman Thomas? "I have trouble comparing him with anyone," says Turner, "because he's a little bit of everyone."

Emmitt is Emmitt. He's just very hard to tackle. "Busy," he calls his style. "They said he wasn't fast enough," Turner says. "But he runs four point five [in the 40-yard dash], which is fast enough. And he runs four point five in the fourth quarter." He'll run by you, around you, and—if he senses you're vulnerable—over you. He is powered by one of the team's, if not the league's, strongest pairs of legs. Coaches wish he would spend more time in the weight room and hit the designed hole more often.

But Emmitt is Emmitt. He lives in his own special world. In the off-season he lives at home with his parents in Pensacola, Florida. He's naive about lots of things and he knows it. He trusts almost no one outside his family. He idolizes Michael Irvin's street smarts and cool. Bejeweled Irvin belongs at least in the Ear-Ring of Honor. Irvin says he suggested to Smith that he get an ear pierced and add an earring to his appearance. "But this boy went out and got 'em both pierced," Irvin says, laughing. "No, no, no, Emmitt."

Jimmy Johnson doesn't care what Smith looks like as long as he's healthy and happy. Johnson gives Smith more room than any Cowboy. Smith wasn't happy in '91 when Johnson spelled him with 245-pound running back Ricky Blake. Johnson says Smith even seemed threatened when Johnson, in May of 1992, traded for journeyman running back Keith Woodside. "He kidded me about it," Johnson says, "but I don't think he was completely kidding."

The trade fell through when Woodside failed his physical.

Blake was released when he had trouble recovering from a hip injury and lost too much weight because of a thyroid condition, trainers said. So as camp approached, Johnson decided that it would be Emmitt or bust. He didn't want to acquire a backup who would eventually campaign through the media for playing time and possibly upset Smith's equilibrium. But what if Smith was hurt? The question made Johnson testy. "No matter who we'd put in there," Johnson said, "we'd lose something. So we'd just have to ask more of the quarterback."

Johnson was "hanging out," as he calls it. Risking. Tempting fate. He was going with second-year man Curvin Richards as his backup running back. Richards, originally from the Bahamas, was just talented and mellow enough to provide insurance without threatening Smith. But if Smith fell, so probably would any Super Bowl hopes.

And here Smith was down, clutching his . . . knee? Had the season ended even before the first exhibition game? Trainers and doctors hovered. No, Smith had caught a helmet in the thigh just above the knee. It was just a deep bruise. You could hear the sighs all the way to Pasadena.

Three plays later, Emmitt Smith ducked back into the huddle and told Curvin Richards he could go back and sit down. The franchise was safe.

★ ★ ★

Nate Newton had gone off the deep end again. "I'm no longer big enough to play tackle," said Newton, the most famous fat man this side of William "the Refrigerator" Perry. Newton had been nick-named the Kitchen when he rolled into Thousand Oaks in 1986 from the United States Football League. But now Newton looked more like the Breakfast Nook.

"Two ninety-six," he said, and sniffed. Yes, the same Newton who weighed 404 just twelve weeks earlier was down to 296, he said. Feast or famine? Wasn't it just a few years ago that the Fridge captured America's imagination because he played for the champion Bears weighing three hundred pounds? Newton had hit the big four oh oh—then had somehow dropped a hundred or so pounds since May 1.

He talked about his May Day distress as he walked out of the St. Edward's chow hall with only a turkey sandwich on wheat, light on the mayo. Players constantly complain about camp food, but it isn't bad: sandwich line, hot-food line, salad bar, pasta bar, desserts galore—all you can scarf. Newton refused to subject himself to the buffet gluttony. He grabbed a sandwich and went straight to his dorm room. He had worked too damn hard to get small enough to tuck in his practice jersey again.

"He's even wearing those pea-sized shoulder pads," line coach Wise said with sigh. "If you figure it all out, please let me know."

During the off-season, Newton had let Cowboy success go to his stomach. "I'd be lookin' at TV late at night and see a Burger King or McDonald's ad and go right to Burger King or McDonald's." Before a May 1 minicamp, he knew he was in big trouble. He went to Johnson and asked to take a three-week leave to work with a personal trainer in his hometown of Orlando who had shrunk Jerome Brown and Cortez Kennedy. Brown and Kennedy had played for Johnson at Miami. Johnson let Newton go under one condition: that he return at 330 or less.

In Orlando, Newton went on an intense walking and aerobic weight lifting program of light weight and high reps, combined with a chicken-vegetable-fruit diet. "No beer, no frieds," Newton said. Newton not only lost the weight, but he lost much of his team-best strength. And now, on August 24, Wise was wondering just how much more Newton would lose. Can a 300-pounder be called anorexic? On one night off, Newton had stayed in the St. Ed's gym playing one-on-one basketball with a member of the women's team so he wouldn't be tempted to drink beer with "the fellas," as he calls them.

For Wise this was a delicate situation. Newton swings a lot of figurative weight in the locker room. He can be the team clown, with his Santa Claus laugh and Richard Pryor wit. But when he's crying on the inside, Newton can cause enormous problems. Newton has some Sir Isaac in him, some intellect. Beneath the booming one-liners and the 'boys-in-the-'hood lingo—"Yo, homies!"—Newton has an angry wisdom. He is the team's best interview, the one reporters flock to when they need a says-it-all quote about an issue or a game. Newton is a regular on a TV and a radio show.

For better or sometimes worse, he can be a leader.

He's also an underrated athlete and "a very, very powerful man," says Wise. "I've seen him just give it this [a quick forearm shiver] and knock a man down."

About all Wise, age forty-one, has in common with Newton is that Wise, too, fights his weight. Wise, about five foot nine, says he was a "shitty" athlete at Ithaca College in upstate New York. He played lacrosse, hockey, and some football. He began coaching at Albany State. At Central Connecticut State, working part-time in a diner, he once bused the table of the linemen he coached. At Washington State, he lived in the basement of current Cowboy secondary coach Dave Campo. At Pitt, as a graduate assistant making $200 a month, he slept in a stadium office, fighting the security guard for the couch. There he met defensive coordinator Johnson, who often let Wise use his car and or asked him to come along for a beer. Wise also enjoys an occasional cigar.

"I was just the court jester, I really believe that," Wise says.

"Jimmy just thought I was funny." Not one-liner funny; Wise just gets worked up and says or does funny things. Frumpy, dumpy Tony, lifelong bachelor, was a lovable character.

Johnson on Wise: "Tony wants to be the best offensive-line coach in the country. He cares deeply about players, and that sometimes gets in the way."

One afternoon during the second week of camp, Johnson and Wise and several other coaches went for a three-mile jog around Town Lake. Johnson fell in with Wise and made a strong suggestion about a move he wanted Wise to make. This is Johnson's version of coaching the coaches. Jerry Jones says, "Maybe Jimmy's greatest asset is surrounding himself with good coaches who can communicate his feelings and beliefs to the players."

Johnson gives assistants as much freedom in their areas as any coach, says Jones. He rarely directly coaches a player during practice. During game week, Johnson doesn't follow a set schedule; he free-lances, dropping in on assistants individually or in meetings to see what they have in mind for the next game plan. He mostly lets his coordinator plan strategy. Johnson occasionally vetoes or modifies an assistant's idea by making a "suggestion." But mostly, he lets them handle the Xs and Os while he handles the media and big-picture personnel moves involving cuts or trades. Likewise, during games Johnson lets Wannstedt call defenses and Turner call plays, though Johnson occasionally overrules, telling Wannstedt to, say, get out of a prevent defense or telling Turner to change a pass to a run. But only occasionally. Mostly, Johnson handles the CEO decisions: when to go for it or punt, whether to play Aikman or Beuerlein, when to pull starters in what's becoming a blowout, when to replace starters permanently.

Johnson wanted Wise to move Newton to left guard, where he would be more effective in his new svelte body. But Wise balked at benching Kevin Gogan. Just as important, Johnson wanted second-year tackle Erik Williams installed at Newton's old spot. Williams was "blotting out" people in practice, said Wise. Williams had star potential. But Johnson wanted Wise finally to decide it was his own idea to make Gogan odd man out. "Then the coach is happy and I'm happy," Johnson said.

Wise said, "I know I drag my feet on these things, but I just hate telling a guy who busted his ass for me that he's been demoted. I just knew he would ask why. Jimmy said, 'You don't have to give him a reason.' But I would have wanted somebody to give me a reason. Jimmy has some interesting sides. He can be as big-hearted as anyone I know. But when he makes a move, he just makes it regardless of anybody's feelings. He finally said, 'The move will be made by Monday.' "

★ ★ ★

Following his run, Johnson returned to his dorm room, which was as immaculate as his Valley Ranch home. Johnson is the Felix Unger of coaches. He cannot stand the sight of crumbs or clutter.

Johnson says he spends almost all his time away from football at his house watching his fifty-inch, satellite-dish TV—and his fish. Water calms the rage in Johnson. He grew up in Port Arthur, on the Gulf of Mexico, about three hundred miles from Dallas. If he had his choice, he says, he would live on the beach in Miami. To relax he used to put on sunglasses, so fewer people would recognize him, and walk for miles on the Miami beaches.

From the start, Johnson didn't seem to care much for landlocked Dallas. Dallas and its high society took itself too seriously for Johnson, it seemed. He left Miami for Dallas only for the opportunity to dominate pro football. He brought some Miami with him to Valley Ranch, buying six saltwater fish tanks—two for the kitchen, four for the den. "And he didn't just go out and buy them," says his friend and attorney Nick Christin. "First, he read every book he could get his hands on. He knows everything about tropical fish and aquariums."

For a while at Arkansas, Johnson majored in vertebrate zoology. During an interview in his room at training camp, as Johnson began to list all his fish and detail their relationships, it was clear he missed watching them. He says he often rises at four-thirty A.M., watches his fish for two hours, then goes to work. "It's extremely relaxing," Johnson said. "The water gurgling, the sound of the generator."

Johnson's son Brent told *The Dallas Morning News*, "The fish—they may be the perfect things for him to have around the house. If he had a dog or a cat, they might bug him, expect something in return. The fish—they don't want to know him. They leave him alone."

The fish: eleven sea anemones, one hundred and fifty different starfish, shrimp-eating lionfish and dwarf lions, clowns and tomato clowns, marine betas, pencil urchins, tube worms. Deeper and deeper Johnson went into his one hobby. He is fascinated by the ways his fish interact—the predators, the hermits, the teammates, the parasites.

Johnson watches another school of fish on the practice field each day. He moves them from tank to tank, mixing blacks and whites, old and young, producers and pretenders, timid and cutthroat, feeding or starving them to see how they'll react. Would Kevin Gogan go into his shell when Wise benched him? Would he be devoured? Or would he survive and be ready as a quality backup when someone went down? Johnson the master manipulator watched.

The fish that amuses Johnson most is the biggest lionfish, more than a foot long. Johnson says it knows him. He feeds it shrimp. If he walks past and the biggest lion is hungry, it will spit at him, Johnson said, chuckling his throaty, hearty chuckle.

Johnson also chuckled while telling another vintage Jimmy story. The previous camp, in '91, he took several assistants out for beers. Johnson's Cowboys were going to make their first "Monday Night Football" appearance and Johnson decided he wanted to hear the band in the bar do Hank Williams, Jr.'s "Monday Night" theme song. "I'd had a few," Johnson said, "and, well, I don't like to talk about this, because it's not important. But I do give people money sometimes, and I gave this bartender a hundred bucks and told him to get the band to play 'Monday Night Football.' The singer said he didn't know 'Monday Night Football.' Now I'm getting pissed. I said [raising his voice], 'I want to hear "Monday Night Football"!' So the owner of the bar calls this guy he knows who owns a record store and gets him up and tells him to go to the store and get the Hank Williams, Jr., tape. Meantime, [special-teams coach] Joe Avezzano, who fashions himself a singer, gets up there and teaches the band the song and he sings it and we're all happy. And as we're leaving, this guy [the record store owner] comes running in with the CD of Hank Williams, Jr."

When Johnson is hungry, he will spit at the world. If he wants to hear "Monday Night Football," people scurry because he's Jimmy Johnson. He's the biggest lion in the sea simply because he wins. If you win, you can pretty much do or say whatever the hell you want. You rule, as long as you win.

Well, you rule everyone but your boss.

Going Everywhere and Nowhere

JIMMY JOHNSON ABSOLUTELY DID NOT WANT TO TAKE HIS TEAM to Tokyo to play the same Houston Oilers the Cowboys had just scrimmaged twice, in San Antonio and Austin. Johnson hates being cooped up on planes for three hours, let alone the sixteen hours—plus a three-hour layover in Los Angeles—it would take the Cowboys to get to the NFC Far East. Johnson says he never sets an alarm, and now his body-clock routine would be shattered. Sleep patterns of his players would be turned upside down as they went back and forth across sixteen time zones. Dolphin coaches warned Cowboy coaches that Miami had suffered a plague of injuries after playing in Tokyo the summer before.

In fact, the Cowboys would have to turn right around and play at Miami five days after playing in Tokyo. Most NFL teams play four preseason games; for Dallas, Tokyo was an added fifth. But wouldn't you think some players would look forward to an all-expenses-paid trip to Tokyo? Very few did, perhaps because their coach was all over newspapers and TV saying what a nuisance the trip was.

Johnson also blamed it for the continued absence of eight holdouts. Sure, he said, why not wait to sign until the Tokyo ordeal was done? For Johnson and many of his signed players, it was thirty second-guesses over Tokyo. Babe Laufenberg, who played quarterback for the 1989 and '90 Cowboys and now works as a Dallas radio and TV commentator, said, "This team really responds to what Jimmy says publicly. As soon as he said he didn't like going to Tokyo, it was open season on Tokyo."

This did not please Jerry Jones. Johnson suspected that Jones's enthusiasm for the trip resulted from a yen for Japanese currency. Jones associates confirmed that Jones was using the trip to explore potential personal investments in Japan, as well as to sell the Cowboys in every way possible. "The Cowboys are huge in Japan," Jones said. "There's an establishment [the NFL Experience/American Sports Bar] that's modeled after Texas Stadium on the inside. You look up through hole-in-the-roof construction, and the sides are painted to look like you're in the stands at Texas Stadium. It's incredible."

Jones also responded to coach and player complaints about the trip in his *Dallas Morning News* column. Jones wrote, "This may be a good time to break from routine. We've had grueling workouts and scrimmages, including six workouts with the Raiders that were as physical as I've ever seen." But Jones ended the column with: "Besides, all expenses are paid, and the Cowboys will receive in excess of $300,000 from ESPN for this appearance."

Exactly, said several coaches and players.

Highlights of coach and player complaints from the trip: Couldn't sleep going over. Couldn't stay awake in Tokyo. Food was terrible and terribly expensive ($54 American for a steak, $8 for a beer). Traffic was worse than the worst in America. Humidity was even worse than Miami or Houston. Everything was overcrowded. Nothing but concrete. Almost nobody spoke English. Troy Aikman told the *Fort Worth Star-Telegram*: "Tokyo is . . . buildings built on buildings as far as you can see. It's so big that everything has to be small, if that makes any sense. Their cars—even their trucks—are almost like toys. They don't have enough room for full-sized driving ranges or baseball fields, so they make them shorter and put fences around and over, so the balls won't go onto the highway a seven-iron or foul tip away. It was everything I didn't like about Los Angeles to the tenth power. It makes L.A. look like Henryetta, Oklahoma."

Much later, Jones commented, "The Tokyo trip really destroyed the season, didn't it?"

But on August 2, even the game turned into a Godzilla movie. The year before, the Cowboys hadn't been able to stop the four-receiver attacks of Houston, Atlanta, and Detroit, and in Tokyo the Oilers again ran-and-shot up and down the field. They led 24–7 before winning 34–23. During the telecast, ESPN analyst Joe Theismann picked the Cowboys to go 8-8, "because their defense is too young and they beat eight backup quarterbacks last year."

Cowboy coaches quietly fretted that they lacked a dominant pass rusher and a play-off-caliber safety, if a Super Bowl was the immediate goal. Jones was working frantically to acquire both, no matter what his head coach might think of some of the choices.

★ ★ ★

Donald Harris, the 1989 first-round pick—fifth overall—of the Texas Rangers baseball team, was a 1992 twelfth-round pick of the crosstown Cowboys. In football Harris had been an all–Southwest Conference safety at Texas Tech, a fierce hitter with "great instincts for the ball," said Tech secondary coach Carlos Mainord, who had coached under Johnson at Miami.

The new Cowboys had taken a flier on Harris the way the old Cowboys had made future picks of Roger Staubach, before his navy hitch, and Chad Hennings, before his air force tour. Hennings, an eleventh-round pick in '88, had returned for his first training camp in '92. Harris began the '92 baseball season at Class AA Tulsa, but was called up by the Rangers in July. He was in the starting lineup for a while and quickly proved, as Ranger general manager Tom Grieve said, "he's the best center fielder this organization has ever seen. He will absolutely run through a wall to make a catch." But the catch was Harris's bat. Would he ever be able to hit above .230 in the big leagues? He needed more minor-league at-bats, the Rangers decided, and when they sent him back down to Tulsa, a disillusioned Harris went home to Waco for a couple of days.

It was there that Jerry and Stephen Jones, who had been avidly following Harris's baseball career, found him by phone and soon offered him a $35,000 bonus up front and $225,000 a year if he made the Cowboy team. Harris, now down to a minor-league salary in baseball, jumped at the chance to compete for a starting job with a potential play-off team. Jones sent his private jet to Waco to take Harris to Houston—the only place to get a visa quickly—then bring him back to catch the Cowboy plane to Tokyo. By the time Harris landed in Tokyo, his head was surely spinning like a curveball.

Harris soon felt he had been thrown a curve. He found that his visa was fouled up, so while the team went straight from the airport to a light workout, Harris was detained by customs officials. He was also told that no practice sweats had been packed for him. "What kind of fuckin' operation is this?" Harris complained to team officials.

A day later, in his first interview with Dallas reporters, Harris said he would play football for only two years. Harris said, "It's not been as easy as I thought it would be. I forgot about all the practices and sitting in the boring film rooms."

Harris might as well have said *sayonara* to Johnson right there. It was bad enough, said assistants, that Johnson felt Jones had gotten a little carried away and not completely involved the coaches in the decision to pursue Harris after camp had started. "And there was a little resentment," said one assistant, "that Jerry was acting like he now had his Bo Jackson or Deion Sanders, like it was going to be a big PR bonanza."

But on top of that, Harris had complained about what Cowboy coaches value most—practice and meetings. He might as well have made fun of Johnson's hair. If Harris had been immediately sensational, Johnson would probably have swallowed his singed pride and kept Harris. But though Harris, at six foot and 185 pounds, threw his weight around during practice, coaches found he didn't have the burst of speed that safeties Kenny Gant, Robert Williams, and Darren Woodson did.

"He's a talent," Johnson soon said, "but he's too far behind." Knowing I had spoken at length to Jones about Harris, Johnson made a point of telling me, with satisfaction, "You're wrong about your boy Donald Harris."

One afternoon back in Austin, Harris ignored Johnson when Johnson yelled for his attention during practice. Harris slept through an afternoon meeting. He also busted a curfew. After about three weeks, Johnson cut Harris, who returned to the Ranger organization.

Part owner Mike McCoy offered this perspective: "How many dicks or outlaws does Jimmy have? None. He kept Jesse Solomon around for a while, but Jesse was a proven NFL linebacker. [Johnson suspended, then traded the mouthy Solomon.] I'm not sure Jimmy knows whether Donald Harris is a football player, because he came in with that when-do-I-start attitude and said all the wrong things, and he didn't really get a chance. He spent a lot of his practice time on the sideline, and he barely played on special teams in games. This was one Jerry got all excited about and basically went to Jimmy and said, 'Have I got a player for you!' Maybe Jerry learned something—to keep Jimmy involved."

Yet Jones insisted he did keep Jimmy involved. Sometimes Jones is oblivious to Johnson's fuming displeasure. Jones said, "I did tell the coaches [before Harris was signed] and they were excited about it. I haven't given up on Donald Harris."

★ ★ ★

Just five days after the game in Tokyo, the zombie-eyed Cowboys played again. But Johnson warmed to this trip; he was making a triumphant return to the beach, to Miami. The tropical sun on Johnson's face recharges him. He agreed to fill every interview request, even the one-on-ones. He was up and he was on, flashing his dimples and his wit. When he wants to be, Jimmy Johnson is one of the best interviews in sports, a highly quotable blend of management philosophy, psychological insight into players, and brazen confidence.

Several in the Cowboy party quietly buzzed about a prediction aired by former Dolphin tight end and current Dolphin radio analyst Jim Mandarich, who said Johnson "will be the next head coach of the Dolphins." Though coach Don Shula had signed a three-year contract, rumors circulated that he was considering retirement after another season or two. In Miami several assistants speculated that, if Johnson soon won a Super Bowl in Dallas, he would want to replace Shula and win another. That way Johnson would have accomplished another shock-the-world first: successfully following two legends.

But that Friday night in Joe Robbie Stadium, a Super Bowl title seemed as far away as Tokyo. Dolphin quarterback Dan Marino missed his first pass attempt—then completed 16 straight before the first half ended, for 163 yards and a touchdown. Marino didn't play the second half. The Dolphins eventually won, 27–24.

Dave Wannstedt said, "Marino had the hot hand. But I came in at halftime and said, 'Come on, you guys got to start breaking on the ball.' Darren Woodson said, 'Coach, we're waiting for him to cock the ball.' You know, they break on most quarterbacks when they cock to throw, and Marino [who fires from a set position] doesn't cock. I looked at all these kids, these fuckin' babies, and what could I say? Woodson said he ran by Marino on a blitz and Marino said, 'You gave it away.' That really meant a lot to him. It was like, 'Dan Marino is talking to *me*.'"

Amazed and amused, Wannstedt shook his head with a growing fondness for his "babies"—Woodson, cornerback Kevin Smith, and middle linebacker Robert Jones. "Don't get me wrong, Woodson's going to be one hell of a strong safety. But he isn't right now. Robert Jones is going to be great, too. He sits right behind me in the meetings and he's all over everything. He said [before the Miami game], 'Coach, are they going to run the no-huddle?' I said, 'Fuck, no.' Of course, they ran it.

"The big decision we're going to have to make in the next two weeks is, do we scrap a lot of things we're doing scheme-wise and just go with the kids? One thing about 'em, they can *run*. So do you go with a lot more blitzes? Do you change the system? It's a huge decision. Where do you get your pass rush? By committee? Maybe. We looked at Sean Jones [the unhappy Oiler defensive end who had "retired" to become a full-time Beverly Hills stockbroker]. He could help, but he has caused some problems. Do you give up a lot for him and he turns into Jesse Solomon?"

Desperation was setting in because Johnson had made a rare error in talent evaluation. The day before the draft, Johnson had overestimated the potential of defensive lineman Chad Hennings, who had been released early from his air force commitment and had flown in for a quick workout for Johnson and the coaches. Even after four years away from football, Hennings was easy to overestimate. He had improved the 40-yard dash time and bench press the old Cowboys recorded on him his senior year at the Air Force Academy, when he won the Outland Trophy as the nation's top defensive lineman. At six foot six he had gained twenty-one well-placed pounds, to 272. Hennings was the ultimate all-American boy—he even had flown escort missions in the final days of the Gulf War. He has Landry's classic jaw. He has Bob Lilly's farmboy good looks. He even has the first name of Johnson's second son. He was too good to be true.

Watching Hennings run solo through drills, Johnson got carried away. Johnson told reporters that Hennings "had fallen out of the sky" and indicated he had Pro Bowl potential. Could Hennings quickly turn into a dominant pass rusher? Johnson later said that Denver called that Saturday before the draft wanting to trade for Hennings. Johnson said, "I told 'em I would commit an unnatural act in the streets of New York before I'd trade him."

The Dallas Morning News did a camp diary with Hennings. *Sports Illustrated* planned a cover story. Fans fought for Hennings's autograph as crazily as they did for Aikman's or Emmitt Smith's. Though Hennings kept promising he would live up to his buildup, the expectations must have been suffocating.

Two weeks into camp, it became painfully clear to coaches that Hennings simply wasn't quick enough to be an NFL force at defensive end. They soon moved him inside to tackle and termed him a project with excellent potential.

Marino: an unhurried 16 of 17.

★ ★ ★

That night on the flight back from Miami, Wannstedt sat in his customary first-row, first-class aisle seat next to Johnson. Johnson needed to talk and he needed Wannstedt to listen. Johnson was reeling, and it had little to do with Marino. The same Johnson who says he "could care less what people think of me" sometimes cares intensely how he is perceived by the public. Johnson needed his conscience, Wannstedt, to tell him he was okay.

In south-Florida newspapers, Alonzo Highsmith had blasted Johnson for not attending the funeral of Jerome Brown, who had been killed in an auto accident on June 25 near his home in Brooksville, Florida. Highsmith and Brown had played for Johnson at Miami. In 1990, Johnson had traded the Oilers a second-round and a fifth-round pick for running back Highsmith, who like Brown was one of his favorites. Johnson cut Highsmith after one season; he was with Tampa Bay when he made these remarks in August of 1992.

Highsmith said in the papers that the day Dallas had beaten Brown's Eagles in Philadelphia, "Jerome had been the first person across the field to congratulate [Johnson]."

The day Brown was killed, Johnson said he was too broken up to talk to reporters. Instead he issued a statement that said, in part, "I'm devastated. There was no finer person than Jerome Brown."

But Johnson doesn't attend funerals or weddings. Well, he has attended two weddings besides his own: Cowboy and ex-Miami PR director Rich Dalrymple's, and older son Brent's. But funerals, no. Not even Jerome's.

"That's all Jimmy talked about on the flight home," Wannstedt said. "What Alonzo said really bothered him. Alonzo was one of Jimmy's guys. I'll never forget the meeting [before a game in Phoenix in 1990] when Jimmy said, 'No, Alonzo's going to be in there!' [A knee that Highsmith damaged with Houston still slowed him more than Johnson had anticipated.] Jimmy said, 'He's a winner!' Alonzo fumbled the first play of the game," a 20–3 Cowboy loss.

Back in Austin, Johnson said, "Alonzo's just a guy frustrated with his life [as a backup in Tampa Bay] and he's lashing out. But, well, I just don't want to go to a funeral and look at Jerome in a casket. I mean, it's over, let's go on. I want to remember Jerome the way I saw him, and that was in the middle of the field in Philadelphia.

"You really have to twist my arm to go to a wedding, too. I went to my son's because—I hate to say this—they made it easy for me. At the rehearsal dinner they had twelve people."

Several insiders were surprised Johnson had agreed to pick up ex-wife Linda Kay at the airport and take her to the rehearsal dinner. Shortly after Johnson took the Cowboy job, he informed her he wanted a divorce. Says a source close to Johnson and Linda Kay, "She was stunned. It came without warning."

Once Johnson makes a decision he doesn't look back, he says. Marriage, funerals, weddings, children—Johnson is at the point in his life where he has no use for any of them.

Wannstedt says, "Hey, my two girls were the first kids Jimmy could stay around very long without getting antsy. That's just the way he is. But if anyone [from Jerome's family] had called to ask for anything—anything—Jimmy would have done it."

Anything but attending the funeral. Wannstedt went. So did several Cowboys who played with or knew Brown.

After returning from Miami, Johnson shook his head over trading for and starting Highsmith. He concluded, "I let my emotions run away with me. . . . The first time he touches the ball, he fuckin' fumbles."

★ ★ ★

JJs alert: Johnson was again miffed at Jones over two small but significant developments. Among the Cowboy cuts released by the PR department was third-round pick James Brown. Johnson thought he had a trade worked out for Brown, but sources said he couldn't get hold of Jerry or Stephen Jones to finalize it. Brown's name was rescinded from the waiver wire, then later that day he was waived again. Tony Wise shrugged and said, "Bob Ackles." Meaning, if Ackles had still been around coordinating personnel moves with Johnson, the Cowboys wouldn't have looked like something out of *Blazing Saddles*.

Johnson was more steamed at Jones about an anonymous quote in the *Fort Worth Star-Telegram*. It came from Jones, Johnson said privately. The anonymous quote said that the Cowboys believed Plan B acquisition Frank Cornish could play as well at center as holdout Mark Stepnoski. Johnson told other staffers, "How can Jerry make a statement like that? How does *he* know? Mark Stepnoski graded out as well as any lineman we've had the last two years. Maybe Jerry's just negotiating, but that's crazy."

In an interview for this book, Johnson said, "I told Jerry, 'I'm not going to lie [to the media].' I'm not going to say we don't need those guys."

When Stepnoski finally signed, two days before the opener, it took him two weeks of practice to get combat ready. Though Stepnoski would make the Pro Bowl, Cornish would play so well in the first two games that Wise struggled with the decision to replace him. "Cornish was better than any tackle who went in the first round of the draft," said GM Jones.

★ ★ ★

The name of the restaurant-bar Hooters fits like one of the tight T-shirts the waitresses wear. Jones and Johnson love Hooters, and probably not just for its world-famous chicken wings.

The Hooters chain has a place in Austin, and Jones chose it for the annual camp-ending media party. The coaches came and went pretty quickly. Jones closed Hooters and led a procession to honkytonks like Dance Across Texas. But standing in the middle of a crowd at Hooters, Jones energized the room with his nonstop smiling and storytelling. He magnetized reporters wanting a little inside info, fans wanting an autograph, and waitresses wanting a picture with "Mr. Jones." He winked at the Hooters girls, flirted with them, hugged them—all in view of his daughter Charlotte and son Stephen at a table not twenty feet away. One of Jones's eyebrow-raising quotes in '89 was, "I love to look at beautiful women." Elizabeth Taylor, in Dallas to promote her perfume line, agreed to be Jones's suite guest for the '89 Washington game. She even participated in the coin flip.

Doesn't Jones's wife, Gene, a former Miss Arkansas USA, flip over such behavior? Members of his family—which is extremely close—don't seem to take Jones's Hooters-style high jinks too seriously. Their attitude: "That's just Dad." Boys will be boys. Jones starts "shooting beers"—a drinking competition with writers—and he gets a little macho, a little mischievous.

Being one of the boys is important to Jones. Johnson tolerates him, shares an occasional beer or pizza with him for business purposes, but won't completely allow Jones to feel he's accepted as one of the coaching staff. But among reporters and front-office staffers at Hooters, Jones is *the* boy. Sometimes in this atmosphere, when Jones really gets wound up, he'll tell a locker-room story about escapades from his past, though it's difficult to tell where exaggeration meets truth.

Gene Jones, a classy woman who tends to roll her eyes at Jerry when he takes himself too seriously, was asked later what she thought about female fans who gravitate to her husband because he's the focal-point owner and general manager of the Dallas Cowboys. "I'm not threatened by it, but I don't like it," Gene said. "It's just Jerry's personality."

A few feet away at Hooters, Charlotte shook her head and smiled at her dad. Charlotte, twenty-six, is a Stanford graduate and honors student who serves as marketing and special events coordinator for the Cowboys. A common trait of Jones's and Johnson's children: brainpower. Jones's son Stephen majored in chemical engineering at Arkansas. Charlotte majored in biology. Charlotte has also done some modeling. She's married and drives a Porsche.

As a high-school senior Charlotte had the grades but not the test scores to get into Stanford. "I didn't test well," she said. Her only hope was an essay Stanford required of applicants on the biggest influence in their lives. Charlotte wrote about her father. "It got me in," she said. "He has always been a source of strength for me."

Yes, says Jones, he can get a little out of hand some nights. "But I've never done anything that would hurt my family," he says.

★ ★ ★

The last full day of camp, August 13, Troy Aikman ate lunch in the chow hall with some of his offensive linemen. Aikman is comfortable with these guys. He calls them Tuey (Mark Tuinei), Nasty G (Kevin Gogan), Stepo (Stepnoski), Gezer (John Gesek), Newt (Nate Newton), Corn Dog (Cornish), Big E (Erik Williams), Vic Vines (Alan Veingrad), and Hell-to-Pay (Dale Hellestrae).

Then Aikman sat back, put a pinch between his cheek and gum, and talked about how the "new Troy" was getting along.

He certainly appeared to be coming out of his less-said-the-better shell. He even was doing his own column for the *Fort Worth Star-Telegram*. In one, he entertained readers with tales of dorm life: "I haven't decided if it's because the walls in old Premont Hall are paper-thin or if the phones are on steroids, but when one rings, the entire floor can hear it. Though I live in 218, I've often reached over to answer my phone only to get a dial tone and later find out that it was ringing in Alfredo Roberts's room, way down in 201. A good night's sleep is a major achievement. . . . I find myself falling between mattresses. They give us two twin beds, which we unsuccessfully try to squash into one queen-size. . . . Music is a popular way to pass time. . . . Unfortunately, it's also a war of the jam boxes . . . not all my teammates have caught on to the latest country craze. . . . I'll just keep clicking my cleats and thinking of home."

At the moment, though, Aikman was dreading what was happening back in Dallas. He had let a writer from *D Magazine*, Eric Celeste, ride shotgun with him on and off for several weeks during the off-season. "Some people said, 'Why are you giving him so much time?' I said, 'Hey, if the guy wants to find out what I'm all about, fine, then let him write what he wants.' "

Fine, at least, until Celeste faxed Aikman a copy of the lengthy cover story before it hit the newsstands. Aikman didn't like the overall picture of him as "basically a lonely guy." But he was particularly fearful of an anonymous quote from a friend about Jimmy Johnson. The quote: "Troy doesn't trust him as far as he can throw him." Celeste then wrote: "Given Aikman's world-class right arm, that's saying something."

Aikman said he considered trying to stop the story legally but decided "you'd just bring publicity to the magazine."

Celeste talked to Aikman about the story, which Celeste considered "pretty glowing" overall. (It was.) But, said Celeste, "because of the unique nature of Jimmy Johnson, [Troy was concerned that Johnson] can focus on something and really make things difficult."

The magazine was due out in the next day or so. Aikman sighed and said he was on his way to prepare Johnson for the story—and to ask if he could spend the last camp night in a hotel, so he could get some sleep.

No problem on either count, said Johnson.

Later, after reading the story, Johnson shrugged it off: "Troy and I are still better than we've ever been." He seemed fully committed to getting along with his quarterback—coexisting at worst. Aikman said, "It did hit me that he kept telling the media what a great camp I had when I didn't think I had a very good camp at all."

Johnson's only concern was how far Aikman could throw this team.

★ ★ ★

The Cowboys fell to 0-3 in practice games by losing at home to the Oilers, 17–16, a forgettable affair that ended with a memorable 66-yard field-goal attempt. It was blocked. But Brad Daluiso insisted, "I could have made it, easy."

Daluiso is the John Daly of NFL field-goal kickers. Like Daly, the longest hitter on the Professional Golf Association Tour, Daluiso is awesomely long but occasionally short on dedication and discipline. Daluiso is a zany Californian from San Diego who wore his cap backward and drove a white Porsche. Several Cowboy assistant coaches feared Daluiso was going nowhere fast.

He had been signed off Plan B to replace Ken Willis. Johnson, intrigued with rare talent, had let Daluiso attempt the game-ending equivalent of a 400-yard drive. The NFL record is 63 yards by Tom Dempsey.

Daluiso dreams of making a 70-yarder and breaking his record for Rows Deep in the Stands on a Kickoff (14 at Buffalo in '91). Coaches were more concerned whether he could be trusted to make a 30-yarder under pressure. The alternative? An undrafted rookie from Texas Tech named Lin Elliott, who drove a white pickup.

As Tony Wise left the locker room late that Saturday night, he was asked about the kicking situation. "Now that's something to worry about," he said. "Steve [Hoffman, the kicking coach] is a guy who's really frustrated because he has always put so much emphasis on the mental, and this guy doesn't seem that dedicated. It's really scary. It always seems to come down to a field goal here or there making or breaking your year."

★ ★ ★

The day before the next home exhibition, against Denver, Johnson did something he doesn't usually do: he put on headphones and went jogging by himself. Then Mr. Punctuality was late for an interview. He came across stunningly subdued, almost defeated. He brightened only for a moment, to show a visitor his son Brent's modeling portfolio. Both of Johnson's sons are stunningly handsome.

Johnson was asked if they got their looks from Dad or Mom.

"With this face," Johnson said of his own, "what do you think?"

This didn't seem like false modesty. Usually, Johnson dresses and acts as if he thinks he's a pretty handsome devil himself. But now Johnson had fallen to the depths of his personal ocean. His father, C.W., a retired dairy supervisor living in Port Arthur, said he had recently talked to Jimmy and that "he's as down as I've ever heard him."

One by one, Johnson's defensive starters had signed and reported with more bitterness than enthusiasm. Vinson Smith and James Washington blasted management. Tony Tolbert, who was about to sign, let Jones have it, too. Johnson said, "The thing I hate about pro football is that decisions have to be made because of money that aren't best for the team."

True, Jerry Jones? "Look, you have to understand the mentality of football players," Jones said a few days later. "Even if they're all upset when they sign, they get back on the practice field and quickly forget about everything but playing football."

Johnson's two best receivers, Michael Irvin and Jay Novacek, were still unsigned and were demanding trades through their agents. So was Stepnoski. Johnson had no dependable pass rusher or safety or kicker. And he had been dropping Super Bowl hints to the media. "Jimmy can't help loading his ass up [by making cocky promises]," Larry Lacewell said.

Meanwhile, veteran defensive tackle Danny Noonan, a first-round pick by the Landry regime in '87, was doing everything in his power to get his rear end traded. Noonan told a reporter, "[Line coach] Butch Davis fucking lied to me, and you can tell him I said that. He said if I performed, I could win the job and that's bullshit. I had a better camp than Russell Maryland, but do you think I can win that job? Come on."

Noonan had put on about twenty pounds, up to 296, in hopes of being traded to a 3-4 defensive team that used a nose tackle, the position Noonan played at Nebraska. Davis called Noonan "the biggest enigma I've had in my ten years of coaching." Davis had started Noonan ahead of Maryland, the top pick in the draft, as the '91 season began. "And I have no idea what happened to him. He'd make one play out of eighteen or twenty. I don't know how many closed-doors [one-on-one sessions] I've had with him, and I can't get through to him."

Johnson had been having closed-doors with Davis over the potentially volatile Noonan situation. Noonan had some brains. He could express himself to the media. He could cause serious problems. Davis said, "It's a very delicate situation."

Little did he and Johnson know that Maryland would soon be hurt. So would the other starting tackle, Tony Casillas, leaving Noonan and Jimmie Jones as opening-night starters. Jones was another enigma, an immensely talented daydreamer "you just about have to beat with a rubber hose to get going," said Davis.

On August 21, Johnson looked like someone had taken a rubber hose to him. Too many holdouts and injuries. Too little progress by injured first-round rookies Kevin Smith and Robert Jones. Too much Jerry Jones. Too many camp disruptions including Tokyo and several fund-raising functions for which Jones had required the presence of players and coaches. Still no Pro Bowl–caliber pass rusher or safety.

On top of all that, Johnson's team opened with four straight games against division foes. First came Washington in Dallas, then the Giants away, Phoenix in Dallas, and the Eagles in Philadelphia. Many experts who weren't picking the Redskins to repeat as NFL champs were going with Philadelphia to at least win the NFC title. By October 5 the Cowboys could be out of the NFC East race, and Johnson believed that winning the East and a first-week play-off bye was almost essential to advancing to the Super Bowl.

Sixteen days before the season opener, a melancholy Johnson sounded as if an 8-8 season were inevitable. "We could have been really good," he said.

Playmaking

FOR *SPORTS ILLUSTRATED*'S PAUL ZIMMERMAN, ALIAS DR. Z, this was a Super Bowl preview. Zimmerman was one of the few national experts who had picked the Cowboys to be in the Super Bowl—opposite Denver, he said. On Saturday night, August 22, at Texas Stadium the Cowboys beat the Broncos, 20–3, in an exhibition significant only because Bronco coach Dan Reeves always points to win the second-to-last practice game. Only for this exhibition does he game-plan, preparing his team specifically for the opponent. He plays his regulars a little longer than usual, then mostly holds them out of the final tune-up.

So this one began as more than just another summer scrimmage. And for the first time since Johnson had come to Dallas, Cowboy coaches saw a flash of dominance. Larry Lacewell said, "What struck me was that we really pushed 'em around in the trenches. That had to tell you something."

All it told Jerry Jones was how close this team was to being something special. He was going to find a pass rusher, a search that was reminding him more and more of the oil-and-gas business. Once, his operation was drilling in southeastern Oklahoma when a pipe broke and cost Jones around a million bucks. Time to retreat and reconsider? No, Jones and Co. moved about fifteen feet and plunged again. They hit what Jones associates call "the mother lode," the well that eventually put Jones in a position to bid for the Cowboys.

Several pipes had broken in Jones's search for a dominant defensive end. One name left on his list was a player who had intrigued Jimmy Johnson for a couple of years. Johnson had voted for Charles Haley in 1990, when he won NFC defensive player of the year. As a fan, Johnson enjoyed watching Haley play for the San Francisco 49ers because "he's one of the few players who can disrupt an offense." Johnson craved Haley's powerful quickness. Johnson had mentioned to Jones several times to keep an eye on Haley, whose sack total had fallen from 16 in '90 to 7 in '91. Through the gossip grapevine, Johnson had heard all the horror stories about how Haley can disrupt his team, too, and Johnson wondered how much longer it would be before the 49ers decided Haley wasn't quite worth the aggravation.

Several teams had inquired casually about Haley—the Broncos, Raiders, Tampa Bay. But when Jones got hold of 49er president Carmen Policy, Jones wasn't shopping—he was ready to buy. "I think we've developed a reputation in Dallas of will-do," Jones said. "I think people respect that we don't have patience for long rebuilding programs, like you see elsewhere. For us, '92 is the year, and I believe Carmen knew that was how I was approaching the deal."

Or, as Johnson says, "Most teams in this league are just afraid to make a deal anymore, afraid they won't get enough and be criticized."

Several times through the whirlwind negotiations, Jones was sure Policy had begun shopping Haley to see if he could top the Cowboy offer and create a bidding war. Now, Jones figures, "I was really negotiating against myself." He and Johnson just couldn't believe nobody else would make a legitimate offer for Charles Haley. The JJs saw Haley as a Super Bowl catalyst.

Apparently, the rest of the NFL saw him as Frankenstein meets the Wolfman—an unpredictable, uncontrollable monster. Haley made Jesse Solomon sound like Beaver Cleaver. And Jimmy Johnson, who refused to coach malcontents, wanted to coach Haley? "I did my research," Johnson said. "I heard all the stories." Here are a few:

• Several Bay Area newspapers reported that Haley exposed himself to Ann Killion of the *San Jose Mercury News* and later apologized.
• Several reporters who cover the 49ers say Haley twice made racial remarks that triggered fights with former 49er Jim Burt. A reporter close to Burt says Burt decked Haley both times.
• Many newspapers in the Bay Area and Dallas–Fort Worth reported that Haley urinated on the black BMW belonging to teammate Tim Harris, who fought with Haley and had to be restrained from seriously hurting him. In the Bay Area, the *Peninsula Times-Tribune* reported that Haley urinated on the office floor of 49er official John McVay, a story many Cowboy insiders also heard.
• Haley openly criticized 49er coach George Seifert during the '91 season for showing the 49er defense a film of the Eagles' defense and praising the Eagles. Several Bay Area reporters say Haley went so far as to say "fuck you" to Seifert, but apologized.
• Former 49er coach Bill Walsh told a San Francisco reporter that he assigned a psychologist to monitor Haley on a daily basis.

But the story most told about Haley was the one that most enlightened Johnson. Haley cherishes the friendship of former 49er teammate Ronnie Lott, who is highly respected around the league as a leader and winner. Haley idolizes Lott, say several Cowboys. In '91, when Haley's 49ers played Lott's Raiders at the L.A. Coliseum, Haley wanted badly to beat Lott's team, perhaps to prove he could match wills with his friend and mentor.

The 49ers lost, 12–6. In the locker room Haley berated quarterback Steve Young and cursed the coaches for playing Young. Haley went berserk and punched a hole in the wall and threatened to punch Young. Haley began crying, curled into the fetal position, and wouldn't move.

Lott had to be called from the adjacent Raider locker room. Clad only in a towel, he came running to soothe the savage beast in Haley.

What did Johnson like about that story? Haley shares with Johnson a rage to win. Sometimes, an over-the-edge rage. Haley's problems were often caused by wanting to win too badly. Yet Johnson's sources told him that nobody practices or studies harder than Haley, who can be wise and funny when the mood strikes him. There's more Haley in Johnson than the coach would care to admit. But of course, there can be only one coach. Would Haley respect that for an entire season? Johnson figured Haley would push him a few times, but how far?

Johnson had previously pursued two other trades for "malcontents," defensive tackle Tony Casillas and quarterback Steve Beuerlein. Both trades had turned into steals because Johnson was able to look beneath the screaming headlines. Casillas, whom Atlanta let go for a second-round pick and an eighth, isn't a bad guy. Johnson knew that from trying to recruit Casillas, who's from Tulsa, to play at Oklahoma State. Casillas just fell into a bad situation: he didn't like coach Jerry Glanville; Glanville didn't like him. It happens. For Johnson, Casillas has been nothing but a model citizen and pillar.

By all accounts, Beuerlein is as fine a fellow as ever wore a uniform, but he stood up publicly to Raider owner Al Davis on a contract matter and paid with a season in exile. At first Jones was more intrigued than Johnson by the available Beuerlein. Johnson said then, "He was a little mechanical when we [Miami] played him [Notre Dame] in college." But Johnson came around when the price for Beuerlein dropped to a fourth-rounder. A fourth for a quarterback who soon proved he could start for probably half the teams in the league?

But the Haley trade was much riskier, given his reputation and physical condition. On March 1 he had undergone arthroscopic surgery on the rotator cuff of his right shoulder, and just two weeks earlier, Haley's right knee had been 'scoped. Super Bowl or bust?

The JJs plunged. Al Davis soon called Jones and said, "Congratulations, you just won the Super Bowl." In Austin, Davis had seen up close just how close the Cowboys were. Now they had added a 6-5, 250-pound, three-time Pro Bowl pass rusher, just hitting his prime at twenty-eight.

CBS analyst and former 49er and Haley teammate Randy Cross commented, "So what if Charles had his shoulder and knee 'scoped? If he decides he's going to play, there isn't a tackle in the league who can block him. But Charles isn't the kind of guy you try to intimidate through the press, which occasionally the 49ers did. He's an extremely nice guy who happens to have some pretty severe mood swings, even with teammates at times. He didn't always take ribbing from teammates very well.

"But he's a huge positive for Dallas. If I'm [Redskin coach] Joe Gibbs, I'm getting even less sleep."

The Redskin-Cowboy Monday-night opener was twelve days away.

Jones was steroid-smiling over the deal—even though Haley now topped the team payroll at $1.4 million for '92 (Aikman made only $1,064,000), and even though Haley would become a right-of-first-refusal free agent at the end of the season, Jones said, "His salary is not out of line with what the top people at his position make." Jones's point: for the right man he would pay top dollar. Jones was so excited that he picked up Haley at the airport.

On this trade the JJs appeared to mesh egos and talents—Johnson's instincts and Jones's supersalesmanship. On this one Johnson appeared to have some respect for Jones's role. On the Casillas trade in July of '91, for instance, Johnson closed the deal by phone with Atlanta officials, he said; yet Jones told reporters he had played an integral role. At that point Johnson said privately, "My girlfriend was right there in the room when I did the deal with [Atlanta personnel director] Ken Herock. Jerry had nothing to do with it. She said, 'Why do you let him get away with [taking credit]? Why don't you go straighten the thing out?' I said, 'Oh, I don't need to be stirring things up.' . . . I can handle Jerry—you know, let him make some calls and make him feel like he's involved. Jerry does have a good heart."

But this time, unless Jones out-and-out lied, he negotiated by phone with Policy.

Policy and many other 49er people were quoted as saying basically good riddance to Haley and good luck to the Cowboys. Haley's comet had flamed out in San Francisco. Jones said the 49ers seemed so sure Haley was no bargain that the Cowboys got a bargain—a dominant player for a second-round pick in '93 and a third in '94. Jones said he closed the deal by making a "little gentleman's wager" with Policy: if the Cowboys finished with a worse record than the 49ers, the Cowboys would exchange places with the 49ers in the first and third rounds of the '93 draft.

"I think it's a pretty good deal," Jones said on August 27.

For once in 1992, Jones was guilty of understatement.

★ ★ ★

Johnson didn't take any special precautions for Haley. No personal psychologist. Johnson just told trainer Kevin O'Neill to "keep tabs" on the newest Cowboy. For the moment, Johnson had more pressing problems. Tight end Jay Novacek had finally signed, but Tony Casillas had been lost during the final exhibition, at Texas Stadium against the Bears. (Though no one in the organization seemed to be counting, the Cowboys finished the preseason 1-4.) Doctors thought Casillas had some ligament damage in his right knee. No surgery, but "at least" four weeks of healing, Johnson was told. Johnson's other starting defensive tackle, Russell Maryland, had a dislocated toe.

Some at Valley Ranch wondered if Johnson had a dislocated brain when he kept as his placekicker rookie free agent Lin Elliott instead of recycling one of four or five veterans available. Johnson had agreed with his assistants and cut Brad Daluiso, who quickly was picked up by Denver, but Johnson stuck by Elliott. "He'll be better than Ken Willis," Johnson vowed to reporters. Johnson was betting a Super Bowl run on an untested kid with the nervous eyes of Barney Fife.

Elliott was about as far as you could get from the Playmaker. Just four days before the Washington opener, Michael "the Playmaker" Irvin was still playing hard to get. For Jerry Jones, this was the toughest negotiation emotionally. Said son Stephen, "Dad has a soft spot for Michael." So does Johnson, who coached Irvin at Miami, where the nickname Playmaker stuck because he often made game-changing plays. Irvin was coming off a season in which he led the NFL in receiving yards and was MVP of the Pro Bowl.

Yet as a businessman, Jones couldn't quite forget that before the '90 season, Johnson had decided to trade Irvin. Johnson hadn't been too high on Irvin's speed at Miami. He said he told former Cowboy personnel director Gil Brandt that Irvin was no better than a second-round draft choice. But the Cowboys took him in round one (eleventh overall) of the 1988 draft, and president Tex Schramm told the media, "This will speed our return to the living." Restart the PR machine: Irvin does Irving, home of Texas Stadium.

Irvin came from a family of seventeen children in Fort Lauderdale, Florida. Irvin grew up fighting for second helpings and taped-up hand-me-down shoes. Irvin had vowed at an early age to have money one day—lots of money. In '88, Irvin proudly wore symbols of his new wealth—earrings, gilt-edged sunglasses, gaudy necklaces, designer watches, flashy rings. Irvin's motto: look good, play good. Irvin is always styling, smiling, and jabbering, though you can never remember much of what he says. Irvin lives to appear from the back of a limo at the hottest Dallas nightspot after taking over a game.

Irvin wants desperately to be a star.

Irvin's father, Walter, was a twelve-hour-a-day roofer who served as a minister on weekends, and Irvin had pledged to spend his Sundays making millions catching footballs. The one thing Irvin had learned from his father was work ethic. For all his twenty-four-karat braggadocio, Irvin is an overachiever, says Johnson. Stylish substance. "Nobody on this team works harder," says Johnson. Irvin is the football equivalent of a gym rat, a guy who will sweat through route after route as long as the third-string quarterback will throw them. Irvin drives himself out of fear his success and jewelry will vanish and he'll somehow wake up poor again.

On October 16 of Johnson's first season in Dallas, Irvin lived his worst nightmare. He tore up his knee against the 49ers.

Irvin attacked the rehabilitation the way he does practices. But during the next training camp, Irvin appeared to have lost a step off his already average speed. Former personnel director John Wooten says Johnson asked him to shop Irvin on the trade market. Wooten says Johnson nearly pulled the trigger on a deal, then reconsidered when Wooten and other assistants were so fearful of giving up on Irvin.

For all his solo ego, Johnson seeks input before making moves. He listens, to a point. He freely gives public credit to assistants in their areas. But he won't share credit for big decisions and rarely admits publicly to bad ones, such as trades he did make for Alonzo Highsmith, Dan Stubbs, and Terrence Flagler. Johnson detests the negative thoughts that sometimes infiltrate his psyche and send him into a tailspin. He constantly battles to convince himself—and the world—he's invincible.

He made the right move by not moving Irvin, who in many ways was made to play for Johnson. Irvin shares that positive gene. On the field Irvin can talk trash with the worst of them. Teammates say he's mainly trying to convince himself he's unstoppable. Irvin speaks of Johnson as if he's some sort of ghetto god—the truth and the way out. "I believe in Jimmy," Irvin says. Irvin views Johnson with an emotion between fear and love. Most black players seem to.

Of Johnson's rapport with black players, Irvin told *Sports Illustrated,* "He'll sit there and listen—I mean, really listen. You know he's in your corner, no matter how the media caves in you." Johnson proudly notes that he was the first coach to recruit a majority of blacks to Miami. "Before then, they had mostly white teams," Johnson says. John Wooten says it's important to remember that Johnson grew up playing sports and hanging with lots of "slick, shrewd" blacks in Port Arthur.

Jimmy's hip. Unlike Tom Landry, Johnson is bilingual; he can speak fluent "press conference" and fluent "locker room." Johnson at age forty-nine seems more comfortable speaking the players' language, including the black players'. Johnson is cool using the f-word and the mf-word for humor and emphasis. Through locker-room joking and practice-field whip-cracking, Johnson communicates the message to players that if they work and play hard for him, he will give them the chance to win games and glory. Johnson won't overcoach or suffocate talent. He almost always lets talented players play. Johnson says, "They know I'll pull the trigger on 'em [cut them], and they know I'll put the game in their hands."

This unspoken bond is critical to Johnson's success as a head coach and leader. Few coaches have Johnson's rapport with players, especially blacks. Johnson seems more comfortable dealing with his black players than, say, with Troy Aikman. He relates easier to the blacks, the cockier performers.

Dr. Don Beck, a psychologist who worked closely with Landry and has studied Johnson, says, "No way could Tom have dealt with today's sophisticated, coming-of-age black athletes. Tom dealt with black athletes who were angry individuals. Jimmy makes them all part of the team—all just football players. There is freedom of expression. But they know he has the hammer—the velvet hammer. Jimmy's ability with the black athlete has been essential to his success."

And Michael Jerome Irvin is the leader of Johnson's black players—and lots of whites, too. Says Norv Turner, "Mike's the one everybody looks to and feeds off." Mike is the one they glance at in the locker room before a Redskin game and think, "I'm glad he's on our side." Mike is the one who will make the big play and refuse to lose.

Then again, Irvin fed off the offense Turner installed in '91— Aikman-Turner Overdrive. In '90, Irvin caught 20 passes. In '91, he caught 93 for 1,523 yards and 8 touchdowns. Working mainly against All-Pro cornerback Darrell Green, Irvin caught 9 for 130 yards in Washington. So off one great season, did Irvin deserve to be the NFL's highest-paid receiver? You bet, Irvin told Jones. Was the guy Johnson nearly traded suddenly better than the best, San Francisco's Jerry Rice? Without Turner's scheme, which is made for Irvin's medium-range, shove-and-cut routes, would Irvin turn back into living proof of the old Gil Brandt line? Brandt once said, "You can find receivers on any street corner in Harlem."

Turner pondered Irvin's value. "I didn't realize how much it meant to be so big and strong and be able to jump so well," Turner said of the 6-2, 200-pound Irvin, who won slam-dunk contests in high school and college. "Michael's arms are just so long, and he's just so physical. He just overpowers a lot of corners.

"When I first got here, he dropped some balls. Jimmy told me, 'He's going to drop some balls.' Mike had been through a tough time when he wondered—a lot of people wondered—if he'd ever be the star he wants to be. But last year he got on a hot streak catching the ball, and even in minicamps he didn't stop. We'll go for days without him dropping one. It's uncanny."

Michael Irvin wants to be the NFL's Michael Jordan. Irvin took his receiver coach, Hubbard Alexander, to Chicago to see Jordan vs. Portland in the NBA Finals. "Ax," as the players call Alexander, all but idolizes Irvin. The longer Irvin's holdout lasted, the more Alexander agonized. "The whole season could hinge on this," he said. Alexander kept in touch with Irvin. Alexander knew the factors tearing at Irvin's soul. He knew Irvin felt some pressure to bring Jerry Jones to his contractual knees and impress one of Irvin's best friends, Deion Sanders. Alexander also knew Irvin could be beaten down by Jones, lose the confidence he had rebuilt after his injury, and never quite regain it after missing the entire preseason.

Yet Jones said the problem simply was this: Irvin began negotiations asking for what Jones called Michael Jordan money—somewhere up around $3 million a year. "I mean, I might as well give him part of the club," Jones said.

But on Thursday afternoon, September 3, Irvin contacted Jones and said it was time to get something done. Later that night Jones bumped up an incentives package and Irvin came down to around $1.25 million base for '92, and they agreed on a three-year deal. Irvin produced a $125 Mont Blanc pen he had purchased for the occasion.

"I'm rich!" he said, beaming.

He told the *Fort Worth Star-Telegram,* "Now I can take care of my mother. I can take care of my people [Irvin helps subsidize many of his sixteen siblings and their families]. They are about to arrive at the promised land, just like Martin Luther King used to talk about. It's too bad my father [who died of cancer in '83] isn't here to see it."

Of course, by Michael Jordan and Deion Sanders standards, Irvin's contract wasn't much more than limo tips. But for a poor kid from Fort Lauderdale, even one with so many family hands in his cookie jar, Irvin was filthy rich. Irvin believed he had won; Jones knew Jones had. Irvin hadn't lost any locker-room face. The Playmaker was on fire to play some football.

★ ★ ★

Center Mark Stepnoski was the last holdout to sign, on Saturday, two days before Washington. He received an about-right $600,000 base salary for '92. After he and Jones agreed, and while the contract was being drawn up, Stepnoski hustled to line coach Tony Wise's office. Stepnoski, a long-haired, twenty-five-year-old curmudgeon from the University of Pittsburgh who enjoys shock jock Howard Stern, actually appeared ready to hug somebody. Wise was in no mood to hug back.

Though Wise hadn't seen Stepnoski for about two months, Wise barely shook his hand. Wise had described Stepnoski as a guy who went to a school that produces lots of NFL offensive linemen. "This," Wise had said, "is strictly a business to Mark."

Wise, from Ithaca College, had little use for coaching big businessmen. "Is that all this is about, money?" Wise asked.

Stepnoski wanted to know if he would be activated for Monday night's game. "I'm not sure," Wise said. "Probably not."

Wise was in the middle of an interview. He told Stepnoski to come back in an hour. Wise told the interviewer he was more concerned about a bunch of other guys who had "busted their ass for me" through a long, hot camp.

★ ★ ★

Offensive coordinator Norv Turner and defensive coordinator Dave Wannstedt are the yin and yang of pregame moods. Turner usually worries about how talented the opponent is, what he probably won't be able to do, what could go wrong, and how overconfident some of the other coaches get. Though realistic, Wannstedt usually talks about new wrinkles he's sure will work and ways he can thwart a star back or receiver.

Two days before the Washington game, Turner said, "They are very, very sound on defense. Every game I've ever coached against them, they've always had a new look—a blitz, a coverage, a front. So I don't know what to expect. I have no idea how Michael and Jay will do. You just hope they don't get hurt. We are not near where we were offensively for Cleveland last year [in the opener]. We just haven't had any continuity. At least [Washington quarterback Mark] Rypien has only been there ten days [after holding out]. He's a slow starter, anyway. Maybe he'll throw a couple to us. Maybe we'll play their run well and it'll just be slow death."

Wannstedt said, "We've always been able to shut down their run. Hey, Danny Noonan and Jimmie Jones [subbing for Casillas and Maryland] had the two best camps of any of our linemen. Kevin Smith just hasn't been healthy enough to win the job from Ike [Holt], but we'll get [Darren] Woodson in there on the nickel. Robert Jones will be okay. We'll be okay. It'll come down to whether Rypien can beat us or not, and we will go after him."

Yet, for this book, Turner and Wannstedt were asked if they thought the Cowboys had a chance to win the Super Bowl. Both responded with versions of, "You've got to be kidding."

The morning of the Washington game, Jerry Jones provided some insight into the pregame yin and yang of Jimmy Johnson, Mr. Positive vs. Mr. Negative. The previous November 24, the 6-5 Cowboys had played the 11-0 Redskins at Washington's RFK Stadium. On the field an hour or so before kickoff, said Jones, Johnson was about ready to call it off. "I'd never seen him just write a game off like that," Jones said. "Jimmy was worried about what getting destroyed would do for us against Pittsburgh [four days later on Thanksgiving]. Dave [Wannstedt] was there saying, 'Hey, we're not going to give up. We'll hold 'em some, get 'em to punt, win a few battles, see if we can hang in.' Jimmy was just beside himself."

For Jones, the amusing point of the story was that Johnson then came out swinging. Just when you thought he was ready to throw in the towel, he threw it in Washington's face. He called for an onside kick following a second-quarter touchdown, and the Cowboys recovered. The Cowboys hit a Hail Mary touchdown pass as the half ended to lead, 14–7. Going for it at every opportunity, Dallas won, 24–21. Johnson was hailed all week in Dallas as the NFL's emerging genius.

In the locker room afterward, flushed with victory, Johnson animatedly told the team about how, when you're up against the big gorilla, you don't just tap him. "You hit him with everything you've got!" Johnson yelled, inspiring whoops and hugs.

Fortunately, of course, the team didn't hear Johnson talking to Jones and Wannstedt before the game.

This time, though, Johnson was feeling good about a home opener against the defending Super Bowl champs, said Jones. Feeling good and cocky. "Jimmy thinks we'll win. He's more worried about getting ready for New York [at Giants Stadium after a short week]."

Any new strategy for the Skins? "Watch," said GM Jones. "We're gonna blitz the shit out of 'em on the first play."

That's exactly what happened. In fact, that max blitz set the reverberating tone for the entire season. With that opening surge, a spectacular lightning storm on a hot, clear Texas night, lots of doubts and distractions were forgotten. The Tokyo trip, the injuries, the holdouts, the youth—all of it went up in the smoke you could almost see coming out of the Cowboys' earholes.

On Washington's first offensive play, first and 10 from its 20, fifteen or sixteen Cowboys appeared to be blitzing. Linebacker Vinson Smith blew through unblocked and sacked Rypien for an 11-yard loss.

And roofless Texas Stadium turned into an echo chamber. Johnson said he had never heard it that loud. Privately, the following day, Redskin coach Joe Gibbs said, "That was Texas Stadium?" Then, half-kidding: "Where was Tom Landry when we needed him?"

Gibbs, of course, has enormous respect for Landry, professionally and spiritually. But this wasn't the sanctuary atmosphere Gibbs had come to expect when he brought his teams to play Landry's. This was like, well, an Arkansas Razorback crowd. On Labor Day night, with the "Monday Night Football" cameras trained on Texas Stadium, these Cowboy fans seemed hell-bent to show the world they no longer sat on their manicures. They made NOISE, damn it.

Washington coaches and players said they were caught completely off guard. The offense couldn't hear Rypien's audibles or snap count. Washington had 8 penalties for 80 yards. Said All-Pro tackle Jim Lachey, "I had to watch the defensive man to know when to move."

What detonated the noise? Was it in part the pent-up anticipation caused by Jones's relentless preseason hyping? Was the crowd just responding to the highly visible emotion of a defense that Johnson and Wannstedt had brought to a boil back in Austin? Was it the red-line rpm level of Charles Haley? No Cowboy defensive lineman had played with such crazed intensity since Randy White in his prime. Haley appeared 100 percent healthy, physically and mentally. Lachey struggled with Haley. Haley made a difference. Cowboy coaches thought other linemen fed off Haley's fury.

"It was the best effort the defense has given since I've been here," Wannstedt said, saying a lot. "It was effort, guts, and speed."

The Redskins weren't quite prepared for the speed with which the Cowboys attacked in the 86-degree heat. Gibbs said, "Our defensive line got blown off the ball, and our offensive line was handled like it hasn't been since '88."

On the second Washington play, Jimmie Jones threw Earnest Byner for a 3-yard loss. On the third play, Haley was all over Rypien, whose pass missed Byner badly. On fourth down, Ike Holt broke free and blocked Kelly Goodburn's punt for a safety; yes, the team so suspect at safety had forced one. Cowboys, 2–0.

The following week, Cowboy coaches marveled at how many receivers Rypien had open in—or behind—the secondary. But Rypien, the Super Bowl MVP, never seemed to recover from that opening sack. He overthrew. He underthrew. The Rypien of '91, who routinely completed 60-yarders as if he were tossing his jersey in the laundry bin, might have hit three or four TD passes.

Instead, the Cowboys were off to the races, 23–10. Though he did drop a couple, Michael Irvin hit midseason form with 5 catches for 89 yards. Emmitt Smith was in postseason form with 139 yards on 26 carries. The defense allowed only 75 yards rushing. The Redskins weren't able to exploit rookie middle linebacker Jones. Rookie kicker Elliott didn't have to attempt a field goal. So what if the 'Boys were the NFL's youngest team, opening the season at 25.3 years per player?

Norv Turner said, "I really didn't think we could run the ball like that. That was the key. Nate [Newton] was great. I mean, their defense was ranked third in the league last year and we got three hundred ninety yards."

Had the Cowboys blitzed the Skins more with emotion than talent? Was Johnson right to be worried about regaining a similar pitch for the Giants in five days? In '91, the Cowboys lost an emotion-packed home Monday-nighter to Washington, 33–31, then got buried at home by Philadelphia, 24–0.

"Nothing to worry about, man," said Newton as he tore the tape off his ankles. To Newton, the team's youth was a strength. "We got too many young motherfuckers on this team who'll be out there running around like crazy at New York. They don't know any better."

For sure, they didn't know their head coach was saying just a week earlier that the season looked bleak at best.

Safety Net

THE MORNING AFTER, JERRY JONES'S EYES LOOKED AS IF THEY hadn't been closed for about forty-eight hours. He said he hadn't slept much if any the night before the Washington game, and he was seen about two hours after the game, maybe one A.M., leading a party of family and friends into the Dallas night. "We're just getting warmed up," he said, grinning.

So the next day Jones's eyes looked a little like maps of red Arkansas two-lanes. Jimmy Johnson is more of the two-fisted drinker, but Jones intoxicates himself talking football, which he'd rather do than sleep. Jones celebrates victories, but he isn't a gloater like Johnson. Johnson says, "Wins hang with me longer because I like to gloat. I'm just being honest. I don't dwell on losses. The media and fans dwell on losses. But a win I hang on to for a while."

As Jones spoke with a few reporters in the hall at Valley Ranch, he was trying not to gloat about his little victory over Johnson and the assistants and players who thought he had ruined the season. "Oh," Jones said, "maybe I was feeling more responsibility for the

Tokyo trip and the holdouts than I needed to. There sure would have been some excuses available if we had lost, wouldn't there?"

Jones gave it one of his "Know where I'm heading?" smiles. The Cowboys had won, and won impressively for all the country to see. Everything worked out, just as Jones kept saying it would. "I do have a plan," Jones said.

That week, Jones's plan included another manhunt.

Jones, son Stephen, and part owner Mike McCoy continued to brainstorm about what else the Cowboys needed to win the Super Bowl. Of oil-and-gas partner McCoy, a forty-four-year-old geologist by trade, Jones says, exaggerating for emphasis, "If Jimmy has a genius IQ, double it and you have Mike." McCoy is a funny, clever, even-keel, camera-shy counterbalance to Jones. He has stylish waves of combed-back hair and a stylish new wife, an ex-flight attendant named Joni. McCoy says he would like to own his own team someday, but for now is content to operate quietly in Jones's giant shadow. McCoy has no football background but absorbs everything the coaches and personnel people tell him and has significant input into major decisions, especially those regarding a player's financial worth. "It isn't brain surgery," McCoy says. "It's just common sense." McCoy did Jones's first major Cowboy negotiation, with rookie Aikman's agent Leigh Steinberg, who was no rookie. Representing many of the league's marquee quarterbacks, Steinberg has matched egos and wits with the league's toughest negotiators. Steinberg called McCoy "whip smart."

Yet the Cowboys were ridiculed in the media for overpaying Aikman.

In '92, as Aikman enhanced a reputation as the most valuable young quarterback in football, he made $3.236 million less than Dan Marino, who made $4.3 million. Aikman probably was the NFL's best bargain in '92—Aikman or Emmitt Smith, who made $465,000 base. Yes, McCoy was invaluable in the '90 Smith negotiation, too. Feed the right data into his mental computer and he'll give you amazingly accurate reads on football decisions.

The day after the Washington win, McCoy helped convince Jones that the Cowboys had to have a safety.

"We have problems at safety," McCoy said in a one-on-one chat, "and I'm sure the other teams know we have a problem. I give [starting free safety] Ray Horton an A-plus for effort. You just wish he could run a little faster, jump a little higher, be a little bigger and stronger. James Washington [the strong safety]—you keep seeing somebody run by him on replays and he looks at the other guys like, 'I thought you were going to take him.' We all [Jones, Stephen, McCoy] sit around saying, 'Where is that surplus safety who might be available?' Would we love to trade, say, Danny Noonan for [Denver backup] Alton Montgomery? You bet, but Denver doesn't need Danny Noonan. We're still looking."

Horton was listed at 5-11, 190 pounds, but played smaller. He was a tenth-year vet out of the University of Washington, a former second-round choice of Cincinnati's and the JJs' first Plan B signee, in '89. His strength was his savvy, though coaches sometimes wished his mental computer activated some 4.4-second 40-yard-dash speed. Washington was slightly faster, but sometimes considerably slower instinctively. Washington was a Plan B acquisition from the Rams in '90, a 6-1, 197-pounder from South Central Los Angeles and UCLA known for big hits and misses. Washington occasionally blasted receivers and ballcarriers; coaches occasionally blasted Washington for attempting the big hit and giving up the big play. Especially against smart quarterbacks and pure passing attacks, the Cowboys were none too safe at safety.

So it was that week, in the second-to-last paragraph of my syndicated sports column, that I wrote, as gently as possible, "Would you trade Noonan, who could start for several teams, for a proven safety who can run a little faster than James Washington and Ray Horton? I would. Washington and Horton have underestimated strengths. But only a furious pass rush will save them from being isolated and beaten deep occasionally."

What happened the following day may provide some insight into the delicate writer-player relationship in the locker room. The Cowboys open their locker room to the media between noon and one P.M. Team officials ask players to make themselves available, at least for a few minutes, though some players often leave for the entire lunch hour or avoid the media by staying in the trainer's room. I didn't know Horton well because he refuses interviews to most media members, especially writers. During training camp, I asked him to be interviewed for this book. He said, "Why do you want to talk to me? The coaches tell you guys everything. They don't tell us anything."

In Austin, Horton and I did speak for a half hour only after I agreed not to quote him.

But that Wednesday after the Washington game, Horton spoke to me unconditionally. He called me over to his locker, the first one on the left after you push through the entrance curtains. The Valley Ranch locker area is a giant expanse of plush blue carpet, about twenty yards square, bordered on four sides by locker cubicles. Through the blue curtains next to Horton's locker are the equipment room and shower area. Through another curtained entrance on the far side of the locker area is the lunch lounge. The lockers form walls that separate the dressing area from a series of individual meeting rooms for each assistant and his players and from one large theater-style hall for team meetings and press conferences. Tex Schramm had designed the Caesars Palace of football facilities.

Originally, Schramm grouped the cubicles into several culs-de-sac, but Johnson felt they lent themselves to cliques and divisiveness and had them pushed back into a giant rectangle, facing each other. So now, if Horton was sitting in his cubicle, he would have to shout to carry on a conversation with, say, Tony Casillas, sitting in his cubicle on the opposite side of the dressing expanse.

Soon, Horton was shouting at me. Teammates and reporters later said they'd never heard him shout at anyone, but from what I could gather, Horton was enraged that I wrote what I wrote after what he considered one of the best performances of his career. Horton was thinking in the present; I was writing big picture. I was writing with input from management and coaches, and Horton indicated he knew that. Was he blasting the messenger? In part, perhaps. Was he sending a message back to my sources? Maybe.

As Horton's voice rose, teammates began to gather. Twenty, thirty, listening with awe and some amusement to this tirade from this quiet, proud little man. Charles Haley, who usually won't talk to the media, either, took a ringside seat in the next cubicle, grinning wider and wider as Horton's temperature rose. Haley later joked that the scene should have been videotaped by the PR department to teach young players how to handle the media.

"Did I get beat the other night?" Horton demanded of me. Though I knew this was his stage and nowhere to discuss my contention logically or rationally, I said in a normal tone I was thinking more of several preseason touchdown passes for which Horton was at least partly responsible, not to mention several '91 games in which he was clearly torched. "But what about the other night?" he kept yelling. "You show me where somebody ran by me." He challenged me to watch the Washington tape with him. I agreed to, though I tried to explain that wasn't my overall point.

Then Horton said, "I don't talk to you. You don't write about me."

Even if Horton won't talk to the media, he is a highly paid entertainer. He is part of the story readers want to read about, isn't he?

Then Horton turned his wrath on the many media members who had also gathered. "A lot of you media people come in here because you want to look at athletes, because you couldn't be one in high school."

Then, back to me: "Come with me tomorrow at three. I'm speaking at a grade school. You'll see what I'm all about."

Obviously, Horton's community involvement has little to do with his ability to prevent touchdown passes. But I did watch the Washington tape with him. He played exceptionally well. But so did Haley. Under Haley's rush and disrupted by the noise, Redskin quarterback Rypien played exceptionally poorly.

Jones was on the move to find a replacement for Horton, and Horton seemed to know or at least sense it. Horton had challenged Jones once publicly, the season before, threatening a walkout over a contractual matter after an October 6 game in Green Bay. "We didn't do a thing and it blew over," said Jones, who seemed unconcerned about any noise Horton would make. To Jones, Horton was short-term. "Maybe he keeps pushing his role of 'quarterback' back there [in the secondary] to keep his job."

★ ★ ★

Horton's uncharacteristic blowup didn't cause much more than a blip on the local media screen that week. But Jimmy Johnson's private life had sparked a public debate on talk shows and in letter-to-the-editor columns. Johnson had made a calculated decision to open to the world his Valley Ranch sanctum—his house a mile or so from the office. First he agreed to let Ed Hinton of *Sports Illustrated* hang out for several days with him and his girlfriend,

Rhonda Rookmaaker, who lives nearby. Hinton even attended a family gathering in Port Arthur with Jimmy and Rhonda.

Then, under some political pressure, Johnson allowed *Dallas Morning News* reporter Barry Horn similar access. The *Morning News* learned the *Sports Illustrated* story was in the works, said Johnson, and well, he decided he owed the Dallas paper an equal opportunity.

"I thought both articles were fairly accurate," Johnson said in an interview for this book. "But a lot of people might not see things the way I see them. That's the danger of opening up your private life. You don't mean to offend anybody, but I'm not going to apologize for it, either."

In the *Sports Illustrated* article Johnson talked about why he sprang a divorce on Linda Kay, his wife of twenty-six years, soon after accepting the Cowboy job. Their second son, Chad, was graduating from college, and Johnson said he was "to the point in my life that I ought to be able to do what the hell I want to do."

The *Morning News* story said, "Jimmy Johnson never enjoyed a Thanksgiving meal with his family, never celebrated Christmas, never exchanged gifts with his family." Johnson's comment to the *Morning News:* "The only way I could have gotten . . . to this point in my life [career-wise] is to have lived the way I lived." Rhonda's comment to the newspaper: "There are so many different sides to him that I still haven't seen and would like to think I will see. A lot of people write things about Jimmy that make him seem like a beast. It's not true. It's just that he's the most honest man I've ever met. He is not afraid to say what he believes. Some people think that's rude. I think that's terrific."

But many Cowboy followers did not think the two stories were so terrific. Johnson, of course, followed Tom Landry. Compared to Landry, Johnson came across as Satan's Coach.

"I have great respect for Tom Landry," Johnson said, then shrugged. "But I'm not Tom Landry."

Amazingly, until the two articles appeared, Dallas-area media and fans had rarely compared Johnson to Landry. During his first training camp Johnson was asked the inevitable questions about the enormous pressure of following a legend. But Johnson quickly made it clear Landry was Landry and he was Jimmy Johnson. He respected what Landry had accomplished, he said, but now he was concerned only with 1989. He was going to do it his way, take it or leave it. No comparisons, please. No more Landry questions.

But this second week in September, many talk-show callers were incensed that Johnson presented such a poor role model. A letter to the *Morning News* from Barbara Schmidt of Stephenville, Texas, blasted Johnson for his "winning-at-all-costs mentality that says moral responsibilities including marriage, children, and family be damned and discarded." Christina E. Seeley of Garland wrote to the *Morning News*, "If ever there was a misfit who had the good fortune to be born during the right historical epoch, Jimmy Johnson is that man. Had he lived during any other time, he would have had to go out and invent the National Football League in order to survive. Here is a man so consumed by his fear of being out of control that he is physically shut out from the rest of the world. There are no family relationships from which to draw comfort or love, no intimate relationships based on trust and loyalty, no healthy work ethic that gives definition to the words *leisure* and *play*."

Yet the "workaholic" tag perplexes Johnson. He isn't a slave to football; he chooses to live it because he loves it. He said, "I spend more *time* at it than working at it." Where would he rather be than watching tape, game-planning, overseeing practice, laughing and talking with Michael Irvin and Emmitt Smith, drinking beer and sharing gossip with assistants, and making decisions that shock the world? What man, asks Johnson, wouldn't want to go home whenever the hell he wants and watch games or movies on cable, watch the fish, or invite his girlfriend over?

"I'm at peace," Johnson said. "Everybody who knows me knows I'm very happy being by myself. There are certain things I'm very selfish with—one is me. I'm not selfish with my money or with things or with praise. But I'm selfish with myself."

Johnson admits he neglected his two sons while they were growing up: "I barely knew them." But now, he said, "I have a better relationship with them than a lot of fathers probably have with their sons. I love them very much. We've become very close friends."

Johnson just doesn't want the traditional responsibilities of being a husband: the social occasions, the functions, the dinners. Of the *SI* and *Morning News* stories Johnson said, "The little old ladies dragging their husbands to these dinners, they're the ones it pissed off. Of course, their husbands say to them, 'Oh, dear, isn't this terrible?' But off to the side they're saying, 'Yeah-yeah-yeah.' "

Johnson did his impression of the henpecked husband quietly clapping with envy for Jimmy Johnson, bachelor role model.

Johnson said, "Some of the most miserable times of my life were having to sit next to some blue-haired lady at some function and having her ask, 'What's the quarterback do?' "

So just this once, said Johnson, he opened his door and laid his lifestyle and beliefs on the kitchen table, right there next to his Heineken and microwaved Mexican food for all to see. Take him or leave him. But why now? Why after three years in Dallas did Johnson suddenly decide to go stunningly public? Some at Valley Ranch believed Johnson had read and heard enough about Jerry Jones, great American success story, and that a part of Johnson was competing for attention. Johnson scoffs at that notion.

PR director Rich Dalrymple's theory was that Johnson had won the right to receive some attention. Dalrymple said, "Jimmy is very comfortable with who he is right now, and a lot of people can't say that. But he was comfortable enough to do the stories because he's more comfortable with where the Cowboys are. It's getting to be like the good old days in Miami. The way we played Monday night, you could almost see some orange and green [Hurricane colors] out there. You saw flashes of the way Miami plays defense— fresh linemen in and out, dominating, speed and hitting.

"I also think Jimmy wants people to know he's a Texan through and through, like Coach Landry. You know, a whole lot of people identify with Jimmy just like a whole lot identify with Coach Landry. I warned Jimmy he'd get a bunch of cards and letters, but that didn't faze him."

Who knows? Maybe the real reason Johnson did the stories was no real reason. As he told the *Morning News*, "Most people think they know me. I like it to be that way. Let them think. But I can't really let people know me. I don't want people ever to know me well enough to predict what I'll do. That way, I always remain in control."

★ ★ ★

In one way Johnson is utterly predictable. When the itinerary said the team plane would leave at ten A.M. Saturday morning, it left at ten. The team's American Airlines charter flights always left from a hangar area on the far side of the Dallas–Fort Worth Airport grounds that required a map to find. The departure site is so remote that, as you make the final left turn, a cotton field is on your right.

Then you follow a two-lane road between air-freight offices and warehouses about a half mile to a fenced-in parking lot, used for players' and coaches' cars. The plane is parked just a few yards away, ready for boarding. The area doesn't allow much room for fans who might want to greet the team as it returns, but very few Cowboy fans had ever been so fanatical that they went driving all over creation late on a Sunday night to find the team's arrival area.

On Cowboy charters the coaches occupy part of first class and the first two or three rows of the coach section. That depends on whether Jerry Jones and/or his wife decide to go on the charter or in Jones's private jet. An occasional top-dollar sponsor gets two first-class seats, too. In the coach-section seats behind the coaches sit more sponsors, team officials, and thirty or so TV and radio reporters and camera people. The players get an open seat between them beginning in about row fifteen of coach to the back, where team doctors, trainers, and equipment men occupy the last seats.

On one three-hour team charter, enough food is served to last a normal human three days. Goody bags are waiting in every seat before takeoff. They usually hold a giant submarine sandwich, a brownie, several cookies, several candy bars, a large box of M&M's, raisins, two packages of nuts, a piece of fruit, assorted cheeses, and two packages of chips. Then, an hour into the flight comes the real meal, usually a choice of seafood or steak with all the trimmings and an accompanying shrimp-cocktail plate that's a meal in itself. Dessert is usually an ice-cream bar, or three.

The players are quiet on outbound trips, eating, sleeping, reading paperbacks or game plans. Many are lost in headphone music. Others talk in low voices among themselves or to assistants. On the way up players dress in coats and ties. On the way back, no dress code. "That's the way Jimmy likes it," Emmitt Smith said. "He makes it very clear we're on a business trip. We can celebrate on the way back, if we win." On some return trips up to sixty cases of beer are consumed, not to mention the hard stuff smuggled onto the flight by some players in need of liquid painkiller. Smith and

Irvin have been known to share a few sips of Tanqueray or Crown Royal on the way home.

Just for Johnson, the crew always stocks Heineken.

On the Saturday flight to Newark for Sunday's game at Giants Stadium in New Jersey, the loudest noise was the hum of the engines. Perhaps the most talkative passenger was scouting director Larry Lacewell, who knew Jimmy Johnson before he became *the* Jimmy Johnson. Lacewell is a loquacious little rooster with a mesmerizing Southern tongue. "Lace," from Bear Bryant's hometown of Fordyce, Arkansas, began his coaching career under Bryant at Alabama and became known around college football for his ability to spot talent and coach defense, and for his stormy breakup with Barry Switzer at the University of Oklahoma. Johnson coached under Lacewell at Wichita State ('67), Iowa State ('68), and Oklahoma ('70–72). Johnson has an affinity for Lacewell because he has always been part of winners—at OU, Arkansas State, and Tennessee, where as late as 1991 Lacewell was named the nation's top collegiate linebacker coach by *The Sporting News*.

On the way to Newark, Lacewell talked about the Johnson he knew and knows.

"I called Jimmy [from Wichita State] when he was down at Picayune, Mississippi [as a high-school assistant], and I told him we couldn't afford to move him and couldn't afford to pay him very much, but that we had a job for him. I said, 'You better talk to your wife,' but before I could hang up, he said, 'I'm comin'.' He and Linda Kay packed up the U-Haul and here they came. I knew right from the start that Jimmy was different. When he didn't have a penny to his name, he was driving a Corvette. When people didn't drive motorcycles, he had a motorcycle—drove it all around Norman, Oklahoma. Took me frog-giggin' on the back of that motorcycle. We'd drive down in the river bottoms and shine the lights in their eyes.

"We'd lose a game at Wichita State, and Jimmy would say, 'That's it, I'm getting out of coaching.' And you'd think he was serious. He used to drive me nuts in meetings because he'd never take a note. Kept it all right here [Lacewell tapped his head]. Never forgot a detail. We'd talk defense for hours. We'd flare up at each other, but we'd come right back the next day and all would be forgotten.

"He always wanted to attack, and I was always more conservative, more sit back and read. Jimmy loves to bring those [defensive] ends and really disrupt blocking schemes. He doesn't want them pausing to think, 'Is it a run or a pass?' Jimmy's linebackers, they ain't nuthin' but strong safeties. Speed and quickness. Listen, people don't understand, but with Haley this defense is just a hair away from being hellacious good. Just one glaring weakness." At safety, whether Ray Horton wanted to hear it or not.

Lacewell, who works closely with Jones, was asked if Jones and Johnson could hold their relationship together long enough to win more than one Super Bowl.

"Who says Jimmy wants to win more than one?" Lacewell asked. "I'm telling you, he's different. He's exactly what came across in those articles—and he's not that at all."

★ ★ ★

Back in the spring Johnson quietly predicted the Giants would be the NFC East team that would slide slowly into the '92 sunset. Now Johnson had the opportunity to hasten the demise of a team that won the Super Bowl two years earlier. Minutes after that game, former Cowboy Everson Walls hugged Giant coach Bill Parcells, who whispered, "Power wins." Johnson respects Parcells—they're friendly—but Johnson believes more in defensive quickness and ball-control passing than in Parcells's big bad powerball.

Not only were the Cowboys the league's youngest team, they were the lightest, too, at 223.6 pounds per man. Already, ex-49er coach Bill Walsh had been widely quoted as saying the '92 Cowboys reminded him of his old San Francisco teams. "They're more cut down as opposed to the NFC East style of huge overpowering teams," Walsh said.

After the '89 season Johnson dumped Walls, one of his first captains, because Walls was too slow and insolent for Johnson. So Walls had joined another Johnson castoff, linebacker Steve DeOssie, in New York and won a ring and a *Sports Illustrated* cover shot celebrating Super Bowl XXV. Walls and DeOssie were still starting for Giant coach Ray Handley. Though the Giants had lost their opener at home to San Francisco, 31–14—to chants of "Ray must go!"—DeOssie predicted New York's proud old warriors would get back to basics and teach this upstart Dallas team one more lesson.

"You better not count us out yet," said DeOssie. "We do still have a guy named Lawrence Taylor, you know."

The Cowboy coaches were much more worried about young running back Rodney Hampton and the Giant offensive line. "Their secondary isn't too good in spots," Norv Turner said. "We'll be able to move the ball against 'em—if we have the ball." Dave Wannstedt said, "We hear that the Giants are just going to try to run the ball down our throats and control the clock."

That did not happen.

What did happen nobody would have predicted. The Cowboys were about to play a doubleheader in a football-only stadium on a perfect afternoon for baseball, 71 degrees and calm.

NFL teams are usually sluggish and often awful when forced to play on the road after a Monday-night game. The body and mind just don't have enough time to recover and reload. All week Johnson and staff had challenged—if not begged—the team to respond just the way it had against Washington. Johnson told the team, "Don't let what happens to everyone else in this league happen to you. You are better than this team."

And before you could say turn out the lights, the young Cowboys punched the lights out of the old Giants. The Cowboys attacked and overwhelmed the Giants just the way they had the Redskins. The Cowboys blocked another punt and deflected yet another. In the first half Troy Aikman was 16 of 24 for 177 yards, while the Giants rang up 53 yards total. Halftime score: Dallas 27, Giants 0.

Wannstedt said, "I went in there at halftime and told 'em the key to the game was the first series of the third quarter. I said, 'Stop 'em there and we'll win this thing.' "

On New York's second play of the second half, Phil Simms's pass was intercepted by James Washington. Three plays later Aikman hit Michael Irvin for 27 yards and the 34–0 touchdown. Imagine: the Cowboys were leading the Giants 34–0 at Giants Stadium. Ray must go!

Following his own advice, Wannstedt backed off a little, calling more conservative zone defenses. Simms took the Giants 80 yards in 9 plays. Cowboys, 34–7.

Five plays later, the Cowboys faced third and 2 at the Giant 46 and called time-out. Later, Turner was furious at himself. "I let myself get talked into something," he said. "That won't happen again." Turner had called a pass. Other coaches sitting beside Turner in the press box, with headphone input from Johnson, lobbied for a running play. Fullback Daryl Johnston was stopped a yard short of the first down. The Cowboys punted.

"We could have put 'em away right there," Turner said.

Instead, the Giants went 80 yards in 12 plays, including a 28-yard pass on fourth down and 10, to cut the lead to 34–14 near the end of the third quarter. The Giants held, then went 62 yards in 8 plays for another touchdown: Dallas 34, New York 21. The Giants held again, then took just 5 plays to go 55 yards: 34–28. Throats grew ever tighter when the Cowboys managed just one first down before having to punt again.

With 3:42 left, the Giants had the ball first and 10 at their 19 with a chance to make NFL history. One more touchdown and they would pull off the league's biggest comeback; in 1980, the 49ers had come from 35–7 down to beat the Saints, 38–35.

In the '92 play-offs the Buffalo Bills would come from 35–3 down to shock the Houston Oilers and the NFL world. Wiping out that 32-point lead set the league record—but it wouldn't have if the Giants had scored one more touchdown against the Cowboys. The game that people would have talked about all season—the one that could have destroyed the '92 Cowboys—would have been played on September 13. Tony Wise said, "We were dangerously close to losing a game we might not have gotten over the rest of the year. On the sidelines it was utter frustration. I know this: we've got a lot of young guys with shit stains on their underwear."

But the point—the one the Cowboys could pack up and put on the plane—was that they did not lose. "We showed a lot of character right there," said veteran defender Bill Bates. Charles Haley shifted into psychodrive and pressured Simms into an incompletion. The Cowboy defense swarmed on the next two plays, gang-tackling receivers for gains of 1 and no yards. The Giants punted.

On third and 7 at the Cowboy 46, with 1:40 left, Turner called for a pass and nobody objected. When some staffs would have played not to lose, Johnson let Turner throw for the win. Aikman hit Irvin on a quick slant for 12 yards. Game over. From that point forward, going for it would become a trademark of the '92 Cowboys. On September 13, a young coaching staff learned a relatively painless lesson as well as its team did.

Grinning with relief, Wannstedt said of his defense, "How can I blame 'em? They did just what I told 'em they had to. Then the Giants started running their two-minute offense, which we didn't have much time to work against because it rained [in Dallas]. Then we started missing tackles and lost all the momentum. But you know what? If you told me three hours ago we could get out of here with a one-point win, I would have taken it."

The Cowboys were 2-0. Danny Noonan was starting at defensive tackle for the injured Russell Maryland and playing well, perhaps even enhancing his trade value. Good things were happening. Lucky things, though Johnson wouldn't admit that. Various Cowboys had blown assignments that resulted in a wrong-place, right-time punt block against Washington and a punt deflection in New York. Was it turning into that kind of year?

Despite the scare, it was a raucous return flight to Dallas, one that called for an extra nip of Tanqueray.

★ ★ ★

Jerry Jones wasn't in a "Ray must stay" mood. Jones was trying like crazy to trade Noonan for a safety, probably to replace Ray Horton. But by Monday, Jones declared Noonan untradable. Other teams said he wasn't quite worth what he was making, said Jones. At Johnson's urging in '91, Jones had agreed to pay Noonan a $615,000 base salary in '92. And now, at Jones's urging, the JJs accomplished perhaps another NFL first: they cut a player who had been starting for a 2-0 team. They cut a former first-round draft choice, a defensive lineman. And Jimmy Johnson believes you win with defensive linemen—that you can't have too many good ones.

"This is very frustrating to me," Johnson said at his weekly press conference, on Tuesday in the Valley Ranch auditorium. "I saw a comment in the paper from another general manager who said we were trying to trade Danny so long he lost his luster."

Each Tuesday, Jones holds his press conference immediately after Johnson's, over lunch in the players' lounge. (The players are off on Tuesdays.) "Look," Jones told the media, "barring injury, Danny would have been on the bench the rest of the year [Russell Maryland was healthy enough to play again]. The only legitimate criticism is, 'What would happen in an injury situation?' But the coaches believe Jimmie Jones and Leon Lett can do some things that Danny just doesn't bring to the table. And don't forget, Chad Hennings made this team. We certainly could've made a trade for Hennings. We feel we made a mistake when we negotiated Danny's contract only because we made him less marketable in a trade. We learned a lesson."

Behind the scenes, Johnson and his assistants were ticked. Johnson said, "Why doesn't he just be honest and say we cut Noonan because of the money?"

In his office Jones responded with unusual heat: "Jimmy is wrong about that. Candidly, we will cut people for financial reasons. But too many times Danny just wanted to collect a check and stand over there on the sidelines and take it easy. We had a numbers problem in the defensive line, and that wasn't the guy we wanted for our chemistry. If he weren't playing, he might be over there causing problems.

"Listen, I've heard people back there [in the coaching department] say, '[Noonan] just doesn't like playing football.' I don't know if anybody really *likes* playing football. I mean, even in my little o' bitty time playing, I'd sit there in the locker room five minutes before the game and I'd think, 'Man, why am I doing this?' In five minutes, my ol' head was going to hurt. I'd look up there in the stands at all those people having fun, and I'd think about being up there. But for some reason, I just had to play. I honestly don't know why. But I had to play.

"With Noonan, something would click when it was time to make the team or time for a contract. Then he'd level off again."

Jones made sound points. Jones was coaching the coaches again. Here, he overruled them.

Signed by Green Bay, Noonan was cut in early December. The Redskins contacted Noonan, but according to a source in Washington, Noonan told them he wanted to wait and start fresh next season. The Cowboys would not miss Danny Noonan.

Still, assistants said the front office was suffering without veteran personnel men John Wooten and Bob Ackles. They said with more information he could trust, Johnson could have jumped in and pulled off a trade for Noonan. Jones, they said, just didn't have the contacts or savvy, and Johnson just didn't have the time.

Tony Wise said, "Jimmy can't be the guru all the time. When John Wooten and Bob Ackles were here, they were on the phone all day finding out what was really going on with other teams."

Now that was Jones's job.

★ ★ ★

During an NFL owners' meeting that week at a Dallas–Fort Worth Airport hotel, Jones whispered a little small talk to Pittsburgh president Dan Rooney, who mentioned the Steelers were about to cut safety Thomas Everett. Jones immediately left the meeting and called Johnson.

Everett was a five-year starter from Baylor who had recently built a home in Far North Dallas. Decent speed; huge heart. Dynamite in a small package (5-9, 183 pounds). A ballhawk (16 career interceptions). Good character. Warrior's pride.

Contract holdout. Everett had refused the last Steeler offer of three years at $1.75 million. Everett had joined a lawsuit against the NFL for unconditional free agency. He was content to pump his bodybuilder's body into contest shape at a Dallas health club and wait.

Jones said, "I first got the idea on Everett last summer in a conversation I had with [San Diego general manager] Bobby Beathard. I was asking about [rookie safety] Marquez Pope, who was behind Stanley Richard [on the Charger depth chart]. Beathard said, 'The best free safety on the market may be Thomas Everett.' I asked [Cowboy and former Pittsburgh scout] Walter Juliff and he really liked Everett. But Jimmy was cool to the idea."

Part owner McCoy said, "The coaches kept saying, 'Give us someone before camp or not at all. There's too much to learn. It's too hard to fit someone in.' Jerry kept pushing Thomas Everett through camp, and Jimmy wasn't interested."

Jones said, "So on my own I called [Pittsburgh director of football operations] Tom Donahoe, who said [during camp] they'd had an injury in the secondary and that Everett would not be available [via trade]. But we said we'd keep talking. So when Dan Rooney told me at the meetings that the price would be a whole lot cheaper, I called Jimmy and he perked up and said he'd start working on it. He called John Fox in San Diego [who had coached Pittsburgh's defensive backs before joining the Chargers] and got a very good report. I said, 'Jimmy, I'm not going to pay this kind of money to have him come in here and be a backup. He's either going to have a chance to play or we're not going after him.' "

Johnson said, "John Fox told me Everett is a good player who wanted great-player money and that Pittsburgh just doesn't pay that way."

Jones said later, "You have to force these coaches to make a decision. Not just Jimmy, any coach. It was obvious we were deficient [at safety], but even Larry Lacewell said, 'The coaches are going to be hesitant to do anything until we lose a ball game because of it.' That's just coaches. But it was time to know what they had or didn't have in Robert Williams [a sixth-year defensive back from Baylor who had been tried as a starter in camp]. Of course, Jimmy said, 'How about IR [injured reserve for Williams]?' Robert has that nagging knee [injury]. But the NFL is cracking down on IR. We had another player [defensive end Tony Hill] who had to go to an independent doctor to get checked out. IR is no longer an option. It could cost us a second-round draft choice [if the player isn't really hurt].

"I was handling the negotiating. Pittsburgh did come back [from an initial agreement to trade Everett for a ninth-rounder] and want a fifth. But I told Jimmy, 'That's because the draft might only be five rounds next year.' [It was eight.] If we draft at the bottom of the fifth round, we'll just be a player or two away from the entire free-agent pool. So a fifth was not a lot. And we were able to sign Everett for less than Pittsburgh was offering because he wanted to play here. We sold him on having a chance to start for a potential Super Bowl team in Texas."

What a deal: two games—both wins—into the season, the Cowboys had their final Super Bowl piece, Jones believed.

Of course, several other NFL GMs were quoted as saying Everett wasn't worth even what Jones had paid him. The knocks: Everett played the run so fiercely that he sometimes bit on play fakes and he too often injured himself making big hits. Everett definitely came COD—crash on delivery. Former teammate Delton Hall said, "Thomas is the type guy who, when the game is going bad, always came up with the tide-turning hit."

Jones said, "He's just what *we* need."

Johnson sounded reasonably pleased to have Everett. But this time he was so incensed over credit he believed Jones was taking for the trade that Johnson called me at home to set me straight. In my syndicated column I did not use any of the above quotes from Jones, but I did say Jones had "nagged" Johnson through camp to consider Everett.

Johnson told me, "I don't know why these things would be said. We had three conversations total [about Everett]. All it was, was just a name [to Jones]. He'd never seen a tape of the guy in his life. That's what I'm dealing with. . . . He [Jones] is getting recognition he never dealt with. It's an unsatisfied hunger that's getting satisfied."

Johnson cooled only when I suggested his working relationship with the GM might be worse in lots of other organizations. He said, "Yeah, it's probably better than it would be with twenty-seven other clubs. Anyplace else the guy might actually *try* to meddle."

The inference was that Jones really wasn't that aware of what he was doing.

Johnson sighed and said, "Well, the way some of the things [in this book] will be structured will be erroneous. But the only person who will know will be me. Well, me and one other person."

96 Tears

THOMAS EVERETT SPENT SUNDAY AFTERNOON IN JERRY JONES'S air-conditioned suite at Texas Stadium, looking down on a steam bath of a game. It was 99 degrees on the field with unusually high humidity for the three P.M. kickoff, and for the Cowboys it would get much warmer. Jimmy Johnson's coaching staff dreaded playing Phoenix. The Cardinals are soundly prepared by head coach Joe Bugel and coordinators Jerry Rhome (offense) and Fritz Shurmur (defense). Rhome coached Troy Aikman during Johnson's first season in Dallas. Shurmur and Norv Turner coached together for six years with the Los Angeles Rams. The Cardinal coaches know the Cowboys.

"We know Phoenix, too," said Tony Wise. "We [as a team] are better than they are, but the thing about Phoenix is that they always play us so damn hard."

Collisions in Cowboy-Cardinal games are among the most violent of the season for Johnson's team. The Cardinals take their proud pound of flesh. For the Cowboys, the '92 season would be made or broken in Phoenix on November 22, in the coaches' later view.

But this was Phoenix in Dallas on September 20, Cowboys favored by 14. A bye week awaited, then the Eagles in Philadelphia on Monday night. The coaches were hoping the starters could somehow build a first-half lead so lots of backups would take the second-half pounding.

The starters did build a 28–10 lead midway through the third quarter, thanks mostly to Michael Irvin, who did a Michael Jordan. Said receiver coach Hubbard Alexander with awe, "Michael said before the game, 'Ax, I feel it. I need the ball. These guys can't hold me.' It was like Michael Jordan in that first first NBA Final game [attended by Irvin and Alexander]. Mike was in the zone. The ball was looking bigger than a watermelon. I've never seen him come out of his breaks as quick as he did today. People don't realize how he can just explode in and out of his breaks and separate from defenders."

Nate Newton said, "Mike was so far in the zone today that he quit talkin' in the huddle. Usually you can't shut him up."

Irvin: 8 catches, 210 yards, 3 touchdowns, one suggestive Elvis-like pelvis dance behind the end zone. A blowout?

No. In the second half the Cowboys could have used Everett. Technically, he wouldn't be Cowboy property until the following day, though news of the trade had broken in Dallas–Fort Worth newspapers. It had been broken by the Cowboys, said Johnson, to make it a little more difficult for the Steelers to back out, in case they reconsidered. Laughing, Johnson said, "We know the best way to leak something, if you really need it leaked." In other words, let Jerry leak it.

But speaking of leaks, the Cowboy pass defense again resembled Texas Stadium—one big hole in its roof. In the second half at Giants Stadium, Phil Simms had completed 18 of 28 for 227 yards and 3 touchdowns. In this game, Phoenix quarterback Chris Chandler went 28 of 43 for 383 yards, the seventh-highest total of passing yards ever allowed by a Cowboy team. Chandler was playing only because starter Timm Rosenbach was hurt. What's more, the Cardinals had more total yards than the Cowboys (438–413) and more first downs (24–21). The Cardinals cut the lead to 31–20 with 4:47 left, then recovered an onside kick and drove to the Cowboy

8-yard line, where they faced fourth and 1. Cowboy defensive end Tony Tolbert basically ended the game by chasing down Chandler for a sack.

Dave Wannstedt was as visibly upset after the game as he would be all season. "We're in place to make plays and we don't finish them off," he said. Then he almost yelled to a group of reporters, "This is just not acceptable."

Wannstedt caught himself. He was supposed to be the rock. He was sounding more like his head coach. He glanced at the ceiling and smiled. "We did win today, didn't we?"

Yes, 31–20. The Dallas Cowboys were 3-0 for the first time in nine seasons.

★ ★ ★

Dr. Don Beck is a psychologist who writes a provocative weekly column for *The Dallas Morning News* sports section and operates out of the National Values Center in Denton, about a half hour's drive from Valley Ranch. Beck worked closely with Bum Phillips when he coached the Oilers and Saints, and for years Beck counseled Tom Landry and Tex Schramm. During the '92 season, he communicated periodically with Jimmy Johnson, offering suggestions or reading material. (A book given Johnson by Beck would have a highly publicized impact on Johnson's psyche during Super Bowl week.)

But a few days after the Phoenix game, Beck was concerned about Johnson's team. Beck had read Johnson's weekly column in the *Morning News* that ran the Friday before and ended with, "We need to keep pushing that much harder." Beck thought it dangerous for Johnson to ask more and more of his team each week.

"Especially before a big game," Beck said, "sometimes it's better to back off and let the team build back up naturally. Jimmy has told me the only way he's ever known is to step back up to the chalkboard. But Jimmy listens. Jimmy is a learning coach. He will try things and see if they work. I never really could get Coach Landry to try things."

That week Beck sensed a potential void in Johnson's relationship with his players. Beck often marveled at Johnson's ability to motivate and communicate with talented athletes—not a Landry strength—yet the psychologist cautioned that Johnson has "a tendency to exploit people." Beck said, "Something is not happening in the second half. When players reach into the well, will there be anything there? Will a sense of loyalty be there? This was why Landry didn't replace a veteran until the new guy was judged vastly superior. I don't really know Jimmy, and I'm not around the team, but I wonder about this."

Had Johnson, without remorse, run off too many vets too quickly? Was Johnson creating more fear and distrust than love and devotion in the players he kept? What kind of character would this team find at the bottom of its well when it got darkest on Monday night in Philadelphia?

Beck mock-moaned when he heard that on Wednesday everybody in the Cowboy coaching department celebrated a birthday. Assistants, secretaries, everybody. Instead of celebrating staffers' birthdays as they happen, Johnson prefers one big party once a year. Get it over with.

Johnson stuck his head in on this one, in the coaches' meeting room, smiled, and said, "Happy birthday, everybody!" Then he went about his business.

★ ★ ★

As another Cowboy-Eagle game approached, writers in both cities put a fresh coat of ink on everybody's favorite love-to-hate images. This was the Eagles' pit-bull defense clamping down on the Cowboys' pretty-boy offense, right?

Nate Newton, Cowboy offensive guard, knows all about pit bulls. Twice he has run afoul of the law while involved in pit-bull fighting. He says he paid his fine. He says that's all in his past and will not happen again.

However, Newton still owns two pit bulls, Nikki and Ice-T.

Newton has a deceptive image: jolly giant. Most Cowboy fans know Newton as the hilarious radio and TV personality, the good ol' black guy who'll play along while white sportscasters laugh with him or occasionally at his backwoods grammar and expressions.

Nate's a great actor. He makes lots of extra money playing good ol' Nate. But Newton has a mean streak.

That's one reason why, after three games, Newton was playing at a Pro Bowl level. His weight had leveled at around 315. He was destroying defensive linemen. His knee occasionally locked up on him, but Johnson asked him to wait for minor surgery until the season was over. Doctors weren't sure they could do much for Newton's knee, which had been ground into arthritic sawdust during too many desperate three-mile jogs by a man weighing up around four hundred.

Now Newton was heading for Philly, infamous for its inner-city pit-bull fighting.

One night that week on a radio talk show, a caller who said his son had been mauled by a pit bull asked Newton how such a "jovial, fine athlete" could have once participated in pit-bull fights.

Newton's answer: "The American pit bull terrier is a fighting style of dog and bred to go into combat against another pit bull terrier. . . . What makes me upset is people who get these dogs to portray how they want to be. This isn't a dog you let run free. Any man who lets 'em run free, the dog don't need to be shot, the human do. Any animal I own who shows any aggression toward a human, I will have him shot."

Newton said he has had one pit bull, a "people-biter," destroyed. But he keeps pit bulls because "they're incredible athletes—I've seen 'em climb five-foot fences." He has watched them display extraordinary courage in the face of death. Nate Newton, who battles the undisciplined quitter deep inside him, draws strength from being around Nikki and Ice-T.

★ ★ ★

One day that week Johnson walked from his office to Jerry Jones's office, in another Valley Ranch wing. "He marched in," said Jones, "and said, 'We need a backup running back.'" Against Phoenix, Curvin Richards had been injured—lacerated kidney—and lost for at least the four weeks he would spend on injured reserve.

Jones said, "We went over the possibilities. I said, 'Would the new running back play if Emmitt goes down against the Eagles?' No, he said, Tommie Agee would play because it wouldn't be enough time to prepare someone else. So I said, 'Would the new running back play against Seattle?' Yes. Kansas City? No, Jimmy said he hoped Ricky Blake would be ready to play again by then, and Curvin shortly after that. So we're talking about adding somebody for one game? Whose spot are we going to take on the roster? Jimmy thought about it and got up and said, 'We don't need a running back.' He had answered his own question. He basically just needed someone to talk to about it.

"Jimmy and Stephen and I are constantly talking, day and night, without any formal meeting time. Formal meetings make you make decisions you might not want to make. This way you can call back and say, 'You know, I've rethought that.' Or Stephen will pop back in and say, 'Maybe you could discourage the coaches by saying this.' Just sitting around talking with Jimmy and Stephen is good for me, too. If I say something and they roll their eyes and say, 'What have you been smoking?' I'll think again. I'm constantly trying to get better. I call people around the league all the time and ask them to critique our games. I called [New Orleans general manager] Jim Finks and asked him to give me a three-point critique of the second half of our Phoenix game. People are honored to do that, and it's invaluable to me."

A day later Jones couldn't make the weekly taping of his TV show at the KDFW studio in downtown Dallas. So he asked Larry Lacewell to sit in for him, with cohost and Cowboy play-by-play announcer Brad Sham. As they finished taping, Brenda Bushell had an idea. She was originally hired in Miami by Johnson to produce his TV show. But now, as director of the Cowboys' in-house television operation, she worked closely with Jones and thought she knew him well enough to try something.

"You know how Jerry loves a joke, especially at his expense," she told Lacewell and Sham, who proceeded to tape a second opening to "The Jerry Jones Show." This one would serve as a practical joke.

This time Sham opened with, "Jerry Jones is too full of himself and couldn't be here this week." Then a grim Lacewell announced, "Jimmy and I have decided to let Jerry go, and he should take it the way Landry and Schramm took it. Jimmy and I are going to run the team now."

Was this a little too close to the truth to be amusing? Bushell took that risk. She gave Jones the practical-joke tape as if it were the real show and asked him to review it.

Jones thought it was so funny that he invited a group of writers into his office to view it on his VCR. In fact, Jones thought it was so good he asked Bushell to air it as the opening to his show. Jones, it appeared, wanted to show the world he could laugh at himself.

Stunned, Bushell felt the joke had gone far enough and firmly advised Jones against airing the "Jimmy Fires Jerry" tape. He finally agreed not to.

★ ★ ★

Herschel Walker was big in Dallas, much bigger in 1989 than Jones or Johnson or even the Cowboys. In his first two seasons in Dallas, '86 and '87, Herschel had become a "good" Tony Dorsett, a superstar running back who said and did all the right things. While Dorsett always seemed to be clashing with management and making wrong-place, wrong-time headlines away from football, Walker danced with the Fort Worth Ballet and conducted clinics for kids who viewed him as a cartoon superhero. Walker said he one day wanted to work for the FBI. Walker, a world-class sprinter, said he did a thousand push-ups and a thousand sit-ups every night.

Walker loved being a Cowboy in image-crazed Dallas. He still maintains a home not far from Texas Stadium and says he'll make Dallas his home when he's through playing football.

But all Johnson cared about in September of '89 was that Walker said he wanted the ball more after the Cowboys opened Johnson's pro career with a 28–0 loss in New Orleans. For Johnson, New Orleans was a shocking, welcome-to-reality loss. The NFL would not be the Big Easy. Johnson realized he couldn't control Walker, who wanted the team rebuilt around him. "You cannot build a team around any one player," Johnson says now.

A month later Jimmy Johnson, coach of the hapless 0-5 Cowboys, traded his one star, Herschel Walker, to Minnesota.

As personnel director, John Wooten watched Johnson suffer through the '89 season. Wooten, now a scout for the Eagles, says, "That season almost destroyed Jimmy. He told us, 'I will not go through that again.' He said, 'I've got a ten-year contract, but I promise you, I will go back to teaching school or selling insurance before I will go through another one-and-fifteen season.' The Herschel Walker trade saved him. Without it, Jimmy might have lost it. That allowed him a ray of hope. He'd just sit back and look at that list [of draft choices]. So he and those coaches never quit working just as hard, trying to get to the Super Bowl. I've never seen a staff work so hard so closely—holler and scream and love each other.

"And I've never seen anyone who could evaluate talent any quicker than Jimmy. Jimmy immediately saw that for all his talent, Herschel didn't have what the great backs have—the vision, the running skills, the ability to make you miss. Jimmy saw a guy who ran straight up."

It took Minnesota management about two seasons to see what Johnson had and hadn't seen in Walker. After the '91 season, Minnesota cut Walker. The Eagles, in need of a star back to take some pressure and focus off quarterback Randall Cunningham, signed Walker. Now the Eagles had their very own pretty-boy Cowboy. To many fans Walker would always be a Cowboy. Somehow, he didn't look quite right in Eagle green. But with him the Eagles were 3-0, and the city of Philadelphia was bracing for "the biggest sporting event that has ever taken place," according to Angelo Cataldi, the loudest of many voices on the city's all-sports radio station, WIP. The Eagles and Cowboys were about to play for the championship of the world—after just four games.

★ ★ ★

The Cowboys spent an endless Monday at a downtown hotel in the City of Brotherly Shove. Kickoff wasn't until nine P.M. Many of them amused themselves by reading the nuclear buildup for the game in the Philly papers and by listening to WIP, whose pregame show started at six A.M. When a brave Dallas fan brought his dog dressed in Cowboy colors to WIP's remote broadcast site near Veterans Stadium, Eagle fans began chanting, "Burn the dog! Burn the dog!"

Chuckling, veteran Bill Bates said, "The way the Eagles are talking, this is the last game of their lives. It's like they're not sure they'll be together next year or if they'll get a little too old. So this is *it*. For us, it's just our second of three Monday-night games this year. That's just the way this team is."

And that's just the attitude Eagle fans despised. *Philadelphia Daily News* columnist Ray Didinger told the *Fort Worth Star-Telegram*, "That's one thing that's always hacked off the Eagles' fans. It's like, 'We hate you, why can't you hate us?' Philadelphia has always been there, poking Dallas in the chest, and the Cowboys have always been looking over the Eagles' shoulders at the Redskins, saying, 'Yeah, yeah, just wait a minute, fellas, we'll get to you after we take care of these other guys.' "

The JJs: Jerry Jones and Jimmy Johnson. Their contentious relationship was the untold story of the 1992 season.

Troy Aikman looks downfield against the Rams.

Offensive coordinator Norv Turner, whose scheme brought out the best in Aikman.

Nate Newton (61) and Mark Stepnoski (53) combine for the block on Nolan Harrison of the Raiders.

The enigmatic and
awesomely talented
Charles Haley.

Michael Irvin gets off
the line against the
Rams.

Five Cowboys, includ-
ing Ken Norton (51),
Robert Jones (55), and
Larry Brown (24), com-
bine to gang-tackle
Herschel Walker.

Jimmy Johnson with best friend and defensive coordinator Dave Wannstedt before the NFC championship game.

Thomas Everett, whose acquisition did much to help anchor the secondary.

Three of the Wise Guys: left to right, Mark Stepnoski, Mark
Tuinei, and John Gesek.

Offensive-line coach Tony Wise.

Lin Elliott, in a typical scene from the
life of a kicker, early in the Bears
game.

Emmitt Smith scores the winning touchdown
against Denver.

Jerry Jones introduces Prince Bandar bin Sultan to Gary Busey
on the sidelines during the Bears game. This sideline visit
triggered one of Jimmy Johnson's biggest explosions.

Darryl Johnston makes his way toward the wet Candlestick Park field for the NFC championship game.

Troy Aikman on the sidelines during the San Francisco game.

Emmitt Smith races by a Bills defender in Super Bowl XXVII.

A blizzard of confetti and an unruly throng hail the emergence of the Cowboys as Dallas's Team after their Super Bowl triumph.

In his column Didinger quoted Eagle safety Andre Waters: "It's personal with the Cowboys. I learned that my rookie year ['84]. It was a different atmosphere in the locker room that week. I could feel the electricity. I heard the veterans talking 'Dallas this' and 'Dallas that.' They were just so emotional. It rubbed off on me."

In his hotel room that Monday afternoon, Norv Turner was worried. True, Turner might worry if the Cowboys were playing SMU or Rice. But this time Turner was more worried than usual. Can't-sleep, can't-eat worried. Turner, forty, had more NFL coaching experience than any other Cowboy assistant, having spent six years with the Rams. Turner had learned that winning in the twenty-eight-team NFL just isn't that easy. On a cocky staff he often tried to provide a quiet voice of reason and patience and was often a voice in the wilderness.

Turner said, "Sure, we could get lucky and win. But you have to think about getting out of there without getting anybody hurt and making sure you take care of Seattle [six days later at Texas Stadium]. That's basically what Denver did."

The Eagles had pounded their chests and Denver, 30–0. Total dominance. Denver managed only 82 total yards. Quarterback John Elway was 8 of 18 for just 59. "They only sacked him three times," Turner said, "but he ran around a lot and just tried not to get killed."

A year before at Texas Stadium, Turner had watched hopelessly as the Eagles sacked Troy Aikman 11 times and won, 24–0. Total dominance, men and boys. "You just can't get behind these guys," Turner said. "They're just too good on defense. If you get behind quickly, you have to make a decision. I know it's 'Monday Night Football,' but do you want to get Troy hurt?"

After his first game against the Eagles during his rookie year, Aikman had his knees, hands, right shoulder, and elbow x-rayed. Though nothing was broken or torn, Aikman said, "I've never hurt so bad in my life." In 1991 at Veterans Stadium, Aikman was driven into the artificial turf by Eagle defensive end Clyde Simmons, No. 96, on the game's fifth play. His shoulder was separated. For Aikman, the Eagles had been "96 Tears." In a '92 camp interview, Aikman said, "I told my sister before camp started, 'I'm really tired of all the pain. I just don't know if I want to hurt anymore.' "

Turner didn't want to see Aikman carried off the field again, not in the fourth game of the season.

"We just don't match up well with the Eagles," Turner said. "We don't have the three wide receivers to spread 'em out the way Washington does." Neither Michael Irvin, Alvin Harper, nor Kelvin Martin has the kind of speed a rival coordinator must game-plan for—Alexander Wright speed—and Wright was going nowhere fast. "He hurt his back late in camp," Turner said, "and when he came back, it was as if he'd never played before. It was almost like he had those great practices against the Raiders and said, 'That's it. I did it.' Now he's lost his edge, his confidence."

Turner continued on the Eagles: "Their linebackers are really good because they're so physical and they can really run. Byron Evans has done a nice job on Jay [Novacek]. Seth Joyner can really help out in coverage. Our best chance will be getting Alvin singled on [cornerback] Izel Jenkins. That's the matchup you look for. But it will be tough. They want to beat us thirty-one to fuckin' ten."

Well, closer to 31–7.

★ ★ ★

For all his trepidation, Turner tried something on the game's opening play that would haunt him the rest of the season. "It was a horseshit call," he would say again and again. He would smile, shake his head, and say, "But wouldn't you think on the first play of the game Reggie White might be thinking a little bit about the run?"

Turner opened with the "boot"—bootleg—Aikman rolling right and looking for tight end Novacek or perhaps even keeping himself and running out of bounds after a nice gain. Normally, this would be a reasonably low-risk call. Turner had opened successfully with it before. But this was the sold-out, whacked-out Vet, howling with rabid fans. These were the Dallas-hating Eagles, who massed behind the end zone before the game pounding on each other's shoulder pads with such fury that, on the sideline, line coach Tony Wise said to himself, "Jesus, I've never seen anything like that." This was Aikman, who still hadn't played in a play-off game or many big games and admitted he still had "lots of butterflies" just before kickoffs.

The "boot" probably was too much to ask of Aikman on the first play of a Monday-night game with a play-off buildup. Aikman wouldn't quite recover the rest of the long, loud night.

Instead of holding his ground and looking for the run, All-Pro defensive end Reggie White exploded upfield—right into Aikman's path. When White wants to be, he's the most uncontrollable force in football. "Troy," said Turner, "probably should have gotten rid of the ball a little quicker. But Seth Joyner was all over Jay and . . ." Aikman was called for intentional grounding. The Vet became one big primal scream. The Eagles pounded on each other and pointed at the Cowboys. Fresh meat.

Emmitt Smith ran into a green wall for no gain. And on third and 25 from the Cowboy 15, Aikman forced a throw over the middle to Kelvin Martin, who was covered. Nickel back John Booty cut underneath Martin and intercepted. Four plays later, the Eagles led, 7–0.

Wise said, "Norv's thinking on that first play was to at least come out and do something that said, 'Hey, we came here to try to win.' I mean, why give it to Emmitt for no gain? But it's like Jimmy always preaches to the team: 'I don't care how many great plays you make. Just don't make bad plays.' Especially against Philadelphia. One bad play and you send 'em into what Jimmy calls a feeding frenzy. I know a lot of people don't like Philadelphia. But the point is, they should be in the Super Bowl. If they're not, you should ask, 'What's wrong?' "

Still, shortly into the second quarter, the Cowboys trailed only 10–7. Third and 2 from the Eagle 2-yard line. Aikman rolled right and attempted to pull a Randall. Cunningham is the Michael Jordan of NFL quarterbacks, especially when he rises to Monday-night occasions. Instead, Aikman pulled a Richie Cunningham, forcing another throw back into the teeth of the Eagle zone coverage. It was tipped and intercepted.

Still, the Eagles led only 10–7 at the half. But in the third quarter Aikman, blitzed by Joyner, threw another interception, to Evans. Eight plays later: Philly, 17–7.

Then Aikman made another poor decision, jamming a pass in to Novacek, who was immediately blasted and separated from the ball. Cowboy lineman John Gesek caught the carom, but was immediately stripped. Philly recovered and soon scored the 24–7 touchdown. After that, it appeared the Cowboy defense tackled halfheartedly, letting the Eagles have their night in the spotlight, 31–7. "Their Super Bowl," several Cowboys said in the locker room.

Herschel's revenge: 86 yards on 19 carries and 2 touchdowns.

Wannstedt was at a loss. "We had a good plan, we had guys in position all night, and we just didn't make the play. How do you explain that?"

Linebackers Ken Norton and Vinson Smith missed key tackles on Cunningham. Kenny Gant dropped an interception he could probably have returned for a touchdown just before halftime. Ray Horton dropped an interception in the end zone that would have stopped the 17–7 Eagle TD drive. Wannstedt said, "Hey, Randall didn't hurt us throwing [11 of 19 for 124]. We always play Randall good."

Remarkably, in losing by 24 the Cowboys had beaten the Eagles in total yardage, 311–266. Remarkably, the more the Cowboy players talked about the game that night, the prouder they were of what they had accomplished. Sounding more like the game had been a tie, Nate Newton said, "We proved we could bang with the best. That's what you have to take away from this game. They didn't kill Troy. They didn't put Emmitt's fire out. Sometimes, the bad guys win. You can't let one game ruin your whole season. One thing you can never forget about the NFL: nothing is ever as bad or as good as it seems."

Pride wounded, Irvin said, "Just write that it was the turnovers. That's all. Just the turnovers." Several players said, in effect, "How can you beat the Eagles in their backyard when your quarterback gives it to 'em four times?"

As Turner left the locker room, he vowed, "We are going to fuckin' beat those guys. It may not be this year. But we'll get 'em."

Wise was angered by the ethics of Eagle safety Waters—otherwise known as "Dirty" Waters. Wise said, "He did play well [a team-leading 7 tackles]. He caused us problems. But it's like he breaks the bond between players: 'I won't try to end your career if you won't try to end mine.' He came in late a lot. He's a good player but he's a rotten bastard."

The flight back to Dallas was long, quiet, and dark, with the main cabin lights turned off. Some players slept. Many spoke quietly, replaying the game and sorting through their bruised emotions. Newton, whose bullhorn voice and laugh can usually be heard all the way up into the cockpit, smoldered quietly until the plane touched down in Dallas at three-forty A.M.

Then, in a bass growl that grew louder and louder, he said to the six or eight rows of reporters just ahead of him, "All right, motherfuckin' media. What kind of motherfuckin' shit are you going to write tomorrow? 'I told you so?' Is that what you're going to say? You're going to hop right off the fuckin' bandwagon.

"But you're going to be back on it next Sunday. I can promise you motherfuckers that."

Go West, Young
Men

DOUBTS MOUNTED AT VALLEY RANCH. AT LEAST AROUND THE coaches' offices, it seemed more like Death Valley Ranch the week after Philadelphia. Norv Turner still had trouble sleeping. One night when his wife, Nancy, awoke to find him awake, she said, "But it's Seattle."

Yes, it was only 1-4 Seattle. But for three straight games the Cowboys had turned from contenders to pretenders in the second half. In three straight second halves they had been outscored 59-17. Had they blitzed the Redskins in the opener with raw emotion and shocking noise? What if they blew a game to Seattle? The Seahawks had nearly beaten Miami in Seattle. If the Cowboys weren't quite ready for the Seahawks, then came Kansas City—a potential Super Bowl team—then a trip to play the Raiders in L.A., then the Eagles again. The coaches seemed to know they were sitting on a talent-packed powder keg. But they weren't sure whether it would blow up Valley Ranch or soon explode on the NFL.

The Cowboys were still too young and, in spots, too average or even old—or so several coaches feared.

One afternoon, as he talked in the hall outside the coaches' offices, tears came to Turner's eyes as he said, "You keep hearing Super Bowl, and you have to ask, 'Is that realistic?' My biggest problem here is control, just trying to control the expectations."

Cowboy doubters mounted. One NFC East personnel director said, "Aikman just really looked nervous [against the Eagles]. The Cowboys tried to get cute and trick 'em on the first play, and you don't do that in their backyard. But you could see fear in Aikman's eyes. They baited him into that first interception. He saw two deep [safeties] and didn't see Booty underneath.

"Troy just isn't Jimmy's kind of guy. Jimmy likes his quarterbacks to be cocky and outgoing. That's Jimmy's style. Troy just doesn't have that charisma or fire."

The only ones who didn't appear to be doubting were the Cowboys themselves. John Gesek, a sixth-year guard who came via trade from the Raiders, sat in his locker cubicle on Wednesday with a look of peaceful amusement. Gesek is a Bible study leader who was becoming a team leader—"the one I want my guys to emulate," says Tony Wise.

Gesek said, "I just don't think it's time to call off the season. We have three games against AFC West teams, and I can tell you from experience, we match up well with the AFC West. Their offenses aren't so complicated that they'll cause a lot of problems for our defense. And we're physical enough we should be able to run the ball on them. So, we win three, go six and one, and get Philly back here." That simple.

Even Jimmy Johnson wrote in his weekly Friday column, "From the minute we hit the practice field Wednesday, there has been a positive atmosphere with no emotional hangover. If anyone was hanging their heads a little at midweek, it was me and a few of the coaches. Our players' spirit and energetic attitude have taken over and had a contagious effect."

★ ★ ★

The Seattle Seahawks were in the wrong place, Texas Stadium, at the wrong time, noon on October 11. Suddenly, they were small animals in the lights of a semi that had barreled all the way from

Philadelphia. The Seahawks were the first to feel the four-quarter power of a deep, emotion-driven defense that would overpower lots of unsuspecting teams.

From the Eagle loss and a week of media negativity sprang the first Cowboy regular-season shutout in fourteen years. Seven sacks. Two fumble recoveries. An interception returned for a touchdown (late in the game, by Ray Horton, who had been replaced in the starting lineup by Thomas Everett).

The fewest yards a Cowboy team had allowed an opponent was 63, by Green Bay in 1965. The Seahawks totaled 62.

After Cowboys 27, Seahawks 0, Dave Wannstedt said, "Our guys motivated themselves. A coach can get players up to that 'frenzied' level only so many times in a season. This time, the players had to do it themselves."

Said linebacker Ken Norton, "We're just going to keep taking it out on people until we get the Eagles again."

The next day Norv Turner was actually worried that the Cowboys had taken it out on Seattle for too long, after the Seahawks had basically waved a bloody white flag. After all, the Seahawks had opened with a quarterback, Dan McGwire, who was making only his second NFL start. McGwire was blasted on a blitz by rookie middle linebacker Robert Jones and lost for the season. McGwire was replaced by Stan Gelbaugh, not to be confused with Sammy Baugh. So on Monday Turner called a Seahawk assistant he knows and basically said, "Sorry if we got a little carried away."

But on Sunday, as the clock ran down, Turner had found his dry sense of humor again. Through the headset, he kidded Johnson that "it's time to get ready for another Game of the Year."

In Kansas City, the Chiefs were just finishing a 24–17 grounding of the Eagles. Kansas City, here they came.

★ ★ ★

Bill Bates, a Tom Landry favorite, plays football the way Jerry Jones plays life. Bates willed his NFL success. It began in 1983, his rookie training camp. "There I was, one of about a hundred free agents in Thousand Oaks," Bates says, "and I wanted it so bad that I'd lay in my bed at night and visualize running down on a kickoff, making guys miss me, and making the tackle. I'd see it again and again and again, and then after games I'd watch myself on film and

I started realizing things were happening just the way I visualized them. It was kind of spooky."

Until then, Tennessee's Bates was best known for getting run over on national TV by Georgia's Herschel Walker—a Herschel highlight shown repeatedly after he won the Heisman Trophy. But Bates, a 6-1, 205-pound safety, made the '83 Cowboy team. Landry admitted Bates reminded him of himself as a New York Giant cornerback—tough, dedicated, and not very fast.

Bates is so driven it's spooky. For games he works himself into a crazy-eyed state that scares even teammates. "I have utter disregard for my personal safety," he says. "That's what it takes for me to be a success in pro football. I've played as hard as anyone has ever played. I've laid in front of my locker and felt as much pain as anyone ever could have felt."

The obsession began one afternoon when Bates was eight years old, playing backyard football against two brothers who were neighbors. The younger one, age seven, "beat the snot out of me. Got me down with his knees on my shoulders and just started fisting me. I said right there that would never, ever happen again."

For ten years in the NFL, mostly as a special-teams star, Bates had knocked the snot out of people. Ballcarriers, blockers, teammates, himself. In Dallas, No. 40 went from rookie cult hero to what Jones calls "the most popular player on the most popular team in America." Bates fed off the adoration, as he returned it by doing probably more charity work than any other Cowboy, even Troy Aikman. "I'm a person who really tries to please everybody," Bates says.

He tried so hard in his early pro seasons that his visualization technique began working overtime. "I'd fall asleep doing it and my subconscious would just keep doing it." Bates began tackling road roommates in the bed next to him. Bates was eventually given a room by himself. At home Bates sleep-tackled furniture, sometimes skinning elbows or knees. But one night his wife found him poised to tackle a second-story window.

"That's when I decided to see if I needed some help," Bates says.

He tried small doses of medication but didn't like the aftereffects. He tried sessions with the team psychologist. That helped a little, says Bates.

But nothing could have prepared Bates for the psychological

ordeal he underwent in the days following October 11, 1992. Incredibly, until that day, Bates had never had a football injury that required major surgery. For ten years he had stayed so healthy that, before camp had opened, Jones offered Bates a risky new contract. Bates would make a little more in base salary (a boost to a reported $450,000) if he would agree to forfeit about $200,000 if he had to be placed on injured reserve. Bates readily agreed. Jones said the team just wanted some protection, but that "with Bill we know an injury is highly unlikely."

Covering a kickoff against Seattle, Bates was shoved off balance. As he planted his left foot, his knee exploded. Two ligaments burst. After thousands of kamikaze crashes, William Frederick Bates sustained a major injury without running into anyone.

Bates jogged off the field with as severe a knee injury as Cowboy doctors have seen.

Two days later Bates tried to talk the doctors out of surgery. Hey, he wasn't limping all that badly, he said. Maybe with a week or two of rest . . . No, said the doctors. One more blow to the knee and Bates might have a permanent limp. It had to be fixed, now. Team officials, assuming Bates's career was finished, talked about having a halftime ceremony to honor No. 40. No, Bates vowed, he would return to play in '93.

One afternoon before his surgery, as Bates walked without crutches out the locker-room door, tight end Alfredo Roberts shook his head and said, "He's in denial."

Roberts, fatefully, would be the only other Cowboy to know that feeling in 1992.

★ ★ ★

For days, weeks, and months Jimmy Johnson had been defending receiver Alexander "Ace" Wright. Just a few days earlier he had snapped at reporters that Wright "is a good player" and would not be traded. But the day after the Seattle game, Johnson basically admitted Wright, the twenty-eighth pick in the 1990 draft, had been one long wrong for the Cowboys.

With the trading deadline just a day away, Jones presented a proposal from Al Davis and the Raiders. Do it, said Johnson.

Jones said, "I had talked to a couple of teams who had some interest. *Some* interest. So I called Al to ask, number one, should we be doing this, and number two, did he know anybody he thought would be interested? He said, 'Jerry, I can't believe it. You're reading my mind. I just came out of a meeting with our coaches and we've lost [receiver] Sam Graddy. We need some speed.'

"Al agreed Alexander was never going to turn into a player for us. But it got a little sticky trying to keep the Raiders thinking we had some other interest, which we did, but not for a fourth."

For Wright the Raiders did give a conditional fourth-round pick, which could become a third if Wright contributed significantly. Also, said a Raider source, Davis encouraged ex-Raider Derrick Gainer, who had been waiting to return to the Raider roster, to sign with the Cowboys. Gainer would turn into a more dependable and versatile backup running back than Curvin Richards or Ricky Blake.

So trading Wright for a fourth and, in effect, Gainer was a pretty good deal. Considering the Cowboys had picked up quarterback Steve Beuerlein from the Raiders in August of '91 for a fourth, some in the front office viewed the overall deal as Wright for Beuerlein. Also from the Raiders the Cowboys had acquired Gesek in 1990 for a fifth-round pick, and one of the league's best long snappers, Dale Hellestrae, in '90 for a seventh-rounder. Not bad for a GM who had learned just about everything he knew about the NFL from Al Davis.

Not bad for a team that now considered Kelvin Martin a far more valuable receiver and kick returner than Wright. Martin, while gaining five pounds to 167, had accomplished something in the off-season that few NFL players do: he got faster. Through weight training, he improved his burst. Norv Turner said, "I also think it had something to do with Kelvin feeling better about himself and his situation here."

As a third receiver, Martin was getting the playing time Wright had in '91. Martin, in his sixth season out of Boston College, just kept proving to Johnson's staff that he was the one thing Wright wasn't: a football player. At the University of Miami, Johnson's staff overlooked Martin, who played high-school ball in Jacksonville. A Miami player from Jacksonville named Willie Smith kept telling receiver coach Hubbard Alexander, "You missed this guy."

Remember the Doug Flutie Game? B.C. shocking Miami at the

Orange Bowl on Flutie's last-second touchdown pass? Martin introduced himself to Johnson's staff that day by returning a punt for a touchdown. In 1987, the Landry regime took Martin in the fourth round.

Hubbard Alexander says, "K Mart feels nothing [no pressure] on the football field. He has the attitude that he can run through a mountain, but he's very bright. He really *thinks* the game. And he really gets up for big games. He tells Michael and Alvin, 'I don't know about you, but I'm going for broke.' He surprises people with his quickness because he's so smooth.

"Let me tell you, he's like chewing gum stuck to the bottom of your shoe. He will not go away."

In the battle for the coaches' respect, it was Wright who went away. Martin soon would stick to the bottom of lots of teams' cleats.

★ ★ ★

Mrs. Jerry Jones said it was her fault. The week of the Kansas City game she sat in the lobby lounge of the luxury high rise in which she and her husband live, not far from downtown Dallas on Turtle Creek, and took the blame for that infamous night of February 24, 1989.

On shopping excursions from Little Rock to Dallas, Gene Jones had discovered "this little hole in the wall over by Love Field." So that night, as her husband neared a deal to buy the Dallas Cowboys, she encouraged him and Jimmy Johnson and Johnson's wife, Linda Kay, to get out of the hotel and enjoy some Mexican food. Johnson had flown in for the day mainly to meet potential investor Ed Smith, who owned part of the Cowboys with Bum Bright and did not want to continue as a minority owner if Tom Landry continued coaching. Smith, who would initially own 27 percent of the Cowboys with Jones, wanted eye-to-eye assurance from Johnson that he would indeed leave Miami and coach the Cowboys. Jones has since bought out Smith.

That Friday night, Johnson did not think it was a good idea to eat out in public. The deal wasn't done yet. Though optimistic, Jones warned it could still fall apart the next morning. Johnson warned that he would probably be recognized. Johnson voted to order room service.

"But the four of us hadn't been together for a long time," Gene said, "and I thought since Jerry and Jimmy were going to be working together, it would be fun to go out." Gene and Linda Kay had been pretty good friends at the University of Arkansas. Their relationship had grown in their senior year because they were both married to football players and entering motherhood.

But after that, as Gene and Linda Kay drifted apart, Jerry kept in touch with Jimmy. "Jerry was always someone Jimmy listed as a reference," Gene said. "Jerry recommended Jimmy heavily when Jimmy got the [head-coaching] job at Oklahoma State. Jerry wanted Jimmy to get the job at Arkansas [in '83]."

Once, in fact, Jones gave Johnson a ride to Oklahoma State in his private plane and it flew into a bad storm. It got so bad, says Jones, they feared the plane was going down. Wouldn't that have changed Cowboy history?

That Friday night of February 24, 1989, the Joneses and Johnsons went down, down in Cowboy history. At a popular Mexican restaurant called Mia's, they were spotted by a *Dallas Morning News* reporter, who called a photographer, who took a picture of the four of them having a good time. The following day, it ran on the front page of the *Morning News*.

"No one in our family had any idea what a high-profile position it would be to own the Cowboys," Gene said. "It's still surprising how Dallas is so interested in the Cowboys."

Jerry convinced Gene to move to Dallas in '89 because their third child, Jerry, Jr., was graduating from high school and heading off to Georgetown and Jerry, Sr., was "feeling an emptiness." The older children, Charlotte and Stephen, aren't sure their father or their family would have made it through that first season in Dallas without Gene.

Says Stephen, "He couldn't function and we as a family couldn't function without her. She holds it all together." Indirectly, a woman who isn't exactly head-over-high-heels about the Cowboys or living in Dallas helps hold the team together.

"She's a great listener," Stephen says. "Dad doesn't like to listen. I don't know what he would do without her."

Gene, a former Miss Arkansas USA, remains a beautiful, dark-haired woman, five foot eight with a contest figure and posture. The daughter of a prominent Arkansas banker, she carries herself regally. She has made best-dressed lists in Dallas, though only recently. At first, she said, she and Jerry were informed they would have to become active in Dallas society to be accepted. "We did some things," she said in a tone that added "reluctantly." But by 1992, Dallas was trying to keep up with the Joneses. Now that the Cowboys were winning, the Joneses were at the top of all the right party lists.

Gene, who still has some sorority girl in her, said she enjoys entertaining in the owner's suite on game days, mostly family and old friends. But she worries about her husband. In a way, he's not hers anymore; he belongs to Dallas and Cowboy fans. She finds it impossible to have a quiet dinner at a restaurant with him. He's constantly approached by fans, constantly preoccupied with the next Cowboy move. Sometimes after a big win, in the midst of a celebration, you can catch Gene Jones staring into space with sad eyes.

"This just consumes him," Gene said. "He starts working on a trade and he just doesn't sleep. He and Jimmy get edgy, and now Stephen's getting edgy. The pressure just keeps building on them to prove they can do it. Now it's hard for me to see Jerry ever giving this up. But if he keeps going at this pace, his life will be short."

★ ★ ★

The Cowboy coaches were edgy all week. "Kansas City's a year ahead of us, maybe two," said Norv Turner after breaking down Chief tapes. Though Johnson called Philadelphia "the most talented team in the league," he told the media that Kansas City was "the most complete team in all three phases [offense, defense, special teams]."

Jones said, "The coaches are very, very nervous about this one." Left tackle Mark Tuinei had hurt his back lifting weights. Backup Alan Veingrad would have to deal with Derrick Thomas, Kansas City's Charles Haley. The Chiefs led the NFL with 23 sacks.

Jones said, "Jimmy's saying, 'It's going to be just like New Orleans' "—a game the Cowboys won in December of '91 by playing conservatively. "He said, 'Get ready, we may have to run it up the middle three times, punt, and play field position.' "

Yet the respect wasn't reciprocated, or so several Cowboys and coaches said after the game at Texas Stadium. Sometimes it was difficult to tell whether players and coaches imagined things or exaggerated minor slights into major insults out of desperation for motivation. But the Cowboys said that during warm-ups, the Chiefs were cracking jokes and cutting up, apparently thinking this would be a laugher.

Defensive lineman Jim Jeffcoat said, "It was obvious they thought they could come in here and run the ball down our throats. People still look at us as some ragtag unit. But we have a whole lot of guys who can play."

Turner said, "It was pretty obvious they didn't take us all that seriously. The big key was that they went right down [with the opening kickoff] and got three [points], and we came right back and got six."

The Cowboys scored another touchdown on their second possession to lead, 14–3. Kansas City cut it to 14–10 at the half. The Cowboys pushed their lead to 17–10 with 7:24 left in the third quarter. And that was the final score.

The Cowboys acted almost offended that, in a surprise move, the Chiefs didn't play All-Pro cornerback Albert Lewis, opting instead to start rookie Dale Carter. Lewis, it was announced, had sore ribs. "I was really looking forward to playing against Albert," Aikman said. "I heard [from Chief players and officials] they held him out because they have a bye week coming up and that would give him two full weeks off. But that's all the more reason to let him play this time."

Aikman was pleasantly amazed he had been sacked only once— and hit only once. Subbing for Tuinei, Veingrad had done a beyond-the-call job of neutralizing Derrick Thomas. Tony Wise said, "That's how you get to a Super Bowl, guys like Alan stepping in cold and having a game like that." Veingrad had some help from 240-pound fullback Daryl Johnston. "As relentless a blocker as I've ever seen," says Turner.

Johnston fit Johnson to a T—a nice, polite young man with a daredevil streak and the pain threshold of a Sioux brave. Johnston needed surgery on a shoulder, elbow, and knee, but kept putting it off and running into Derrick Thomases and even catching passes. Johnston isn't very fast, but his hands are among the team's surest. Against the Chiefs, Johnston caught 5 for 29 yards and a TD.

An hour after the game Aikman leaned back in his locker cubicle still wearing his game pants and eye black and spoke with a manual laborer's appreciation of Johnston. Aikman, who used to help his dad lay pipe, said of his fullback, "Great fuckin' football player. And they said in 1990 [when the Cowboys took him in the second round out of Syracuse] that DJ was a bust."

The locker-room mood: the game hadn't been as close as the score. Several coaches said it should have been 27–10 instead of 17–10. Jeffcoat said, "We controlled the game. The key was that they couldn't run on us." The Chiefs had only 91 rushing yards and 230 total. A new Cowboy trend: the Chiefs didn't score in the second half.

Yet they did have their opportunity, with 6:32 remaining. Aikman's sideline bullet for Michael Irvin was intercepted by rookie Carter. Larry Lacewell, who coached at Tennessee while Carter played there, says he encouraged Johnson to draft Carter, who was eventually voted defensive rookie of the year (AFC and NFL) by several news agencies and publications. The Cowboys passed Carter for Kevin Smith. "I know Jimmy wants to build with character," Lacewell says. "But there comes a point where you have to take a chance on a Dale Carter. It was obvious he had a chance to become a great pro, while Kevin Smith was a very solid choice. Kevin is a very solid kid. Dale didn't always pick things up quickly and he was unstable emotionally, but he is a talent."

The Cowboys had taken advantage of Carter's youth several times in the first three quarters. But this time, said Aikman, "he guessed right. Norv said he almost called a pump [and go]. Wish he had." Aikman spat into a snuff cup for emphasis. If Aikman had pump-faked as Irvin broke toward the sideline, then gone deep, Carter would have been in trouble. Instead, the Cowboys appeared to be in some. Kansas City, down 7, had the ball at the Cowboy 47.

Six plays later, it was third and 8 at the Cowboy 22. Charles Haley time. He took his quickness into another dimension and was all over quarterback Dave Kreig before he had time to set or scan the field. Kreig cut loose a desperate wobbler.

Intercepted—by Ray Horton, one of six substitutes sent in as part of a nickel pass-defense package.

It was more of a poor underthrow than a great play. The ball pretty much found Horton. But he did catch it. He did make the play that saved the day.

And afterward, he chose to speak to the media, drawing quite a crowd around his locker. The Texas Stadium locker room isn't nearly as spacious as Valley Ranch's. The tall wooden cubicles run along the walls, but are also grouped back-to-back in the middle of the locker room, narrowing walkways and making postgame media traffic a shoving, sweating gridlock around the more important players. Some players, including Horton, sometimes duck out a side door before the media is allowed through the main entrance. But this time, Horton seized the stage.

Defiantly he said, "I had a chance to make a play in the Phila-delphia game and I didn't. So off to the bench I went. If guys are going to be punished for a bad game, then half the guys in the NFL wouldn't be here. But I believe in handling these things with class and dignity even though I feel like an outcast and a leper."

Johnson wasn't publicly angered by Horton's critique of the coaching staff. But there was a reason Johnson couldn't be. Even at 5-1, all was not harmony and bliss at Valley Ranch.

★ ★ ★

Dave Wannstedt's Monday-afternoon meeting with his defense left him "as depressed as I've been since I've been with the Cowboys." Horton was upset. Cornerback Ike Holt was upset about being replaced during the second half by Kevin Smith. Safety James Washington was upset about his fluctuating role between strong and free safety, regular and nickel defenses. Several other players were upset over playing time.

Some NFL experts considered Dallas over Kansas City some-thing of an upset, and now it seemed to Wannstedt that half his defense was upset, along with his stomach.

If the Cowboys wanted real problems, how about Philadelphia's? In a 16–12 loss at Washington the day before, the Eagles had lost both starting safeties, Andre Waters (broken leg) and Wes Hopkins (knee), perhaps for the season.

But Wannstedt and his coaches—Butch Davis, Dave Campo, and Bob Slowik—were substituting more and more players in more and more situations. Six or seven running on, six or seven running off nearly every play. Johnson's staff relies on computer printouts of opponents' tendencies at least as much as the NFL's original high-tech regime, Tom Landry's. Wannstedt studies percentages for each down and distance. The idea was to keep juggling the perfect combinations of tacklers (Everett, Kenny Gant, and passing-down linebackers Ken Norton, Godfrey Myles, and Dixon Edwards), cover artists (Larry Brown, Kevin Smith, Darren Woodson), ball-hawks with decent hands (Everett, Holt, Washington), quick, physical blitzers (Gant, Woodson), and savvy (Horton).

How the Cowboys avoided a twelfth-man penalty or a ten-man crisis was a sight to behold. Campo, the defensive backfield coach, said, "Jimmy turned to me several times on Sunday and said, 'Are you sure . . . ?' "

Are you sure the right guys are in? Somehow, they always were. No penalties. No presnap confusion. Somehow, the Cowboys were 5-1, while surely leading the league in substitutions and sub hub-bub.

David Cross Campo's middle name reflected the mood of his defensive backs. Campo is a decent, dedicated man who knows about family squabbling. He has moved his wife and six children all over the country, from Central Connecticut State to Iowa State to Washington State, coaching defense at eleven schools before joining Johnson at Miami. Campo teaches pass defense with the passion of that high-school teacher you'll never forget. With his thick glasses, Campo looks more studious than athletic, though he was a defensive back and shortstop at Central Connecticut.

Tuesday after the Kansas City game, Campo looked like a teacher out of *Blackboard Jungle*. His guys had been tough on him. He said, "Sure, you'd like everyone to be happy. You'd like to have the continuity of four guys who can line up most of the time. But you have to have productive continuity. We have a blue-collar group—there aren't any white-collar players. They have to accept that. So we forgo continuity to maximize the talent we have and get the best combination of strengths on the field at any one time. To some people, it may look like we don't have any idea what we're trying to do. But we do."

Obviously aware of the Monday conflicts, Johnson delivered a message to his players through the media at his weekly briefing on Tuesday. Volume rising, he said, "It's just what we tell the players to start training camp. Everything we do for the Dallas Cowboys is for the team to win. No personalities come into it. Not mine, not the assistant coaches', not the players'. Whether you're my personal friend or a guy I don't like doesn't matter when it comes to the team. Everybody wants more. But when moves are made, you can deal with it two ways. You can sull up [Johnson's pet expression for becoming sullen] and be negative, or you can adjust. If you approach it the first way, you're out of here."

To fans, this heated speech came from nowhere. But to others at Valley Ranch, it seemed a little ironic, if not hypocritical. To several insiders, it seemed that Johnson had been a little slow to give Thomas Everett playing time. Johnson said before the Philadelphia game that Everett was ready to play on goal-line and short-yardage defenses, if not more. Wannstedt said he wanted to play Everett quite a bit. Yet Everett played very little. Campo said later that Everett just wasn't ready. But some wondered if Johnson was miffed at Jones for taking too much public credit for the trade. Had Everett been stuck in Johnson's craw? And did he stick on the sidelines longer because of it?

Now Everett was playing on the regular defense, but coming out in the passing-down packages. Wannstedt said, "Thomas is picking things up very quickly. He's very intelligent and I really think he's going to help us. But, well, it's a delicate situation with Ray."

Because?

"We did tell him he'd be out [of the starting lineup] for one game," said Wannstedt, "and it was two."

So Horton had known he could get away with using the media to send a message back to the coaches: You lied.

Johnson, in his Tuesday press conference: "It's important for the coaching staff to be up-front and on the table with every individual player."

Players often said Johnson told them he was going to say this or that to the media, to set the week's tone or steer reporters away from a potentially controversial theme. But here Johnson was using his Tuesday platform in reverse, to help clear the air in the locker room. This week, said Johnson, Horton would start at free safety, Everett at strong, and Washington would start on the bench.

On Wednesday, as Wannstedt nibbled on fruit from the lunch buffet just outside the locker area, he sighed and said, "We're just trying to do the best with what we got." Early in camp, coaches agreed that their '92 motto would be, "We got what we got." Quit complaining about what players can't do. Accept them. Play to their strengths.

Wannstedt said, "Jerry Jones came up to me after the [Kansas City] game and said, 'Man, I didn't know you guys were going to gamble so much with so many blitzes.' I said, 'Hey, we were just doing what we had to do to survive and win the game.' We're getting better at mixing in blitzes. We're getting better at protecting our safeties by having the underneath guys hold up receivers. We have to keep trying new stuff. On the [Horton] interception, we just rushed three guys and dropped [defensive tackle] Jimmie Jones into coverage, which probably surprised them."

Wannstedt was still learning about coaching pro football. He said, "You know, you just can't get too close [to players]. It just doesn't work. These guys just aren't going to hug you. They'll come in your office, do this [Wannstedt reached deep in an imaginary pocket], and say, 'How much [effort] do you want? We'll give you all you want.' But they are not going to do this."

Wannstedt hugged the air.

★ ★ ★

For a few minutes the palm trees passed quickly as the Cowboy buses rolled along the Santa Monica Freeway toward downtown Los Angeles. Then: a wall of red brake lights. Welcome to L.A. The Cowboy traveling party was stuck in the traffic caused by Drew Bledsoe's Washington State vs. Southern California at the L.A. Coliseum. The following day, the Cowboys would cause the traffic as they played the Raiders.

On one bus John Weber talked about the message he was planning to give the team the following morning. Weber, who works for Campus Crusade for Christ, is the team chaplain. He's a stout fellow of five foot seven, a former college wrestler who occasionally wrestles with his role in pro football. There's nothing holier-than-thou about Weber, who doesn't take himself nearly as seriously as he does his faith. He has a warm smile and he's cool with many of the players, who turn out heavily for pregame chapel. Jones and Johnson also attend.

One Cowboy who rarely attends is John Gesek, who rarely misses the team's weeknight Bible study, also conducted by Weber. Bible study usually draws eight or ten players and sometimes their wives. Gesek questions the motives of some players who attend pregame chapel but don't seem to need God the rest of the week. "Frankly," Gesek says, "I just couldn't take it anymore."

Weber sometimes wonders if he's really accomplishing the Lord's work within a violent game played on Sundays. "Sometimes I wonder if I'm just part of the problem," he said. "Am I just making it worse? Am I being a hypocrite? Would my time be better spent elsewhere? Am I just doing this because it's fun being around the players and the games? If you go strictly by the commandments, you wouldn't play on Sunday. But do you do what the monk did, sitting up on a pole and having your food brought up to you? There are so many inconsistencies in the world. Hey, I can be a real jerk sometimes. I tell my wife, 'I can be a real jerk, can't I?' "

He chuckled at himself. If only the world had more jerks like Weber. He thought for a moment.

"You know, sometimes I saw more inconsistencies in Coach Landry's life than I've seen in Jimmy's. With Jimmy, what you see is what you get. A lot of the players used to question whether Coach Landry was really a Christian. They'd ask me, 'Do you really think he is?' Some people questioned his greed. Of course, there was much to admire about him. But one thing about Jimmy: he's very close to his sons. On the drive in from the airport [hotel, before home games], he calls them both [on his car phone] and tells them he loves them."

Yet insiders chuckle over one potential inconsistency in Johnson's faith. Several times a season he pays the way of Father Leo Armbrust to Cowboy games. Father Leo lives in Miami, where he helped conduct chapels for Johnson's Miami teams. Sometimes Weber shares duties at Cowboy chapels with Father Leo, who says mass. Johnson, who isn't Catholic, worships with Father Leo, while Protestant players and coaches pray with Weber. Does Johnson consider Father Leo a good-luck charm?

Weber said he has no idea. "I haven't figured Jimmy out. I'm not sure anybody really knows him. But I'll look in his eyes during chapel and I know he's really listening. I sense an intense desire to become more spiritual."

And the players? "Most of them really seem to believe in what we're doing. Of course, I was at the training table at camp and I heard one of the guys [from Bible study] say, 'What is this shit?' And I thought, 'Oh, I'm not doing much good.' "

Weber was told about a similar remark made by Gesek minutes

after the Phoenix game. Normally, Gesek displays as few spiritual inconsistencies as any Cowboy. But as he spoke in the locker room, Gesek hadn't yet come down out of the state of controlled fury required to be one of the league's finest linemen. He was still fuming about what happened after an interception. The man Gesek was blocking suddenly turned into a blocker. As Gesek glanced toward the play, his man knocked the heaven out of him.

Gesek said, "Somehow, someway, I'm going to get that cheap-shot motherfucker."

Weber smiled thoughtfully.

"You know," he said, "people are talking about the Super Bowl and I keep thinking of the Duane Thomas quote ['If it's the ultimate game, why do they play it every year?'] What if the Cowboys win it? I mean, will God redeem everyone's soul in Dallas? I tell people, 'God didn't have anything to do with the Cowboys winning their other Super Bowls, and he won't have anything to do with this one.' "

★ ★ ★

Jerry Jones perched on the edge of his chair in the owner's suite of the Cowboys' hotel in downtown L.A. Jones was trying to do what he does worst: sit still. "Man, is this exciting," he said.

Johnson had been miffed that Jones ordered a bigger plane for this trip, to hold twenty or thirty more sponsors. But Jones shrugged it off, kidding, "What's he going to do, not come? He'll be fine."

Jones was excited because it had taken him thirty minutes to work his way through a lobby jammed with people wearing Cowboy jerseys and caps. Jones must have signed a hundred between the entrance and the elevator. Jones was hearing that lots of Cowboy fans had bought tickets for Sunday's game in L.A. Jones had also been told that the Cowboys had officially passed the Raiders to become the NFL's No. 1 team in merchandise sales.

"In our meeting with [NFL] Properties," Jones said, "we were told we're now by far the biggest seller. I told Jimmy and Troy, just so they'd realize what they're doing is working. Of course, we did have the great tradition to build on."

During camp, Raider owner Al Davis had said in Austin, "Maybe America's Team is back. But we're still the world's team."

"Maybe not," Jones said with a big grin.

Jones also wasn't so sure about his coaches' concerns that Raider Mystique would still be a factor. "They are very worried about intimidation," Jones said. "Are our young guys ready for just how physical a game this is going to be?" The NFL's youngest team was about to play the oldest and most experienced. The Raiders led in average age (28.3) and career length (6.34). "But those last couple of practices against the Raiders, I saw our young guys holding their own. Listen, four or five games down the road we're going to have a hell of a defense. The coaches just love Darren Woodson. Kevin Smith will be in there for Ike pretty soon. We hated to lose Bill Bates's leadership and all the things he did for us on special teams. But Ken Norton is giving us a little more versatility [in place of Bates as a nickel linebacker].

"And our offense—listen, it's becoming a damn ball machine. I just don't think intimidation will be a factor, not the way our guys stood in there against Kansas City."

★ ★ ★

Usually the vast Coliseum turns into a black sea for Raider games. Well, black pond; often crowds reaching only the 50,000 range brave the hair-trigger neighborhood just south of downtown. But on this sunny, smoggy afternoon, the Raiders played before easily their largest crowd of the season, 91,505 in the 92,488-seat stadium. That, in fact, was the largest crowd to watch the Cowboys in Cowboy history. Fittingly, at least a third of the throng—maybe closer to half—came to see the visiting team. Black-clad Raider fans appeared to be matched in number by blue-clad Cowboy fans.

"The Cowboys are one of the most amazing phenomenons in sports history," said team ticket and promotions director Joel Finglass, who had made the trip. "For years people everywhere intensely loved or hated the Cowboys because they had so many great American heroes—Landry, Staubach, Lilly, Randy White—and because they had so many controversial players—a Dorsett or Hollywood Henderson. People found the uniforms fascinating—the shades of blue and silver and the star on the sides of the helmets. Everything was different about the Cowboys, right down to the hitch the offensive line did before each snap. The Cowboys were the first to have the beautiful, sexy cheerleaders. The Cowboys were in Dallas, and the TV show 'Dallas' was number one.

"It's funny, though. This team has very little to do with all that. Troy could be a much bigger national star, but he doesn't pursue it. Maybe he knows it's safer this way, because the national fame can be a double-edged sword."

Part owner Mike McCoy shrugged away all the overblown imagery. He said, "The simple fact is that people everywhere loved the Cowboys because they won [twenty straight winning seasons]. It's just like Notre Dame. The farmer in Iowa adopted the Cowboys as his team so he could tell his neighbor down the road that 'we' won. That's what people want most—bragging rights. All these fans were just dormant for a few years because we didn't give 'em any bragging rights."

Though several of the current Cowboys were Cowboy fans as kids, the team as a whole seemed to have very little sense of franchise history. The huge blue road turnouts seemed to amaze most of the players. Later that afternoon Emmitt Smith said, "All I know was that, as the clock was winding down, all that was left in the stands was about forty thousand Cowboy fans, cheering and chanting. That made me happier than anything, because we sure gave 'em something to cheer about."

What the Cowboys gave them was the new team theme: respond. If they score, we answer. The Raiders took the opening kickoff 83 yards in 11 plays to a touchdown. On third and 5 from the Cowboy 18, Ray Horton was flagged for pass interference on Raider tight end Ethan Horton. Injury to insult: Ray Horton hurt his knee on the play and was out indefinitely.

On first and goal at the 1, Marcus Allen scored for the Raiders. A fumbled snap cost them the extra point. Still, they led, 6–0.

But the Cowboys had the correct answer, 81 yards in 14 plays. The touchdown was scored from 6 yards by Emmitt Smith on one of Norv Turner's favorite plays, the lead draw, Troy Aikman fading as if to pass and slipping it to Smith, who has time to scan the field and let his instincts be his guide. Cowboys, 7–6. Bizarre crowd roar: Irving, California?

That score stood until the Raiders' first series of the second half. Dave Wannstedt called a blitz he had concocted off the scrimmages in Austin. "I was sure it would work," he said. But the Raider line and backs picked it up, leaving cornerback Ike Holt alone on Raider sprinter Willie Gault. Quarterback Todd Marinovich hit him with a 31-yard TD pass. Black jerseys, 13–7.

The Cowboys responded two plays later, thanks to another 911 call by Turner. Ironically, Emmitt Smith was writhing on the bench, victim of a helmet in the back. He would be okay. Daryl Johnston was momentarily hurting, too, and out of the game. How about a backfield of Tommie Agee and Curvin Richards? Time for a quick slant to Michael Irvin? No, the Raiders were the first team all season that double-covered Irvin nearly every play. So Turner called on Alvin Harper, who drew single coverage by cornerback Lionel Washington. Second irony: Harper had been struggling all season, searching for an identity opposite Irvin. Coaches considered him superior athletically to Irvin; at six foot three, Harper had won the Southeastern Conference high-jump title, but he hadn't risen to first-round-pick expectations in Dallas. Harper, who fancied a second career as a model, seemed to be more about glory than guts. He didn't have Irvin's fearless fire. To coaches, he didn't always want to win desperately enough.

But this time, after an Aikman pump fake, Harper took off and caught up to the rope Aikman threw him. The play covered 52 yards and flipped the momentum. Three plays later, Smith scored again.

Visitors, 14–13. That throw to Harper lingers in memory as one of the season's most critical.

"But," said Turner, "Troy threw a couple of other balls in the first half, to Michael and Kelvin [on third-and-longs], that were as well thrown as any you'll see in this league. If we don't make those plays, I'm not sure we win. Every game comes down to four or five plays. Make 'em, you win. Troy [16 of 25 for 234 yards] did some really good things today."

Aikman moved and threw with more authority than usual. He appeared more comfortable with being the star. Something about playing in L.A. did that to Aikman; he was back in his hometown, back where he played college ball at UCLA, back in the L.A. area where he had turned around his pro career against the Rams in 1990. He would be back again in January.

Yet five plays into the fourth quarter, still with a 14–13 lead, Turner faced third and 12 at the Raider 19. And he did it again: another lead draw. Thirteen more yards and a first down that set up the clinching touchdown. Smith capped probably his most dominant day as a pro—152 yards on 29 carries—with a 26-yard run for yet another TD with 3:26 left.

Cowboys, 28–13. Cowboys 365 yards, Raiders 165. Cowboys, 7 of 14 on third-down conversions; Raiders, 0 for eight.

Wannstedt couldn't quit shaking his head and grinning with amazement. "Fuckin' nuts," he said. "Just fuckin' nuts. Norv hit 'em with two third-down draws? And why didn't they ever try any dump-offs [late flips to backs]? We heard Al [Davis] got on the phone and called down to raise hell about it. I don't know, I guess Marinovich had some guys open deep early and they just kept looking for the home run."

Cowboy players heard from Raider buddies that Davis was furious about the blown deep passes. For years the Raiders have lived and died by the bomb. Davis saw four or five potential TD passes on tape that Marinovich failed to see, the Cowboys heard. The Raiders spent the next week concentrating on deep passes.

So was a combustible Cowboy secondary fortunate Marinovich tossed only one match on it? Maybe. What of the defense's inflamed egos and inner turmoil of the previous week? Once again, everything was forgotten on Sunday. "On Sunday," said Nate Newton, "this team is together." This team had beaten its third straight AFC West team. The Cowboys were 6-1 with Philly coming to Dallas.

Tony Wise lingered in the locker room to talk proudly about what he had seen. Raider coaches had paid Cowboy coaches a coming-of-age compliment. "Today," said Wise, "we saw that the Raiders changed a lot of things [strategically] for us. Maybe that means we're doing something right."

On the flight home, several Cowboys listened to one of the hottest rap groups, Boys II Men.

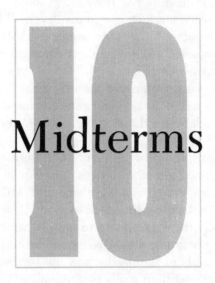

Midterms

JERRY JONES SOMETIMES TALKED ABOUT NOT WANTING THE SEA-
son to go any faster: "You're anxious, but it's like each week is a
new subplot. You want to enjoy the moment." Jones thrives on
striving. He's at his best and happiest dealing with controversy and
dilemma. As the rematch with the Eagles loomed, this week's crisis
was Lin Elliott.

Jones said, "Sometimes Jimmy's afraid the kicker will faint before kickoff."

Elliott, the rookie placekicker, had made 6 of 12 field-goal
attempts. Even on the makes, he hadn't always looked smooth,
tending to jump at and punch the ball without a rhythmic follow-
through. But he did have above-average leg strength. When
matched in camp practice duels with Brad Daluiso, Elliott had
flashed a competitive streak that caught Johnson's eye. Johnson
was building with "winners," guys "who can walk into any establishment and make the eight ball."

But at the moment, Elliott and his confidence were behind the eight ball. His performance in L.A. had left a troubling asterisk on the outcome: with about six minutes left in the Raider game, Elliott could have made it 24–13 with a 48-yarder. Wide right. No big deal—but it could have been. How much longer could the Cowboys get away with a kid kicker who displayed all the bravado of a Woody Allen character? assistants wondered. Management wondered. Fans wondered, loudly. Elliott came off more like a guy who would sink the cue ball.

In his weekly press conference Johnson defended Elliott by saying, "Look, Lin's a rookie. I'd like to see a game where he had the opportunity to kick two or three field goals from short distances, for his confidence."

Privately, Johnson was receiving some subtle pressure from Jones and Co. to consider alternatives. Veteran kicker Eddie Murray was available. Jones, son Stephen, and Mike McCoy were kicking around that possibility. McCoy said, "Everybody's a little goosey about Elliott. We're dying to go to a Super Bowl, and it's obvious most of the good teams have good kickers. It always seems to come down to a field goal in the play-offs, doesn't it? We have a good kickoff kicker—Elliott really booms 'em, which has been a big advantage over Ken Willis. Elliott might make a fifty-four-yarder, but will he make the key thirty-two-yarder? Don't know. Could we have somebody in for a tryout by next week? Yes. If Eddie Murray's just sitting at home, would he come in here for sixty thousand dollars and a Super Bowl share? Maybe."

But Johnson resisted. Near the end of a phone interview for this book, Johnson was asked if he was comfortable with Elliott. "Evidently, because that's what I'm doing," Johnson snapped, and hung up.

Kicking coach Steve Hoffman spoke for Johnson: "Jimmy is really great with kickers. Even at Miami, he never yelled at them. When he got close, he'd say, 'Go talk to Steve.' Jimmy said [about Elliott], 'No way am I going to bring other kickers in for tryouts or we'll lose the guy.'"

Lose Elliott mentally, that is. Johnson's theory on kickers: "They're like golfers—ninety percent confidence, nine percent technical, and one percent ability. If you even hint at a lack of confidence in a kicker, and it gets into his confidence, you've lost him."

Hoffman was asked if it ever seemed a little crazy that NFL

games and even championships sometimes are decided by a guy who really doesn't have much to do with the game of football. "It does," Hoffman said. "The coaches put in all this preparation, these great athletes fight it out, then games are won and lost on field goals. But that's the rule."

Hoffman, thirty-four, was perhaps a little too athletic to be a placekicker. A football and baseball star at Dickinson College, he punted in the USFL. Because the ball doesn't sit on a tee for punters, they're required to be a little more coordinated than most placekickers are.

Hoffman doubles as quality-control coach. "Computer nerd," he calls himself. He runs stacks and stacks of computer printouts for the coaches. For each game, Wannstedt might use up to ten different defensive fronts and fifteen coverages, with up to six variations off each, depending on an opponent's tendencies. By league rule, teams are required to send tapes of their previous three games to each upcoming opponent. Every Monday through Wednesday, Hoffman goes through three tapes while tabulating on a spreadsheet every down and distance, personnel group in the game, field position, number of steps in the quarterback's drop, blitzes, stunts, coverage, and blocking schemes. Cut-up tapes are prepared to correspond with important sequences on offense and defense. Complete scouting reports usually run about one hundred pages.

Though most coaches are in by at least six A.M. each morning, they begin meeting at seven-thirty (Monday through Friday) and rarely leave before ten P.M. Players are off Tuesdays. Wednesday begins with a special-teams walk-through in the morning and practice in the afternoon. On Wednesday nights, coaches break down third-down, blitz, and nickel situations. More special-teams walk-through and practice on Thursday, followed by coaches studying short-yardage, goal-line, and two-minute-offense possibilities. Tapes of practices are also reviewed on Wednesday and Thursday night. Friday mornings, the Cowboys go through a fifty-play scrimmage against the scout team. On Saturday, one more walk-through, along with more team meetings and tape review by players and coaches.

Johnson is everywhere, overseeing, troubleshooting, greasing squeaky wheels. He follows no set schedule, ducking in and out of meetings or popping into an assistant's office for an update or to plant a seed about a move he wants made or a direction he wants to go in the game plan. Johnson says, "I can tell you at every moment of the day exactly what each of my coaches is doing."

Meanwhile, Elliott and punter Mike Saxon don't seem to be around all that much. Comparatively, they don't have a whole lot to do. Other than special-teams meetings and short special-teams periods at practice, they're pretty much on their own. They work with Hoffman on technique, hit the weights, goof around, then win and lose games on Sunday. Johnson believes the kicking game is so critical that he calls special-teams coach Joe Avezzano "my third coordinator."

So all the intense hours of preparation, the dreams of athletes like Troy Aikman and Emmitt Smith and Michael Irvin, the ambitions of Dave Wannstedt and Norv Turner, and the obsessions of Jerry Jones and Jimmy Johnson could eventually hang by a thread of Elliott's unraveling confidence? Some rule.

"It's pretty crazy, isn't it?" said Elliott, who probably took himself less seriously than any other Cowboy. Once upon a time, Elliott was just another starry-eyed kid in the Dallas suburb of Richardson. Elliott's parents used to take him to games at Texas Stadium. His mom still has a picture of Lin at age six or seven in a Cowboy uniform kicking a football. He kicked for hours in the backyard, winning Super Bowls with field goals between two broom handles rising above the fence. And now Elliott's childhood fantasies were coming all too true.

"I'm living a fairy tale," he said as camp ended. But he was also feeling the weight of his Cowboy-crazed hometown on his little kicker's shoulder pads. While eating at restaurants, he could feel people's eyes on him. Elliott's problem was that he knew exactly how much his kicking meant to them.

"I know how bad they want me to do good," said Elliott. He's a good kid: genuine, gentle, humble, friendly. Sharp, but a little naive. More athletic (at six foot, 180) and less goofy than most kickers. Definitely country. During camp his long, thin, light brown sideburns were referred to in the media as "Beverly Hills, 90210" sideburns, but Elliott hadn't let them grow out because of any TV-show fad. Pickup-driving Elliott left them long because he went to school at Texas Tech, out in Lubbock, and long sideburns have been in style for years in West Texas.

Week to week, Elliott would sit with an interviewer for an hour at a time pouring his heart out about a subtle change in technique that was going to mean the difference. On and on he would go, trying to talk himself into it and sometimes accomplishing the opposite. "You know," he finally would say, "I'm going to kick it and it's either going to go through or it isn't." Listening to Elliott reminded you of the country-western line "I don't know whether to kill myself or go bowling." Elliott sounded as if he didn't know whether to kill himself or go practice.

As the Philadelphia rematch approached, it was difficult to tell who was more tormented, the kicker or his head coach. Even Jerry Jones, the unflappable optimist, said, "The kicker worries me."

All the king's horses and all of his men . . .

★ ★ ★

Quietly, several players and coaches were equally concerned about No. 8. It was Halloween week and Troy Aikman was in need of an exorcism. It was time for Aikman to confront his deepest, darkest fears—green monsters. Aikman was 0-6 against Philadelphia. For Aikman, every Eagle game had been a nightmare.

In Philadelphia the Eagles were making statements aimed at the Cowboy bulletin board and Aikman's subconscious. They obviously wanted Aikman to read quotes like this, from Seth Joyner: "If he gets off to a good start, it's kind of hard to hold him down. The thing is to get to him early and get him a little rattled, get him a little uneasy. Shatter his confidence as soon as you can."

In Dallas, Nate Newton made an echoing statement on a radio show. He said, "Don't forget, we have another quarterback. If for some reason Troy can't do it, we have Steve Beuerlein."

Beuerlein had played the previous December, when Johnson's team won its first and only game over the Eagles, 25–13, in Philadelphia. Yes, Jeff Kemp had played quarterback for the Eagles, who had lost Randall Cunningham for the season. But privately, some veteran Cowboys still weren't completely sold on Aikman. They liked him personally. They admired him. They were in awe of his talent and stature. But was he their Joe Montana? Would he rise above the big games and make the biggest plays? Did he have that "winner" intangible? On the field and in the locker room, Aikman hadn't quite seized the leadership role of this team. Beuerlein had come closer to doing that, but Johnson remained the team's leader.

It was obvious Aikman had a more powerful arm and a little

quicker release than Beuerlein. But Beuerlein was more of the back-yard scrambler who on guts and guile could make something of noth-ing. Beuerlein was regarded by teammates as a guy who'll find a way to win. He was a highly recruited high-school basketball shooting guard and four-year starter at quarterback for Notre Dame. He's smart and personable. He's a little more charismatic than Aikman. As the starter, Beuerlein had shown more outward competitive fire, more hand-clapping, fist-shaking body language than the usually emotionless Aikman. The Cowboy huddle broke for the line with more urgency and spark when Beuerlein called the plays.

"He's a little more contagious than Troy," Newton had said dur-ing Beuerlein's six-game winning streak the previous season. Coaches also admitted Beuerlein had a little better arm than they had thought when the Cowboys traded for him in August of '91.

But for now Beuerlein was living up to his '92 preseason vow: "This is Troy's team. There will be absolutely no controversy. I completely accept my role. I promise you I will not make a single wave." He hadn't and wouldn't. Mike McCoy said, "Every time we read those statements from Steve, we say, 'Thank you, God.' Do you realize what a controversy he could create with just one little remark?"

Instead, Beuerlein was using his intangibles to make Aikman as comfortable as possible. Aikman said, "Steve and I have become very good friends. There's a lot of mutual respect."

Beuerlein had made peace with his option of becoming a free agent at season's end. Norv Turner said, "I keep telling him this period will be over before he knows it. He'll get his money. He'll get his opportunity." Of course, Beuerlein also knew that Aikman had been injury-prone. But from week to week, Beuerlein was content to play cheerleader for Troy during meetings and during games, waving a towel to encourage more Texas Stadium noise.

That week Turner lost patience with having to defend Aikman. As a big-brother figure he admitted he sometimes lost perspective. But flashing rare emotion, Turner said, "People just don't appre-ciate how good this guy is and how good he will be." Turner said he was tired of reading quotes about any psychological edge the Eagles had on Aikman: "Psychological edges have nothing to do with it. This is simply a game of matchups. Can we get Jay [No-vacek] open on Seth Joyner? Can we get Daryl Johnston open on

Byron Evans? I'm sure deep down it's bothering Troy that he hasn't beaten these guys. But the point is, Troy isn't the only quarterback who has problems with them."

The combined rating of every quarterback who played against the Eagles the previous season was 52.1, which would have ranked last among all NFL quarterbacks with 224 or more attempts in '91.

Aikman also said he was sick of hearing about how the Eagles had their claws on his subconscious. "If you know anything about football, you know that's a joke," he said. Yet before the first Philadelphia game, it was Aikman who had spoken of not wanting to take another physical beating from the Eagles, saying, "I don't want to hurt anymore."

Sometimes Aikman seemed to be the bravest, toughest guy on the team; sometimes he seemed about to crumble under the pressure of being the Cowboy quarterback in Dallas. Up close, Aikman is a stunningly huge man out of the Li'l Abner mold. At six foot four, 235 pounds he is bigger than any Cowboy linebacker. He has big hands, big forearms, big bone structure, big thighs and calves. But he seems more like six foot two, 210 pounds when you watch him play because he carries himself and throws so economically.

Aikman's lips are at least as full as Mick Jagger's—and the bottom one has been stretched by the almost constant dip of snuff. Aikman has lots of big teeth, seen only when he hikes one side of his mouth into a grin. During most TV interviews, Aikman speaks monotone clichés. Off camera, among friends, he enjoys a good laugh, sometimes about the silliest things.

Even Aikman's eyes are huge. In the past Aikman's eyes have perplexed coaches because they seem almost to be made of glass. If uncomfortable or unsure, Aikman hides behind their dead gaze. One of his coaches at the University of Oklahoma says, "He sometimes had that faraway look in his eyes and you couldn't tell whether or not he was comprehending what you were saying. We never were sure how football smart he was."

Aikman is a walking contradiction: an expressionless stoic and a tortured whiner, fearless and vulnerable, star and reluctant star, what-the-hell and what's-it-all-mean, sex symbol and lonely guy. He sometimes complained about prying questions but seemed to enjoy probing his soul and answering them, almost as if he's living a wistful country song. He's a private guy who can't be out of the spotlight for too long. He says the best times are barbecuing for his few loyal friends; he parties, sometimes in public, with equally big stars from the country group Shenandoah. Close friendships run so deep for Aikman that two of his college friends moved to Dallas to be near him. Yet how secure a leader could Aikman be if he had to surround himself with supporters who constantly reassure him?

Aikman is a jeans-and-boots guy; he has changed his hairstyle more times than Madonna and resists the "country" label. Some women consider him a gorgeous stud; some consider him odd-looking. He's a nineties guy with bedrock fifties values. He isn't sure he trusts the institution of marriage; he's one star who refuses to demand renegotiation of a contract that makes him ridiculously underpaid. His character and principles equal Roger Staubach's. Unlike Staubach, who's widely known for his Christian beliefs and speaking, Aikman doesn't talk publicly about religion or take an active role in team chapel services or Bible studies.

Troy Kenneth Aikman has a rareness about him he can't quite get used to.

As November of his fourth season in Dallas approached, the point about Aikman was this: "I wasn't at all prepared for how much is expected of the Dallas Cowboy quarterback on and off the field. It still overwhelms me at times. I've talked to other quarterbacks in other cities, and I just don't think anywhere is quite like Dallas." The expectations, demands, idolatry. Did he want all that? Sometimes. Did he understand it all? He wasn't sure. "Sometimes I read those little tiny notes [about him] in the sports section, and I'll think, 'How could anyone actually care about this?' I guess they do."

The more Aikman gave to Dallas—more charity time, more interviews, more autographs than any other Cowboy—the more Dallas wanted. He didn't often say no. He wants to be loved. "He cares very much about how he is perceived by people," says Eric Celeste, who wrote the September cover story for *D Magazine* entitled "Aikman Won't Dance."

What still irritated Aikman about the story wasn't so much the anonymous quotes about Johnson. It was the "lonely guy" theme. Aikman said, "Eric just kept going back to the same idea that I'm a lonely guy without a girlfriend. I had a buddy of mine call and say, 'Can I come by so you won't be so lonely?' I have a woman right now who would like to get married. But I'm just not ready.

She says, 'Then I'm not the one.' And I say, 'No, while I'm doing this [football], I'm just not ready.' Besides, I just don't know any couples who have stayed together more than ten years [Aikman's parents had remarried after two years apart]. I told Eric [after reading the article], 'You'll probably call me in ten years and I'll be married with a couple of kids and be completely unhappy.' "

So would beating Philadelphia make him happy? Would winning lots of games? Would realizing all his football dreams? Would that silence all the doubting voices in Dallas? In the locker room? In his head?

★ ★ ★

Outside Gate 8 at Texas Stadium that Sunday stood former Cowboy Jay Saldi, now a Dallas entrepreneur. As a Cowboy assistant, Mike Ditka took a liking to Saldi and eventually signed him to play in Chicago, where Saldi and quarterback Jim McMahon hit it off. The night before, Saldi had had dinner with McMahon, who now backed up Eagle quarterback Randall Cunningham.

Saldi said Eagle coach Rich Kotite had told McMahon to be ready, that he might replace Cunningham. Saldi, via McMahon, said Kotite and Cunningham were feuding because Cunningham often disregarded game plans and had refused to take a pop quiz on the flight to Dallas.

"Sounds like there's some real dissension," Saldi said.

Sometimes, winning in the NFL is all about when you catch opponents. Are they healthy, physically and mentally? The Cowboys had caught the 3-0 Eagles' Sunday punch on that "Super Bowl Monday" in Philly. But now, without safety Andre Waters, the Eagles weren't so sure about themselves at 5-2.

On the Cowboys' side, Ray Horton needed minor knee surgery and was placed on injured reserve, allowing Thomas Everett and James Washington to pair at safety. Washington, who had appeared tight with Horton, now said, "Thomas and I are becoming really good friends. We work really well together." In other words, Cowboy dissension was dissipating.

This game would start similarly to the first one, with an early Cowboy turnover, but would end very differently. It was almost as if the biorhythmic tables had been turned.

Midway through the first quarter Emmitt Smith did something he did only twice all season: he lost a fumble. He would carry and catch the ball 516 times in sixteen regular-season and three play-off games, and he fumbled only 5 times, losing only 2. But this one was quickly canceled and forgotten. Remember the theme: response. On the next play Cunningham threw a short, wobbly interception right to Larry Brown, who isn't known for his hands. (Emmitt Smith on Brown: "He couldn't catch a cold buck naked in Alaska.") Brown couldn't help catching this one. Cunningham had been caught off guard by a scheme the Cowboys didn't often play in '92—"cover two." It's a pure zone. Instead of running with receiver Calvin Williams, Brown stayed put. "Randall was surprised," secondary coach Dave Campo said. "We do a good job of self-scouting and we occasionally try to mix it up."

Six plays later, Lin Elliott tried a 42-yard field goal.

Wide left.

The Cowboys held and moved into position for a 38-yard field goal.

Wide right.

Elliott slapped himself on the helmet with both hands and jogged off the field with his head down as boos rose. Johnson moved quickly to Elliott, grabbed his arm, and said, "Don't worry, you are going to make the one that wins the game."

Johnson deserved a best-supporting-actor nomination. (Larry Lacewell says, "Oh, Jimmy has some actor in him. All the great ones do.") He convinced Elliott he was okay. "That meant a lot to me," said Elliott. "I think I just said, 'What the hell,' and went out and kicked."

Finally, Johnson had willed himself a kicker.

The Cowboys held again and moved into position for a 52-yard field goal. Against a tricky breeze Elliott made it—though it was erased by a delay penalty, the thirty-second clock just nipping the snap. The Cowboys punted and held again. And as the first half ended, Elliott made a 35-yard field goal, which stayed just inside the left upright.

Cowboys, 3–0.

Kotite was desperate enough to make a move that would be debated for weeks in Philadelphia and the Eagle locker room: McMahon replaced Cunningham to start the second half. Eighty yards and 8 plays later, the Eagles led, 7–3.

The Cowboys responded immediately. Aikman to Michael Irvin for 21 yards, to Jay Novacek for 25, and to Kelvin Martin for 11 and

23. The plays by Martin were as spectacular as any made all season. "A great catch [on the first] and a great run [on the second, for a touchdown]," said Norv Turner, who got the matchup he wanted, Martin on nickel back Otis Smith. "He just can't cover K Mart. I said, 'Thank you.' "

Cowboys, 10–7.

But on the next Cowboy series, Aikman reverted. He didn't see linebacker Byron Evans in underneath coverage and threw an interception right to him. After the season Turner said, "If we hadn't won that game and had the season we had, people wouldn't have let Troy forget that interception."

Instead, from first and goal at the Cowboy 3 the Eagles came away with only a field goal—though on a first-down thrust, it appeared on replays that Herschel Walker broke the goal-line plane. It was that kind of day for Dallas.

The third quarter ended 10–10 with Elliott lined up for a 48-yard field goal. Hold it, Lin. Turn around the other way. Wait a couple of minutes for TV to come back from a commercial break. Now try it. Said kicking coach Steve Hoffman, "Having to wait through the quarter break and still making the kick really showed some mental toughness." From Barney Fife to James Bond: Elliott calmly nailed the 13–10 field goal.

Then, after the defense held, Emmitt Smith and his offensive line did something the coaches wouldn't have thought possible. Going into the game, Turner and Tony Wise kept telling each other, "A two-yard gain against these guys isn't bad. Be patient." But now, first and 10 at their 22, the Cowboys wore the Eagle defense down and out. Smith went for 10, 14, 6, 6, and 9. "I've never seen Troy so excited in the huddle," Nate Newton said. "He wanted to kill those guys."

In the wake of Smith's 14-yarder stood All-Pro Reggie White, bent over, hands on hips, apparently exhausted. Bam, bam, bam, 8 plays, 80 yards.

Cowboys, 20–10. That's how it ended.

Tackle Erik Williams, who blocked White most of the day, said he saw "fatigue." With 115 yards in the second half, Emmitt Smith totaled 163 yards on 30 carries. Aikman, sacked 11 times by the Eagles a year earlier at Texas Stadium, was sacked only once. Wise said, "The Eagles came in here thinking they'd win because they're just better than we are. They didn't care if we had gutted it out against the Raiders. They thought they'd wear *us* down in the fourth quarter."

The Cowboys had finally broken the Eagles' will and perhaps their psychological hold. While Emmitt Smith had taken over the game, Aikman had played merely well enough to win—19 of 33 for 214 yards. But that's all that mattered. The big green monkey was off his back. "Looking back," Newton said later in the season, "that second Philly game was when we found out we could play with anybody. Troy found out. Emmitt found out. The offensive line found out."

Wise said all five linemen graded out "very well." But the NFL office gave Williams, the 330-pound tackle, NFC offensive player of the week. Sweet irony: former Eagle coach Buddy Ryan, who often feuded with Johnson, said after the '91 draft that the Eagles blew it by taking tackle Antone Davis in the first round. The best offensive lineman in the draft, Ryan wrote in a *New York Times* column, was a kid from inner-city Philadelphia who played at Central State of Ohio, a big Eagle fan named Erik Williams whom the Cowboys took with their third pick in the third round.

And he had whited-out Reggie White, who was held to just two tackles, one assist, and no sacks.

It was that kind of day.

It ended with Lin Elliott saying he felt "totally confident" and the 7-1 Cowboys leading the NFC East by two games over the Eagles and Redskins.

★ ★ ★

Just two weeks earlier, Dave Wannstedt's defense had been in emotional disarray. Now this.

On Monday, November 2, Wannstedt was informed he had the NFL's No. 1 defense. This was somewhat mystifying to Wannstedt, whose defense finished seventeenth statistically in '91. Now it led the league in fewest yards allowed (242.8) and also in opponent's third-down efficiency (23.9 percent). The Cowboys had shut out Seattle, shut out Kansas City in the second half and held the Chiefs to 10 points, held the Raiders to 82 yards after an opening 83-yard drive (including 0 for 8 on third down), and held the Eagles to 10 points and 1 for 10 on third down.

The last time a Cowboy defense finished a season No. 1 was 1977.

That also was the last time a Cowboy team won the Super Bowl.

Wannstedt said, "We are not the best defense in the NFL, and I guarantee you I will not even mention this in the meetings. All I have to say is 'Lions,' and I hope they get the same feeling I get in the pit of my stomach. It's been gnawing at me ever since January."

In October of '91, the Cowboys played Detroit in its Silverdome and lost, 34–10. But a blocked kick and an interception were returned for touchdowns, and the word *fluke* was muttered in the Cowboy locker room. They got their chance to prove their superiority when they returned to the Silverdome for a divisional playoff game in January.

Detroit, 38–6, thanks to 421 total yards.

The Lions were saying they had the Cowboys' number—48342, the Silverdome's zip code. Running back Barry Sanders said, "It's funny. We can't play Washington, Washington can't play Dallas, and Dallas can't play Detroit."

But Johnson doubted that just saying "Lions" would strike fear in the expanding egos of his players. You could almost hear the Cowboys humming "The Lion Sleeps Tonight." Plagued by injury and tragedy, Detroit was 2-6. So Johnson made a locker-room appearance during the media hour on Wednesday. Johnson seldom if ever shows his face between twelve and one on Wednesday or Thursday; he knows if he did, media people would try to talk to him.

Bingo.

Privately, Johnson was saying, "We're ripe." Ripe to be upset by a dangerous but inferior team. So Johnson wanted to bombard the newspapers and airwaves—and players' senses—with a message. Johnson pulled aside the first two reporters he saw and said, "Hey, listen, Detroit's only missing two offensive linemen [Kevin Glover, Erik Andolsek] from when we played them last year. They didn't have Jerry Ball on defense last year. Now they do. The receivers are still there. So is the secondary. Detroit easily could be five and three. They're plus four in turnovers; we're even. They're still basically running the run-and-shoot, and we know what run-and-shoots have done to us in the past."

Johnson made a point of not making "revenge" the week's theme. Despite the two embarrassments the previous season, revenge would be phony; the Cowboys didn't have any historical hate for the Lions, and this wasn't a game that warranted working the

Cowboys into an emotional frenzy. This was the ninth game of sixteen, not counting play-offs.

So that week Johnson gave his taking-care-of-business lecture to the team. He talked about how important it would be the rest of the season for every man to be on time for everything. Focus. Commitment. Attention to detail. All forty-seven players, dedicating themselves body and soul, on and off the field, to what could become the greatest thing that had ever happened to them.

The punctuality speech, Tony Wise called it.

★ ★ ★

Something was wrong. It was 10:31 A.M. on Saturday and the team charter flight was not moving. It was 10:32 . . . 10:33 . . . 10:34 and the plane didn't budge. Bad weather in Detroit? Air-traffic control problems at Dallas–Fort Worth Airport? When Jimmy Johnson's itinerary says 10:30, the plane leaves at 10:30.

But seat 20C was vacant.

Jimmy Johnson waited seven long minutes before reddening and saying, "Go."

Michael Irvin had missed the flight. He hadn't called. Even his best friend, Alfredo Roberts, said he had no idea what had happened to Irvin. Irvin didn't ever miss the taping of his TV show. How could he miss a team plane?

The closer the flight got to Detroit, the closer Johnson got to the edge. Several players who walked past his seat said Johnson looked madder than they had ever seen him. From Detroit's Metro Airport the team bused about forty-five minutes straight to the Silverdome for the usual Saturday walk-through, a brief mental drill. The players don't even change out of their coats and ties; they just take their places in the formations Norv Turner has chosen for the game and in the personnel packages Wannstedt will use. They get a feel for the turf and check out the locker room, just so there won't be any surprises on game day.

Usually Johnson bounces among the players, joking, encouraging, reminding. Not this time. Through the entire thirty-minute session, Johnson stood at midfield, arms folded, staring off into the empty stands, fuming. Mike Saxon said, "Man, I'd never seen his face so red."

Players often spoke quietly of Johnson's powerful presence. Defensive tackle Jimmie Jones, who also played for Johnson at Miami, says, "First time I walked in a room with him, he was clear over on the other side and I knew he was The Man."

Now Johnson was dominating the entire mood of the walk-through by not moving a muscle.

Jerry Jones watched with CBS broadcasters John Madden and Pat Summerall, then hopped a ride on Madden's personal bus to the hotel just a couple of blocks away. As Jones blew into the lobby, he had the look of a big kid on Christmas morning. "Michael missed the plane and everyone's pissed!" he said with a big smile.

Jones hoped this sobering development—and Johnson's reaction to it—would be just what the team needed. Jones said, "Who knows? Maybe this will help everybody get real serious."

Public relations director Rich Dalrymple agreed, saying, "Oh, Jimmy loves a good crisis. Sometimes I think when we don't have a controversy, Jimmy creates one." Dalrymple laughed. "I'd like to know our record, 'weeks with internal turmoil, on turf.'"

This prompted Jones, son Stephen, and Mike McCoy to debate an intriguing question: Did Johnson and Irvin conspire to create this crisis? Could Johnson possibly have gone to team-leader Irvin and ordered him to miss the plane just a couple of days after his punctuality speech?

McCoy said later, "We sat around and laughed about it. We all doubted Jimmy put Michael up to it, but if anyone could take the heat for something like that, it would be Michael, and neither one of 'em ever would tell or that would ruin it. But you say, 'Man, is Jimmy some Leonardo da Vinci?' Some absolute genius who sits around plotting this stuff? The answer probably is that some of it's calculated and some of it is Jimmy just being Jimmy, just a little psycho."

Tony Wise and other assistants scoffed at the notion that Johnson scripted the incident. Wise said, "Believe me, Jimmy is very up-set—mainly because of who it is. Michael, of all people, the very week Jimmy lectures everybody on the importance of being on time, the very week we're playing in such a creepy place. It's almost comical."

Irvin arrived by commercial flight in the early evening. He told teammates and staffers a story that went basically like this: His wife, Sandy, had gone early to visit friends in Detroit, wives of Lions and former Miami Hurricanes. Irvin relies on Sandy to wake him. He set an alarm, but awoke early and went into the living room to watch cartoons. He fell back asleep on the couch and couldn't hear the alarm.

Irvin angrily refused comment to reporters and didn't publicly apologize. Johnson would say only that Michael Irvin would be punished.

★ ★ ★

Irvin did not start the game. Johnson also fined him $1,000. But without him, the Cowboys' first offensive series had the look of, "Here we go again." Emmitt Smith, one yard. Alvin Harper, drop. Troy Aikman, horrible pass right into the hands of Detroit safety Ray Crockett, who couldn't hold it. Crockett had returned an interception off Aikman 96 yards for a touchdown the season before.

But this was 1992.

Saxon's punt pinned Detroit at its 1-yard line. But the run-and-shoot clicked off gains of 15, 14, 13, and 13 against the NFL's No. 1 defense.

Wannstedt had been so fearful about putting pressure on the Lion quarterback (Rodney Peete or Cowboy nemesis Erik Kramer) that he came up with a defense he called "the Lion Group." It consisted of all "speed guys"—rookie defensive backs Kevin Smith, Darren Woodson, and Clayton Holmes, along with James Washington and linebacker Dixon Edwards—and could be used only when the Lions substituted their "Jade" package of four wide receivers. The Lion Group would put four Cowboys in no-help man-to-man coverage and the rest would blitz.

Week after week, Wannstedt devised risky blitzes, as if he were coaching the twentieth-best NFL defense. Sometimes, on proven talent, he was. He would call these blitzes on a moment's notice— the second he saw Detroit's Jade running toward the huddle, for instance. Wannstedt, in the press box, yelled, "Lion Group," through the headphones to Dave Campo, who immediately had to send the right players into the game. "It gets a little crazy," Wannstedt said, "because those guys have to be standing right there next to Dave, ready to go."

Wannstedt used the Lion Group once in the first half, pressuring Peete into a third-down incompletion. But the key play, stopping the first Lion drive, came when 5-9 Thomas Everett, lurking behind the linebackers, baited Peete into an interception. Key difference between Everett and several other Cowboy defensive backs: when Everett got his hands on a ball, he held on.

As the Cowboy offense hustled back onto the field, No. 88 joined it. Irvin's punishment had ended after one series.

Against the Lions, Irvin caught 5 passes for 114 yards and a touchdown. The Cowboys led 20–3 at the half and 34–3 after three quarters before winning, 37–3. They forced 4 turnovers, including 3 interceptions, 2 by Everett. "Now," Wannstedt half-joked, "we probably won't have another interception for a month."

Detroit finished with just 77 passing yards. "The run-and-who?" safety Washington said as he walked up the tunnel to the locker room. Detroit didn't convert a single third down in seven tries. Detroit really didn't have the ball much, just 22:03 to the Cowboys' 37:57. Another Cowboy trend was gaining momentum: domination of time of possession. With only three penalties to Detroit's ten, the Cowboy offense just kept executing and controlling the ball.

Lin Elliott actually made all four of his field-goal attempts, though after a Lion penalty Johnson wiped the first one off the scoreboard and turned it into a touchdown. Isn't the old saying, "You don't take points off the board?" Johnson's quick response, "That saying goes for normal football teams and normal players."

Johnson was riding high again, feeling cocky, gloating.

Johnson even encouraged a rather silly dance that nickel back Kenny Gant had done after making an interception. It was something Kevin Smith had brought from Texas A&M called the Shark. Smith had started doing it after making plays in practice, but said, "I wouldn't have the nerve to do it in games." Gant had the nerve. Gant, in his third season out of Albany State in Georgia, was called "a crazy motherfucker" by Nate Newton. Reserved during interviews, Gant said, "Sometimes I look at myself on film and I can't believe that's me doing the things I do." He had become a crowd favorite at Texas Stadium because he exhorted fans before kickoffs and after big defensive plays.

Now Gant was creating a dance sensation, the Shark, in landlocked Dallas. With his right hand he made a four-finger dorsal fin alongside his helmet. Then, slightly crouched, he moved forward, somewhere between Groucho Marx and Michael Jackson, shaking his left hand out to the side. Johnson said the Shark was "kind of neat." Johnson liked emotional displays that inspired the team. He did not, however, like what Everett had done after his two interceptions. Everett called it the Incredible Hulk—a bodybuilder flex, fists together at the belt. Johnson publicly said he didn't want to see the Incredible Hulk again. The Shark was more of a "we," the Hulk a "me."

Johnson even did the fin part of the Shark on his TV show. In the coming weeks, women in designer originals would be doing the Shark in Texas Stadium suites. Gant embodied the spirit of the '92 Cowboys—young, fearless, spontaneous, blissfully ignorant about anything more than today's game and tomorrow's practice. Newton referred to Gant when he used his favorite word, *geeked*—a word "from the Negro leagues," Newton said. Newton often said, "We're getting geeked for this game." Getting pumped. Getting psyched. "Nobody," said Newton, "gets geeked the way Kenny Gant does."

Gant said, "You watch film of other special teams and they just don't run as hard as we do."

The Cowboys had been geeked enough for Detroit. "The Lions came out strong," Newton said, "but they couldn't sustain it."

The flight back was as loose and lively as any all season. Seat 20C was again vacant because Irvin flitted all over the back of the plane, celebrating. Had he and Johnson pulled one over on the football world?

Johnson's sarcastic response: "Please."

Newton was so happy on the plane home he even started talking politics with Jerry Jones. Bill Clinton had just been elected president. Jones said, "It's strange when somebody you've known for a long time gets something that big. It's just hard to believe." Perhaps Clinton was thinking the same thing about Jones.

Newton readily admitted he didn't vote for Clinton. "My father called and said, 'You've got to vote for Clinton. He won't tax us black people.' I said, 'Speak for yourself. He won't tax the black people without money. But he'll tax my mo'fuckin' ass. You vote for Clinton. I'm voting for Bush.' "

Newton laughed hugely. So did Jones. Ripe for an upset, the Cowboys had won hugely.

Now they were really ripe. For the '92 Cowboys the real season was about to begin.

Desert Survival

THE WEEK BEFORE THE RAM GAME AT TEXAS STADIUM, TALK-show lines in Dallas were clogged with nickname suggestions. The Cowboys were 8-1 and it was dawning on fans that this defense was indeed pretty good. For weeks it had been fashionable around town to sigh and say, "How can this team realistically think it's a Super Bowl contender with Horton and Washington at safety and Ike Holt at cornerback?"

In Detroit the Cowboy defense had improved on its top-ranked statistics by about 4 yards. It was now allowing 238.1 yards per game. But more incredible, opponents were converting third downs at a rate of just 22.2 percent. Dating back to 1981, when the NFL began keeping this stat, the league's best percentage for a season, 26.1, had been recorded by New Orleans in '91. The '85 Chicago Bears, with their Wrecking Crew defense, allowed 28.8 percent.

So this Cowboy defense deserved a nickname. But what? Landry's great defenses were called Doomsday. Somehow, with its shaky secondary and rookie middle linebacker, Robert Jones, this defense didn't quite seem like a Doomsday machine.

But perhaps the most clever suggestion from a talk-show caller was Doomsdéjàvu. Maybe too clever; it didn't catch on. Some of the best submissions: The Hole in the Roof Gang. The Silver Bullets. The Silver Shuffle. The Bad News Boys. Blue Thunder. The Big D. The Roughriders. Haley's Comets . . .

Cornerback Ike Holt came up with The Who, "because nobody [around the NFL] knows nobody [on the defense]." The starters in the defensive line started calling themselves the Posse, but that won no points for originality: Washington's receivers had been calling themselves the Posse for several years. The second wave of defensive linemen started calling themselves the Lynch Mob. Jim Jeffcoat explained, "We come in and finish off what the Posse started."

The Lynch Mob wasn't bad. But it didn't stick. Nothing did. The Cowboy defense would finish the season without a universally embraced, down-in-history nickname.

Somehow, this defense just didn't strike fear the way Pittsburgh's Steel Curtain once did. This was still a defense without a star. Charles Haley? He had only 2 sacks, though he did lead the team with 32 quarterback "pressures." Dave Wannstedt said, "The guy has been a force. I mean, he's always hanging all over the quarterback, and I'm sure he helps open some things up for other guys. It just rips my guts out that he doesn't have the [sack] numbers to back it up."

This was a defense without a magazine-cover star—a Bob Lilly, a Randy White, a Too Tall Jones, a Lee Roy Jordan. It was a team-concept defense, a group that—on Sundays at least—did exactly as it was told and often played harder for longer than many other pro defenses. That was because of its depth. (How about the Depth Charge Defense? Sorry.)

Wannstedt's strength was in numbers. He and his coaches were running nineteen players in and out for the eleven spots. But there was a difference in the eight-player tag team that played the four line positions. Unlike the linebackers and defensive backs, who were being shuttled in and out in an effort to conceal weaknesses, the line group was loaded with underpublicized talent—maturing, sometimes exploding talent. Even without Danny Noonan, the

Cowboys had better two-deep defensive-line talent than any other NFL team.

To Johnson and his seven former Miami assistants now on the Cowboys staff, it *was* Doomsdéjàvu. They were winning in the NFL with a concept that was born on a steamy November 1984 afternoon in the Orange Bowl, when Miami played Pitt. The Panthers' strength was their muscled-up offensive line, featuring all-American Bill Fralic.

That day defensive-line coach Butch Davis tried something rather radical—a tag-team rush. It was Johnson's first season at Miami, and Davis had come with him from Oklahoma State. Davis played defensive end at Arkansas, where he earned a degree in anatomy and physiology. Davis, thirty-three in '84, had learned that "fresh guys tend to beat tired guys," no matter how good the tired guys are. Davis had several fresh guys who deserved to play—not start, maybe, but play.

Davis says, "It was evident a young guy who wasn't starting was giving other teams fits when he came off the bench. His name was Jerome Brown [then a sophomore]. So we started letting him play eight or ten plays for this guy, eight or ten for that guy, and he was getting thirty, thirty-five plays a game.

"Everybody started accepting it over the next few seasons because no one's stats were diminished. I don't mean any disrespect to the greatest linemen who ever played, but I promise there were eight or ten plays a game they coasted. They'd think, 'I'm not really involved in this play. I'll go through the motions.' They might as well have been resting. Listen, rushing the passer is very physically exerting, and the NFL game is infinitely faster than college. We expect our players to rush all-out, then chase the ball. On the first play the other day, Detroit completed a ten-yard pass and Kenny Norton caused a fumble. Who recovered? Russell Maryland, who had rushed the passer."

At Miami, Maryland learned to share snaps with the late, great Brown, with current Seattle great Cortez Kennedy, and with Cowboy teammate Jimmie Jones. Four talents, four powerful egos; the coach's handbook would warn that the starter would cause problems if you asked him to split time with a younger second-teamer. Yet, that day against Pitt, first- and second-teamers saw the results. Davis says, "Pitt had been practicing in forty- to fifty-degree weather. They truly had one of the outstanding lines in the history of college football, but by the fourth quarter their linemen were covered with ice towels and calling *no mas.*"

Johnson was winning with his Miami Method. Yes, again the former college coach was scoffing at NFL convention. Tell Johnson, "It just isn't done that way on this level," and look out. Burned in Johnson's memory were these 1989 words of former Eagle coach Buddy Ryan: "If you want a good NFL coach, get yourself a good NFL assistant." But now, the only burning was in the second-half legs of some NFL offensive linemen, who were beginning to know that *no mas* feeling themselves.

Haley started at right end, but occasionally lined up at left end. Sometimes tenth-year vet Jim Jeffcoat came in at right end and often at right tackle. "This could prolong Jim's career a couple of years," Davis said. "Now he knows he can maximize his effort every play he's in there, and his production is so much better." Jeffcoat balked at first, then bought the program.

Tony Casillas started at one tackle. "Casillas and the other guys rag on me to no end," says Davis. "They say, 'I'm just getting into the flow of the game.' But if we're ahead, fourteen to three, I can say, 'Take the next three plays off and I'll give you the next twenty.' "

If the Cowboys had been 1-8, Davis might have had an eight-deep line outside his office door. But at 8-1, even Haley and Casillas, who had caused team-rocking problems in other cities, were accepting their roles. Davis himself is a proud, hot-tempered country boy from Tahlequah, Oklahoma. So the fresh-horses approach required patience on everyone's part, including the coach's.

But how would you like to be an offensive guard who had just handled Casillas for a couple of plays? You're feeling pretty good, but as you break the huddle, you look into the eyes of a fresh 6-6, 300-pound Leon Lett. In his second year, the man they called Big Cat had the potential to be even better than Haley. "Freakishly gifted," Davis says of this quiet, polite Baby Huey project. Johnson drafted Lett in the seventh round, out of Emporia State of Kansas. Lett had missed four games of his senior season with a sprained knee, and his ambition had been questioned by NFL people, but Cowboy scout Ron Marciniak raved to Johnson about Lett's potential after watching him dribble the length of the court and dunk in a basketball game. Lett was recruited out of Mobile, Alabama, by

Alabama and Auburn, but he didn't have the grades or test scores to play major-college football.

Lett says Buffalo indicated it would draft him. "I had no idea the Cowboys were going to take me," he says. "But I was a huge Cowboy fan growing up."

What's even scarier about Lett is that he has developed an over-achiever's work ethic. "As hard as Leon practices and studies film," says Jeffcoat, "he could be as good as anybody who ever played this game." And in 1992, he was just another of eight Cowboy linemen, a guy known more by blockers and rival coaches than national media and fans.

Davis's point about Lett: "He knows he's going to get to play. So he doesn't put it on automatic pilot during the week. He prepares just the way the starters prepare." Under, for instance, Tom Landry, with starters set in stone, a Lett could grow discouraged. But this way, says Davis, "if tragedy strikes, we don't have to go cold turkey. A Leon Lett has played enough that you aren't worried about him starting."

The other starter at tackle was Maryland, an undersized over-achiever, affable and humble. Several rival GMs criticized Johnson for taking Maryland with the first pick in the '91 draft because, they warned, Maryland was too small at 6-1 and about 270 and not powerful enough to be a force against brutish NFC East linemen. Maryland still carries the leftovers of a childhood weight problem around his midsection, and he doesn't have much upper-body def-inition. Yet, says Jerry Jones, "When I think of what I want the Dallas Cowboys to be, I think of Russell. The character, the work ethic, the heart." Maryland has what coaches call "slither," an agile knack for squirming through a block. "Explosive change of direc-tion," Davis says.

So about the time a blocker began to get comfortable with Mary-land's tenacious slither, here came tackle Jimmie Jones, an unpre-dictable underachiever. When he decided to, Jones could be as disruptive as Haley. "The most talented backup defensive lineman in the league," Wannstedt called Jones.

The day after the Super Bowl, Johnson told *Sports Illustrated*, "While [Buffalo coach] Marv Levy is over there reading about Harry Truman, Jimmie Jones is on his bed, belly-laughing at Fred and Barney on 'The Flintstones.' "

The starter at left end was Tony Tolbert, whom Johnson drafted in the fourth round of the '89 draft. Too skinny, sniffed rival scouts. At the University of Texas–El Paso, Tolbert was a 6-6, 230-pound outside linebacker. Tolbert had spent much of his first two pro years in the weight room. Now he weighed 265 and had become a quiet force against the run, a cornerstone. Tolbert would also finish second on the team in regular-season sacks with 8½. But Tolbert occasionally gave way to 6-6 Tony Hill, a former high-school basketball star who played football at Tennessee-Chattanooga. Again, Hill fit Johnson's mold: quick, powerful, athletic. Hill had perhaps the most impressive physique of any lineman and, says Davis, "Charles Haley quickness."

Yet as one Cowboy-Raider practice ended in Austin, a Raider assistant was heard to say, "Nothing but little guys."

Lots and lots of little, quick guys. Other than Lett, every lineman was considered a little too small to bang with the big boys in the NFC East. Haley was listed at 6-5, 230 pounds (though coaches said he was closer to 250). But the Cowboys were wearing down the big boys with lots of two-on-one. To fully grasp the quality of the Dallas depth, remember that the ninth man down the list was Chad Hennings. So far there was no room at the inn for the "savior" of early training camp. Moved to tackle, he rarely played, except on special teams.

"Believe me," Davis said, "we could win Sunday with Chad Hennings starting at tackle."

★ ★ ★

The offensive line had a nickname, though the offensive linemen didn't embrace it. The name that had stuck with some media people was the Wise Guys, after Coach Tony Wise. Occasionally you saw WISE GUYS T-shirts in the stands—pretty good for a sorry athlete from Ithaca College who called himself a court jester.

In 1989, Wise had inherited two starters that the previous coaching staff had all but disowned. Former offensive coordinator Paul Hackett had concluded, "You just can't win at this level with Mark Tuinei at left tackle and Nate Newton at guard."

Tuinei made the team in '83 as a free-agent defensive tackle from Hawaii. In desperation, coaches moved Tuinei to offensive left tackle in '85. Left tackle is the most important position for a right-handed quarterback, because the best rushers usually swoop from the quarterback's blind side. A bad left tackle can cause offensive cancer. He can ruin a quarterback's confidence, if not health. He can split a coaching staff into paranoid factions. The left tackle can open the castle gate.

And the old Cowboys started a converted free-agent defensive tackle at left tackle? Jimmy Johnson soon said Tuinei would start for him, too. One of Johnson's most outrageous statements early in his first training camp was: "I feel better about our offensive line than I do any area of the team. I believe in Tony Wise."

Now, in November of '92, football experts around the country were beginning to believe, too. More and more the Cowboy offensive line was being mentioned as one of the league's best. Newton was on his way to a Pro Bowl season. So was center Mark Stepnoski, a third-round choice out of Pitt in '89. Tackle Erik Williams, the Leon Lett of the offense, had the look of a ten-year Pro Bowler. Guard John Gesek, a former tenth-round pick by the Raiders from Cal-Sacramento, consistently graded out as high as any lineman and deserved all-star recognition, coaches said. Wise had untaught Gesek's Raider-style "grabbing" technique and helped turn him into a "puncher," neutralizing the defensive tackle's charge with forearm blows.

And Mark Tuinei had developed into one of the better left tackles in the league. In Tuinei, Wise saw a bright, quiet warrior. "I said, 'Well, he weighs three hundred pounds,' though he always says he's two ninety-nine and doesn't seem that big in his clothes. He's a good athlete. Quick feet. Good coordination. And Tuey's so quiet that people don't realize how sharp he is. I can't get him on anything in the classroom. But the main thing about Tuey is you can't break his spirit. That's what left tackle's all about. If he gets beat, he'll fight you just as hard the next play."

Newton says Tuinei is the one guy on the team he isn't sure he could whip in a street fight. "I would definitely have to kill him to whip him," Newton says.

So what did a fresh-from-college coach teach these guys that the former coaches didn't or couldn't? Wise said, "In an early film session, a guy who's no longer with us [identified by others as Dave Widell, now playing for Denver] says to me, 'Tony, do you know who that is [on film]?' Well, yeah, that's Lawrence Taylor. 'And you're still going to block him that way [with Tuinei]?' Yes, we are.

"Listen, I truly despised that attitude. I still think about it. The key thing we had to get across was this: Lawrence Taylor and Reggie White are not Superman. They're going to beat you some, but many, many plays they can be blocked."

Yet Wise is careful not to take any credit for turning any of his linemen into supermen. "Hey, Tuey is the one who took it to the next level. Yeah, I work hard. I drive 'em all crazy harping on details and technique. I tell 'em exactly what I think needs to be done to block a guy. But after that, don't even let me get close to taking any credit. With my guys, are you shittin' me? They'd never let me get away with that. They're too smart, too cynical."

While Wannstedt's defense was us-against-the-world volatile, Wise's guys were more the yawning, sarcastic skeptics. Just relax and wake 'em on game day. While many defensive players raved publicly about Wannstedt, Wise's guys quietly hinted at some resentment of their coach's media recognition. Some groused about how tough Wise was on them in film-grading, because financial incentives for offensive linemen often are tied to grades. So while the defense spoke with love of Wannstedt, the offensive line avoided saying much about Wise, other than he's "fine."

It was an odd relationship. But it worked.

Asked to talk about Wise, Newton said, "That's the one thing I won't talk about."

★ ★ ★

Friday afternoon, returning from a jog with his coaches, Jimmy Johnson was in dimple city. He was grinning, cutting up, looking forward to the usual Friday night off. He didn't even seem to care that his hair was sweaty and uncombed. The tip-off to a good Johnson mood was the greeting "Whatcha got?"

Perhaps Johnson was unwinding because his team was about to play three games in twelve days that it should win: the Rams, Phoenix away, and the Giants on Thanksgiving. The Cowboys had won five straight to rise to 8-1. The humiliation in Philadelphia now almost seemed as if it had happened a season ago. The offense, defense, and special teams had performed at a play-off level in Detroit. The team had responded to Johnson's rage after Michael Irvin missed the plane. For the moment, Johnson had flipped his switch to "cocky." He could smell 11-1.

Johnson even allowed himself to think about the one sport he enjoys watching almost as much as football: boxing. He was asked whether he liked Evander Holyfield or Riddick Bowe in that night's title fight. He said, "Bowe lost all that weight—what, 272 to 235? But Holyfield is just 205? Oh, I guess I'll go out on a limb and take Bowe."

Johnson asked what time the main event would start. He can't get pay-per-view channels on his home satellite dish, so he was forced to watch this fight at a sports bar.

"Not until nine-thirty?" he said, and began to laugh. Johnson liked to "have a few" on Friday nights. "Oh, I'll be in a stupor by then. I'll have to wake up in the morning and read that Bowe won."

★ ★ ★

Omen No. 1: Back in training camp Norv Turner mentally scanned the Cowboy schedule and said, "You know, the Rams could give us as much trouble as anybody." Turner had helped coach the Ram offense for six years. He knew Ram quarterback Jim Everett had the savvy, experience, and speed at receiver to pierce Wannstedt's camouflage and capitalize on some obvious Cowboy weaknesses. Turner knew his mentor, Ram offensive coordinator Ernie Zampese, would be licking his chops and his game-plan pencil.

Omen No. 2: On Wednesday, Charles Haley pulled his groin in practice. Johnson said, "We don't expect it to be anything major." But Haley—who says, "My whole game is based on quickness"— could barely push off his left leg. He tried it for a couple of plays against the Rams and took himself out.

Omen No. 3: At the suggestion of the league office, Jerry Jones and staff toured Texas Stadium, planning for a potential NFC championship game. Later, Jones said, "I think everyone counted this game as a W. In all candor, I did."

Omen No. 4: Johnson, concerned about mounting distractions and complacency, moved quickly when he heard the offensive line was considering an offer to make a music video. "He nuked it," Newton said.

Omen No. 5: A picture of four Cowboys gang-tackling a Raider appeared on the cover of *Sports Illustrated*, potentially invoking the dreaded *SI* cover jinx.

Omen No. 6: As the Cowboys warmed up before Sunday's game,

Wannstedt noticed that linebacker Ken Norton was "completely drenched with sweat. I'd never seen anything like it. He looked like somebody had hosed him down. I guess it was a big deal for him playing against so many of his buddies [from UCLA]."

Omen No. 7: Completely out of character, Johnson chose not to go for the first down on fourth and inches at the Ram 19 in the first quarter. The 3-6 Rams had taken the kickoff 81 yards in 13 plays to a 7–0 lead. But Johnson opted for the field goal, which Lin Elliott made from 37. Johnson said he felt his team needed "a positive instead of a negative" at that point. What had happened to the coach who said this wasn't a normal football team? Johnson had sent a negative message to his team: against this team we're playing not to lose. It appeared that Johnson thought his team was so much better than the Rams that he didn't want to risk anything that could backfire and give the visitors any reason to think they had a chance.

For Johnson in '92 that was a first and a last. Jones said that after the game, Johnson told him, "This was the first week that, as a staff, we didn't say, 'We've got to find some way to win. One way to win.' "

Back and forth it went, both teams moving the ball. Everett and Troy Aikman would wind up with identical numbers, 22 of 37. But the Rams would have more total yardage, 367–349. The Rams would win the clock, 33:28 to 26:32.

The Cowboys didn't play horribly. They didn't commit a turnover, but they didn't force one, either. The Rams, said Wannstedt, "just played a near-perfect game. Everett put on a clinic. He made all the right choices and all the tough throws in the clutch and kept getting rid of the ball so damn fast. But we also missed an amazing number of tackles. What are you going to do?"

What do you do when a fifth-year leader, Norton, gets called for penalties—holding on a Cowboy punt and a 15-yard facemask—that fueled two fourth-quarter Ram scoring drives? "Kenny played like shit," Wannstedt said. "For the first time all year, they just weren't up for it—until the second half. Then you could really see them scrambling. But the Rams play against a defense just like ours every day in practice. They were reading everything."

So was the Ram defense. Often, said Cowboy offensive players, Ram defenders correctly called out run or pass before the snap just because they were so familiar with Turner's formations. For the Cowboys, this was a bad matchup at a bad time.

Still, they had a chance to win. A good chance.

With 1:50 remaining, trailing 27–23, they had the ball first and 10 at their 24. Aikman hit 5 of 8 passes for 62 yards, the last a $1.25-million catch by Michael Irvin at the Ram 14. Six seconds remained. Time, probably, for two plays.

Plenty of time for Aikman to make the one throw that would prompt people around the country—and the locker room—to say he had officially arrived as another Montana or Marino or Elway. For Aikman all that was missing was a little last-second magic. Step right up, Troy, and win about 4 million women a Kewpie doll.

Aikman threw to the back of the end zone for Alvin Harper. Safety Anthony Newman cut inside Harper and nearly intercepted. Now Aikman faced his first pro opportunity to complete a last-play pass to win. One second left: do or sigh from 14 yards.

Turner called Ace Right 0-44, a play the Cowboys had practiced often for this situation. Irvin and slot receiver Kelvin Martin lined up left and ran "end" routes, basically down and across. Harper crossed from the opposite side of the formation. Aikman drifted left, looking first for Irvin. Several Rams said later that Aikman still had a habit of "locking on" a receiver. Reading Aikman's eyes, Newman broke to Irvin, who was blanketed with double coverage.

Jones said, "Troy did lock on to Michael, instead of looking off the safety. But hey, things are happening so fast, I wouldn't want you or I to have to make that split-second decision. I still say the consistency of our quarterback play has been the story of the year so far."

As Aikman glanced to his second option, Martin, it was too late. Ram rookie Sean Gilbert was in Aikman's face, having fought off Nate Newton's block. Aikman unloaded for where he hoped Martin would be. But Martin had instinctively slowed, ready to work back toward Aikman if he scrambled. No rapport, no shared wavelength. The pass wasn't even close, skipping off the turf five yards from the closest Cowboy or Ram. Texas Stadium groaned in shock. The Rams, who had lost twelve straight on the road, had beaten the Cowboys at home, where they had won eleven straight.

"Remember," Turner said, "only about one in five of those last-second throws work. Sometimes Montana or Elway don't make them. But chance often plays a big part. Improvising." Whirling away from Gilbert, rolling back right, buying time. Maybe lobbing a jump-ball completion to the 6-4 Harper. "Of course," said

Turner, "we know that's not Troy's strength. But after all he has done, I'm certainly not going to criticize him for it. I keep asking myself, 'What could I have done different?' Throw underneath to Emmitt? Go to Jay [Novacek]?"

Wannstedt was asked if the defense missed Haley. He tried to play but couldn't and feared he further aggravated his groin pull. Wannstedt said, "I don't know, he doesn't play the run much at all [Cleveland Gary rushed for 110 yards on 29 carries]. So it probably didn't matter."

But several defensive backs said no Haley was a no-win situation. "With Haley, it's one way," James Washington said. "Without him, it's another way."

Remarks like that would burn in the gut of Jim Jeffcoat until the following Sunday.

★ ★ ★

Later, the Cowboy coaches would say they had never worked harder and felt more pressure than they did preparing for the Cardinals at Phoenix. To many fans it was "just Phoenix." To the coaches, it was just everything. "That was the whole season right there," Dave Wannstedt said. "That was the turning point. That was crucial. I have never, ever grinded so hard for a game."

This week the coaches were grinding because, once again, they didn't trust how good their team was. They were grinding because Phoenix quarterback Chris Chandler had put their secondary through a grinder—383 yards passing in Dallas. They were grinding because Chandler was out of the Jim Everett mold—slick and smart with the arm to match. Worse, Chandler is more nimble and daring than Everett.

They were grinding because the 3-7 Cardinals had upset the Redskins and 49ers at Sun Devil Stadium in Tempe. They were grinding because, if they got lost in the desert, they had to play the Giants four days later, then three tough road games: at Denver, at Washington, at Atlanta. Later, Tony Wise said, "Every year in the NFL, some team's rolling along and it barely loses a game. Then it can't quite get back up for the next one. Then the schedule gets tougher and all of a sudden the team everybody thought was pretty good has lost six in a row. We were in position to lose six in a row."

That week, Wannstedt kept catching himself chewing on the

side of his index finger. "I never do that," he said. "I will not let Janet [his wife] say the word *stress* in our house. Stress is what you put on yourself. But I was feeling stress."

Johnson heated up and walked out of an early-week press conference when he said a reporter was smirking at his answer. PR man Rich Dalrymple said, "Jimmy's just trying to set the tone for the week." Johnson, said insiders, decided to do something dramatic—in effect, to slap players in the face and show them he wouldn't stand for losing. Johnson demoted cornerback Ike Holt and replaced him with rookie Kevin Smith. So now the Cowboys had two rookie starters on defense, and rookie Darren Woodson was playing more and more on passing downs.

The Cowboys would also be without Charles Haley. His groin was so bad, or so he said, that he didn't even make the trip. The coaches were still trying to figure out Haley. Was he really that hurt? Or was he taking a couple of weeks off? Wise said, "I don't know if anybody [coaches or players] has figured the guy out yet. But I'll tell you this: a lot of people around here have just about had enough of him."

Jim Jeffcoat included.

★ ★ ★

Jimmy Johnson used to make jokes to assistants and writers about the "apelike" way Jeffcoat ran. This certainly was no racist reference. Rocking side to side, Jeffcoat simply doesn't look too smooth or athletic when he runs.

But the jokes were made during Johnson's first Cowboy camp in '89, long before he had developed an appreciation of Jeffcoat's subtle talent. It took a while. During the garage-sale days of '89 and '90, Jeffcoat was shopped hard on the trade market. Jeffcoat knew it and didn't like it.

As John Wooten used to tell Johnson, "Sometimes the best trades are the ones you don't make." That proved true with Michael Irvin and Jim Jeffcoat.

Jeffcoat won over the coaching staff with his film study, his off-season conditioning, his role-model influence on young defensive linemen, and his unique knack for making key plays. Often, Jeffcoat materialized in the right place at the darnedest times. He doesn't have massive muscles or a menacing aura. He has had trouble keeping weight on his 6-5 frame. He's a former '83 first-round draft choice who didn't make any all-star teams. He just made memorable plays and, in '92, started wearing memorable shoes.

"I asked Reebok to send me the weirdest, funkiest shoes they had," Jeffcoat said. The speckled Preseasons made Jeffcoat feel young again, at thirty-one.

But to most fans, Jeffcoat's game was as gray as his game-day stubble.

Dave Wannstedt says, "He doesn't look strong when he walks into a room, the way Tony Casillas does. But he probably has the best first-step quickness of any of our guys, and he has natural strength. When you least expect it, he makes plays. If I were starting a business tomorrow, I'd say to him, 'Here, you run it.' That's how much I believe in him."

Jeffcoat, father of three, has a master's degree in business administration from Arizona State. He played his college ball at Sun Devil Stadium. He loved playing the Cardinals at Sun Devil.

At first, though, Jeffcoat did not love it when the Cowboys traded for Charles Haley. Jeffcoat strode straight into the coaches' offices for an explanation. He was promised he would get his playing time, if not at end then at tackle.

Jeffcoat would lead the '92 Cowboys in sacks with 10½ He would also lead in resentment of the credit given Haley. He respected Haley's talent, but he refused to believe "we were nothing" until Haley arrived. "We need him," Jeffcoat said. "But we're still pretty good without him." Several times the week before the Phoenix game, Jeffcoat read headlines such as this one in the *Fort Worth Star-Telegram:* "With Haley hurting, Dallas's pass rush was ineffective." Jeffcoat seethed. He was at his relentless best when he convinced himself he had been slighted.

"Jim," said Wannstedt, "is really pushing the guys to make a stand. Jim is the coach type behind the scenes. He gives us the motivation dimension."

Knowing Wannstedt, he probably taped a mugshot of Haley in Jeffcoat's locker that Sunday in Tempe.

It happened again. The crowd of 72,439 was the Cardinals' largest ever, and it had a blue tint. Several Cardinal staffers, including former Cowboy executive Bob Ackles, estimated that at least half the crowd came to cheer the Cowboys.

They would need all the help they could get.

The desert weather wasn't too hot, 65 degrees at kickoff, but Chris Chandler was blazing. He hit 5 of his first 7 passes, including a 2-yard touchdown flip. Phoenix, 7–0.

Worse for Dallas, safety Thomas Everett had banged up his shoulder on the game's fifth play. His replacement? Robert Williams, who should have been a Cardinal. (Johnson had attempted to slip Williams, a valuable special-teams player and backup safety, through waivers when he returned from injured reserve to take Ray Horton's spot. This way Johnson would save one of his two remaining "free" moves. Knowing Williams might even be able to start for Phoenix, Ackles recommended claiming him. "I knew Jimmy would be pissed," Ackles says. But, says a Cowboy source, "Robert has a new house and a girlfriend, and he was scared to death about going to Phoenix and having to prove himself. He's not real secure. He just wanted to stay here and have a chance to be part of a Super Bowl team. So it was explained to him what would happen if he failed his physical." Somehow, he did. His knee, recently arthroscoped, hadn't completely healed and might require further surgery down the line. But Cowboy doctors had cleared him to play. Strange but true: two weeks after failing his physical in Phoenix, Williams was playing for the Cowboys—in Phoenix.)

Chandler's offense was on the move again. Third and 5 at the Cowboy 46. Gambling, trying to make something happen, Wannstedt threw "the Shark" at Chandler. This was Wannstedt's mad-scientist invention of the week: eight defensive backs, with Kenny "the Shark" Gant as a roving middle linebacker and only three down linemen (Tony Tolbert, Leon Lett, and Jeffcoat). Though only three Cowboys rushed against five blockers, Lett crashed through the middle and flushed Chandler from the pocket. As Chandler scrambled left, Jeffcoat broke free of his blocker and chased down Chandler. As the two of them tumbled and rolled over, the 300-pound Lett bounced on top of them. Chandler was carried off on a stretcher with what turned out to be badly bruised ribs.

That one play was probably as important as any all season for the

Cowboys. Without it, perhaps, the Cowboys would have lost to Chandler's Cardinals, lost confidence, and lost several more games. "That," said Johnson, "was a big, big play . . . in more ways than one."

It stopped another Phoenix drive—and it forced the Cardinals to play former starter Timm Rosenbach, who was covered with rust and soon with Cowboy rushers as well. Said Wannstedt, "We were able to go after Rosenbach much more than we would have Chandler." The Cardinals became basically inept on offense, totaling only 149 yards.

But now the Cowboys' problem was scoring. Said Wise, "They came out in a front we hadn't prepared for, with a defensive end over our tight end." Alfredo Roberts, who often works against linebackers, isn't big or strong enough to handle a defensive end. "So they took away our best play, the lead draw, and it caused a high degree of frustration, with Emmitt and with us," said Wise.

After watching the tapes, the coaches concluded Smith was so frustrated he sometimes didn't run hard. He wound up with 84 yards on 23 carries. Aikman sometimes frustrated coaches (and fans) with his safety-valve swing passes to Smith, who caught 12 for 67. But Aikman throws the swing pass, one of the most difficult to execute because of the touch and timing required, as consistently accurately as any NFL quarterback. At least Aikman didn't force the issue or an upfield throw. He remained patient.

The game degenerated into trench warfare. "That," said guard John Gesek, "was as physical a defensive front as I've ever run up against." Late in the third quarter, Aikman found Alvin Harper alone on cornerback Lorenzo Lynch. Harper made a neat reverse-pivot spin move and was gone 37 yards for a touchdown. That gave the Cowboys a 16–7 lead. They didn't score in the fourth quarter, but they survived in the desert, 16–10, thanks in large part to The Survivor—to Jeffcoat.

He had the game's only two sacks and led the Cowboys with 7 tackles. "This is vindication," he said. "People got down on us without Charles. I think a lot of people forgot how I've played over the years."

Six or eight lockers down in the cramped quarters, a bubbly Michael Irvin best capsulized the team's relief. Irvin yelled for all to hear, "You know what I say about this place? Fuck it! Get us outta here!"

On Monday, Jimmy Johnson told the team, "You're going to have a tough time getting ready this week. It's a short week and you've probably got family coming in [for Thanksgiving] and I can't help you [get motivated]. But if you aren't ready, you are going to lose to a team that isn't half as good as you are."

On Tuesday, Norv Turner admitted to reporters his offense was in a lull, but not a slump. "No, we're just in a lull that teams go through. People are taking away some things we've had success with. They're doubling Michael and committing to stop Emmitt. It's going to be tough from here on out." Privately, he said, "We're a couple of players away from a Super Bowl team. Maybe a speed receiver and a third-down back like [the Giants' Dave] Meggett who can really create problems [as a receiver] with his speed."

On Wednesday, more controversy swirled around Haley. *The Dallas Morning News* quoted a source as saying Haley made the decision not to accompany the team to Phoenix. Johnson said, "I make all personnel decisions around here." In response to a question about his health status for Thursday's game against the Giants, Haley was quoted in the *Fort Worth Star-Telegram* as saying, "I don't have to answer your ------- questions. Who the ---- do you think you are, you piece of ----?"

Tony Wise commented, "Charles's mouth is moving, so he must feel better. Let's just hope he isn't stupid enough to cross Jimmy."

On Thursday, Nate Newton apologized to America for "putting folks everywhere to sleep in front of their TVs." That afternoon the Cowboys paused to give thanks because, again, they caught a team without its starting quarterback. Or, in this case, starting quarterbacks. The Giants were without Jeff Hostetler and Phil Simms. They started second-year third-stringer Kent Graham. Somebody up there was starting to like these Cowboys.

Pass the turkey.

Wise said, "We were just hoping turmoil took its toll [on the fading, bickering Giants]." Later, Troy Aikman said, "We really need this [ten-day] break because we're mentally drained. It seems like for twelve straight weeks we've played the biggest game of the year."

Neither team was geeked. Cowboy highlights of a 9–3 first half were three field goals by Lin Elliott. In danger of losing his job, if not his mind, on November 1, less than four weeks later Elliott set a franchise record for most consecutive field goals. His first of the day surpassed the previous record of nine straight, set by Rafael Septien in 1981 and matched by Ken Willis in '91. Then Elliott made two more in the first half, one with 2:22 remaining from 53 yards, his career longest.

On the sideline, when Johnson yelled, "Field-goal team!" Elliott tapped him tentatively on the shoulder and said, "Uh, Coach, that's fifty-three yards."

Johnson said, "You can make the fuckin' thing, can't you?"

"Well, uh, I'll give it my best."

"Power the son of a bitch."

Elliott did. Elliott believed in Jimmy. Elliott said, "Boy, that was a big-balls call to keep me after that Philly game."

But Johnson did not believe in the team's first-half effort. He unloaded in the locker room, yelling, "You're going to be sick when you lose this thing!" Maybe Johnson was too convincing. The Cowboys played hard in the second half. Maybe too hard.

This team—and its coaching staff—still didn't know its own strength.

What had become a dinking man's offense (107 yards in the first half) continued to dink away through much of the third quarter. Simple, ineffective running plays. Safety-valve flips. But finally, another swing pass to Emmitt Smith gave him enough room to throw a little move on Giant defensive back Reyna Thompson, and Smith was gone 26 yards for the 16–3 touchdown. On the next Cowboy series, Turner resorted to a play called Slant G, which calls for guard John Gesek to pull out and block for Smith. Cowboy linemen rarely pull. "We're basically a straight-ahead power-running team," Turner said.

Slant G sprang Smith 68 yards for the 23–3 touchdown with 3:53 left in the third quarter. For the Giants, the fun was just beginning.

During the next Cowboy drive, Johnson encouraged Turner to go with a pass on fourth and 2. "Are you sure you don't want the field goal?" Turner asked through the headset. Later Johnson told reporters, "We were just trying to kill the clock." Aikman hit Michael Irvin for 5 yards. On third and 3 from the Giant 4-yard line, Johnson again encouraged Turner to call a pass. Troy Aikman hit Alvin Harper for the 30–3 TD with 6:04 remaining in the game.

In came rookie quarterback Dave Brown for Graham. The Giants had the ball for the next 15 plays, though 6 were penalties. Brown was sacked three times and hit four more times. The Giants' net gain in those 15 plays was 10 yards, from their 8 to their 18.

Several Giants were furious with the Cowboy coaches for the fourth-down plays and fourth-quarter blitzes. Veteran Leonard Marshall said, "I was pissed off and surprised. That was one of the unclassiest moves I've ever seen. Like I told some of the young guys here, don't you ever forget that move."

Cowboy coaches appeared genuinely surprised by the criticism. Remember, their team had nearly blown a 34-point lead at Giants Stadium. Remember, too, that they were still unsure just how much farther their team would wobble before the wheels would come off.

Wannstedt said, "I get criticized after the game in New York for laying back and losing all the momentum. Now I pressure them and I'm heartless."

Wannstedt noted that many backups played on the final New York possession. He insisted he called only one all-out blitz. The problem, he said, was that if scatback Meggett stayed in the backfield to block, the two linebackers assigned "bracket" coverage on him were supposed to blitz. That, said Wannstedt, happened three times.

Turner, probably more sensitive than any other Cowboy assistant to rubbing it in, later said, "Oh, come on. Those guys had no right to complain. They quit. They didn't even block Leon Lett."

Johnson considered the criticism for a while and decided it was a compliment. Just four years earlier, he thought teams rubbed his nose in it. But he did not complain. To Johnson, dominant teams dominate. That's the law of the aquarium. "This is what we used to hear at Miami," he said. "The point was, they were throwing at the end and I just didn't want them to score. If they had run, we would have called off the dogs. If they don't like it, screw 'em. We'll play 'em again next year."

Later that evening, at the coaches' get-together upstairs at Texas Stadium, scouting director Larry Lacewell saw a different Johnson.

This one had left his strut and bluster in the locker room. Here, you might say, Johnson was letting his hair down.

"I tried to talk to him after the Ram loss, but . . . ," Lacewell said, and shook his head. "I just decided to stay away from him for a while. But [after the Giant game] he was very melancholy. He was feeling a whole lot of stress. He hugged me and said, 'Lace, this is a tough son of a bitch.' He just keeps putting more and more pressure on himself [by what he says publicly]. He just doesn't know any other way.

"But people forget how much this poor sumbitch has been through. Oklahoma State was no bed of roses. That first year at Miami, that was a mess [a dissension-racked 8-5]. And 1989? Following Tom Landry with a one-and-fifteen? Jimmy has been through an awful lot to get to this point, and he just doesn't want to see this whole thing crumble."

Thin Ice

TUESDAY IS USUALLY THE PLAYERS' DAY OFF. NATE NEWTON always showed up Tuesday afternoons at Valley Ranch to burn some calories and work on his stamina—maybe thirty minutes on the StairMaster and thirty more fast-walking on the treadmill.

Charles Haley sometimes came in on Tuesdays, too, for some extra conditioning.

On the Tuesday before the Denver game, Newton and Haley found themselves alone in the locker room, near Haley's cubicle. Haley had just finished dressing and, in leather jacket and jeans, appeared ready to leave. Newton was wearing Cowboy sweat clothes still wet from his workout.

I happened to walk through just in time to hear Haley say, ". . . your fat ass," and give Newton a little shove. Haley seemed to be playing around. Newton was not smiling.

"You're lucky I like you, motherfucker," Newton said, fists balled at his sides.

Noticing me, Newton motioned me over with his head. Newton

is smart enough to know that a fistfight with Haley in Jimmy Johnson's locker room on December 1 would not be a good idea—not with the team 10-2 and Haley coming off a pulled hamstring and Newton's knee flaring. My instincts told me Newton needed my presence to break the tension. Haley eyed me a moment—another bleepin' reporter —picked up his bag, and walked toward the curtained exit.

Newton called after him, "Your tongue is the biggest muscle in your mo'fuckin' body."

Haley stopped, turned, and said, "You're right, and it gets more work than any muscle in my body."

Then Haley laughed.

Newton managed a little smile.

When Haley was gone, Newton said, "Charles, he somethin'. Somewhere along the line, somebody really bothered him, really made him feel bad about hisself." Several players and staffers said Haley occasionally mentioned that his father had beaten him when Charles was a child, though they were never sure how seriously to take what Charles said.

Newton said, "If Charles can get into *your* head, he will. He will challenge you. But that's his way of keeping you off of him, because his feelings are easy to get hurt. Really, Charles is a nice man. He's smart. People say he's off his rocker, but he ain't nowhere near. He's funny. I mean, he'll say shit you wish you had said. And believe me, the man can play. I don't give a fuck what Jeffcoat and some of 'em say. They *know*. They know we wouldn't be as good without Charles."

To avoid the media Haley often spent noon hours in the training room around trainer Kevin O'Neill, who says, "I think we all learned that you have to respond to Charles the way he responds to you when he walks in the door. If he wants to 'motherfuck' you, you have to 'motherfuck' him back. And if he wants to talk about the stock market, which he's fully capable of doing, you talk about the stock market. It's like he wants everybody to think he's an asshole. He wants to be known as a wild-and-crazy son of a bitch who everybody is scared of. That's all part of his game. He has a very strong side of him that's very good, and he probably doesn't want people to know about that side. For instance, I have an assistant he bought some clothes for. That's Charles, too."

Haley, with his razor-sculpted Fu Manchu, does a great glower.

He walks slowly, toes pointed in, shuffling his feet as if his shoes are too tight and it's *your fault*. Within earshot of reporters, he said a couple of times, "Oh, I forgot to take my medicine." Was he just trying to enhance his psycho mystique? Cowboy officials say 49er officials told them Haley had used a mood-controlling drug while playing in San Francisco. But Cowboy officials say they didn't ask Haley about it and weren't aware that he was using any unusual medication in Dallas.

On the field Haley's game is intensity and NBA quickness. Teammates found him as quick mentally as physically. He's a dedicated film-studier and often beats blockers to the punch. But a tough guy? Other Cowboys were beginning to wonder if he was more bark than fight.

Still standing at Haley's cubicle, Newton was asked what would have happened if he and Haley had come to blows. Could Newton take him?

"Shit, yes, homes," Newton said quickly and seriously. "That is, unless he reached and got hold of something. Ain't no more fair fights. But in here, ain't no place to hide. I'm just going to keep comin'. What you going to hit, the top of my head? Once I get you up against one of these lockers, it's all over. I'm going to fuck you up, man.

"Now, the little guys, the Michael Irvins and Kelvin Martins, they quit fightin' fifteen years ago. Half the guys is packin' somethin' in their car. Today, it's all about . . ."

Newton pulled an imaginary trigger.

"But in a fair fight, I could take any bitch in here. Including Charles. I'm just too big and strong for him, homes."

A few minutes later Jerry Jones sat on his office couch and talked about his annual return to his roots. Most of Jones's interviews and many of his conversations with Johnson take place on the Cowboy-blue couches to the right as you enter his long office. The couches run along two walls. In the middle of the couches and two chairs is a large, low, glass-topped table. Though Jones's desk is a 15-yard completion on down the rectangular office, it is around this table that he often has "a little tea"—iced, of course—and he "visits."

Jones had just returned from his hunting lodge near Stuttgart, Arkansas, in the White River Refuge. Each Thanksgiving he and about thirty family members go for the area's duck-hunting celebration, which includes the National Duck-Calling Contest. "It's the only time I go back to the way my life was before I owned the Cowboys," Jones said. "It's organized chaos, thirty people for fourteen beds, kids running around everywhere knocking over tables. It just blanks your mind out for a while."

But when Jones returned to Dallas and turned his mind back on, it raced to startling new conclusions. "I realized I'm happier and busier than I've ever been. Most people would say, 'You've made your money. Go hunting every day. Go to the beach and sip margaritas.' But that's where I was in '89 and I needed another challenge."

Jones had decided to dedicate his life to running the Cowboys, with or without Jimmy Johnson.

"I know Jimmy's got six years left [on his contract]. But if we won a Super Bowl, there wouldn't be a question of *might* he do something else—*might* he need another challenge. He probably would. That's why I have to be prepared for anything. We can't have an explosion here. I've studied Cowboy history, and the thing you see is that it never stayed the same. It was constantly changing, growing, evolving, like a child. What's happening right now, in 1992, will never happen again. Assistant coaches will leave. Players will come and go. Circumstances will change.

"I've got to keep putting the wood to it."

Jones now considered himself keeper of the metallic-blue flame. This was his calling. He would be the Cowboy constant. He would hire a new head coach, if he had to, and the Cowboys would keep winning and winning and . . .

Somewhere, Jimmy Johnson and Gene Jones just sighed.

★ ★ ★

As close as Johnson said he and Dave Wannstedt were, Wannstedt had constantly been in the job market for two seasons. He wanted to be a head coach, college or pro. In November of 1991 he dropped some public hints he'd be interested in the University of Texas opening. Nothing came of it; John Mackovic got the job. Since finishing second for the Pittsburgh Steeler job in January of '92, Wannstedt had kept his eyes and mind open.

Wannstedt said, "People keep telling me, 'Oh, you'll get a head job.' But that's easier said than done. There are no guarantees."

That week University of Pittsburgh alums contacted Wannstedt. Coach Paul Hackett had been relieved of his duties. "I understand the alums paid off the entire contract," Wannstedt said. The alums wanted Wannstedt to return home to save the day. He's one of theirs, a Pittsburgh guy who played for Pitt.

They were offering a reported $300,000 a year for five years. For about forty-eight hours Wannstedt attacked the decision the way he does a game plan, considering every angle, nearly driving himself nuts. If he took the job, he would have to leave immediately to begin recruiting. Yes, the coach of the NFL's No. 1 defense would have to walk away from it at 10-2. Was he ready to do that? Not quite, he decided.

But Wannstedt hoped Jones would reinforce his gut feeling with a token of his appreciation. As defensive coordinator he was making around $120,000—while some star coordinators topped $200,000.

Wannstedt says, "Jimmy goes over there [to Jones's office] and says, 'Dave can have the Pitt job right now.' Jimmy and I knew I wasn't going to take it. But he says I can have it, at that moment. Nothing. You'd think he'd do something to keep me. Nothing."

No raise. Not even a little, "We need and love you, Dave. Please stay." Of course, Johnson and Wannstedt were trying to run a little scam on a Jones who is no Jethro. He figured to lose Wannstedt to somebody soon and doubted even doubling his salary would keep him as a coordinator. Yet even after he accepted the Chicago Bears' head-coaching job on January 18, Wannstedt insisted that if Jones had been more appreciative of him financially and personally, he would strongly have considered staying as coordinator in Dallas to "see how many Super Bowls we could win." Wannstedt said, "It's not really the money—that's not me. It's the principle."

At that point, however, he was still a little hurt and bitter over the way Jones had treated him before he turned down the Pitt job. It's hard to believe Wannstedt would have turned down the Bears.

Yet for a man who loved being around coaches, Jones rarely expressed to them how much he appreciated the jobs they were doing. Privately, he could be dime-a-dozen flip when talking about their contributions. Norv Turner sometimes said he felt no rapport with Jones and had no idea where he stood with him. Was this part of the ownership style Jones learned from Al Davis? No one coach is bigger than the winning organization sustained by the owner?

Jones's attitude was, they've done a fine job, but the Cowboys will go onward and upward without them.

Maybe so. But without Wannstedt and Turner, the Cowboys probably wouldn't have gone onward and upward quite so quickly.

★ ★ ★

This time the team charter flight left forty minutes late. Michael Irvin was safely buckled into seat 20C. But Jimmy Johnson was up, sticking his head in the cockpit, calling over the flight attendants, wanting to know what the hell was happening and what was being done about it. Especially on team trips, Johnson wants his schedule followed to the second, dammit. Delays or foul-ups can trigger a tantrum.

Heading into a hostile environment, Johnson wants nothing left to chance. He wants to control things other visiting teams often don't. He wants, says Emmitt Smith, "to get in and get the hell outta Dodge with a W." Johnson says he leaves "about fifteen minutes" on the itinerary for players to see family or friends on the road. Players have six off-season months to see family or friends, he says. So Johnson schedules lots of meetings, team meals and snacks, and ten-thirty P.M. bed checks. All business.

Johnson's Miami teams developed a "Road Warrior" reputation. Johnson's friend and attorney Nick Christin, who teaches law at the University of Miami, says, "A lot of people thought those teams played even better on the road than at home." Former Hurricane Melvin Bratton once said, "We love to go into people's backyards and turn over the garbage cans." Johnson's teams won at Oklahoma, Michigan, Arkansas, LSU, and Florida State. Former Hurricane and current Cowboy Russell Maryland says, "The more they screamed at us and poured beer on us, the more we liked it. It was an attitude we had. We went on the road and intimidated people. We could see it in their eyes."

That's the attitude Johnson wanted his Cowboy team to forge in December, in Denver, in Washington, and in Atlanta. But first, the Cowboys had to get to Denver.

A snowstorm had shut down Denver's airport. Cowboy officials even considered flying to Salt Lake City and busing to Denver, as a last resort. The team plane took on extra fuel before taking off. But Johnson's stormy persistence finally had an impact. The plane's crew talked officials at Denver's Stapleton International Airport into allowing the Cowboy plane to land. The airport, it appeared, was closed to commercial traffic. But the Cowboy plane descended through a thick snowfall and found the runway, to a thankful ovation from the players' section.

The Cowboys held their walk-through in the locker room at Mile High Stadium. The forecast called for a low of 7 degrees that night, but Johnson remained near his boiling point. The one thing he hates almost as much as losing is cold weather. "He's pretty uptight," Tony Wise said. How would his Cowboys handle the altitude in a stadium whose very name kept reminding a player his lungs were going to burn?

"I hear you really suck up here," Emmitt Smith said. Literally and for visiting teams, often figuratively.

Norv Turner said he expected the Broncos to shut down Smith, as they had done in the August 22 exhibition game. Turner said, "They're very quick on defense. They'll also put a lot of pressure on Troy."

Dave Wannstedt was more apprehensive than usual. He said, "They have more speed on the perimeter than anyone we've faced all season." Ray Horton was back at safety for Thomas Everett, whose bruised shoulder needed another week of healing. The biggest fear among coaches: two or three deep TD passes, setting off an avalanche of noise at Mile High, one of the toughest places to win in sports. The Broncos were the NFL's winningest home team over the previous sixteen seasons—93-29, 76 percent. In '92, the 7-5 Broncos stood 6-0 at Mile High, which would spill over with its 179th straight sellout. This time, Cowboy fans would not take over an opponent's stadium. Tickets were as scarce as duplicate snowflakes.

How would the Cowboy secondary handle the footing against fast receivers on a snow-covered field? The coaches had no idea. The Cowboys hadn't played in snow since Johnson left Miami. Denver coach Dan Reeves was saying publicly that quarterback John Elway would not play because of a sore shoulder, but Johnson's staff didn't buy it. They prepared for Elway, bombs away.

Were Cowboy coaches continually overreacting to their secondary deficiencies? Not according to one prominent observer. That week, assessing the NFL's best teams, Raider owner Al Davis said in *Pro Football Weekly,* "Everyone likes Dallas. . . . But Dallas's secondary is so vulnerable. You saw our game against Dallas? You remember the couple of post patterns we missed early in the game? What I'm saying is there's no great team out there."

Reeves was also saying his leading rusher, Gaston Green, wouldn't play. Cowboy coaches scoffed. But Green did not play. Neither did Elway. One trend Cowboy coaches didn't seem to appreciate was how million-to-one healthy their team was for Game 13. *Sports Illustrated's* cover story that week was "The Carnage Continues," detailing the NFL's rising injury rate. To that point, 482 players had been hurt seriously enough to miss a game. Yet, with Everett's return the next week, every Cowboy starter would remain healthy through the play-offs. In 1992, not one starter suffered a career-ending injury. Feelings were hurt, especially in the coaches' offices, but not starters.

"Truly remarkable," said Dr. Robert Vandermeer, the team physician. In 1989, Vandermeer operated on seven season-ending knee injuries. Johnson insisted that avoiding injuries was a direct result of the team's commitment to its off-season conditioning program. But it was difficult to believe the Cowboys worked any harder than, say, the Redskins, who had been devastated by injuries.

Vandermeer said, "I have to disagree with Jimmy. I think it's mostly luck. It just goes in cycles. Some years are just meant to be."

Sometimes, the Jimmy Johnson who detested even saying the word *luck* seemed to be the luckiest guy in the world.

★ ★ ★

It did not snow Sunday in Denver. It was 19 degrees and clear as the teams warmed up. The footing was excellent. John Elway was not. The maker of Mile High miracles could not perform one on his shoulder; Elway stood on the sideline in a long-rider coat. For the third straight week the Cowboys were catching a team with one arm tied behind its back.

Norv Turner walked near Dan Reeves at midfield and decided to say hello and maybe break the ice. That week, columnists at both Denver newspapers had called for Reeves's job following Denver's 16–13 overtime loss in Seattle. Through the 1970s, former Cowboy Reeves had served as Tom Landry's offensive coordinator.

"I don't know Dan very well," Turner said. "But I said, 'Hey, Dan, they sure miss your flea flickers and double reverses in Dallas.' " Turner took a beating on talk shows and occasionally from sports columnists for seldom running a trick play. Turner didn't even use screen passes. One of Landry's favorite plays was a double screen.

Reeves responded to Turner, "If we had executed the way you guys do, we wouldn't have needed any of that stuff."

It was a fateful exchange. Dallas vs. Denver became a game of trick plays vs. execution. But behind the scenes the outcome of the game—and the Cowboy season—may have hinged on a halftime gamble by Jimmy Johnson.

Reeves stuck with his announced plan to alternate kid quarterbacks Tommy Maddox and Shawn Moore. Two early interceptions thrown by Maddox set up Cowboy touchdowns. Dallas, 14–0. The game had the look of a rout. But rookie Maddox threw an 18-yard TD pass. Moore turned Mile High's volume even higher with a 40-yard flea flicker, which was misjudged by James Washington. Maddox threw another TD pass, this one 12 yards.

At halftime Dallas was routing Denver, 17–13.

Occasionally Johnson yells at the team in the locker room at the half. But this time Johnson took Charles Haley aside. Reacting on impulse and instinct, Johnson challenged Haley the way Haley often challenges assistants and teammates.

"That," said Turner, "is what being a head coach in the NFL is really all about. It's not Xs and Os as much as knowing how and when to deal with people."

Later, Johnson said, "Charles had been distant, and I just didn't like it. It was time to say something. He had sat at the very back of the meeting the night before, and I wanted him more involved."

So, off to the side but within sight of other players, Johnson heatedly told Haley he had seen and had enough. Witnesses say they were surprised that Haley mostly listened and nodded. How high was Johnson's risk?

"Oh, it was a big deal," Johnson says. "If he blows up at me in front of the team, that's it. It's over. You got to get him the shit out of here. But I just felt it was the right spot. It wasn't that he hadn't played hard in the first half. But in the second half, he played *hard*. He responded."

Haley, with just two sacks all season, had two in the second half.

But even without Elway the Broncos weren't in a moral-victory mood. The kids were having too much fun against that No. 1 defense. Maddox threw another touchdown pass, a 23-yarder. And on third and 11 from its 19, Denver pulled off a double pass—a triple-rookie shocker—with Maddox throwing laterally to rookie receiver Cedric Tillman, who threw an 81-yard TD pass to rookie Arthur Marshall. Landry would have loved it.

Denver 27, Dallas 24.

Night had fallen. So had the temperature. Now the game was being played under lights in St. Bernard cold.

With 9:05 remaining, the Cowboys began a drive at their 23. Perhaps they began a Super Bowl drive. "That drive," Turner says, "is what Super Bowl seasons are made of."

Aikman to Daryl Johnston, 6 yards. Emmitt Smith, no gain. (Turner was right: Smith was held to 62 yards on 26 tries. Frustration mounted as coaches in the press box yelled for Smith to "hit the hole" instead of dancing off-target into gang-tackling Broncos and appearing to give up.)

But Aikman found tight end Jay Novacek for 11. Then 22. Then 17. Novacek is sometimes called Paycheck by teammates because he makes money catches. A true cowboy, a gentleman rancher who speaks mostly with his performance, Novacek is a six-foot-four distance runner who tends to get faster in the fourth quarter. Denver attempted to cover him with linebacker Karl Mecklenberg. "What were they thinking about?" guard John Gesek said.

But guard Nate Newton, who played probably his worst game of the season, was beaten for a sack by Simon Fletcher. Aikman fumbled as he hit the ground, but reached and barely recovered. Novacek, finally covered by rookie cornerback Frank Robinson, couldn't hold Aikman's next throw. And on third and 14 at the Denver 25, Turner called a pass he had borrowed from Redskin tapes and installed especially for this game.

It's called Y option 4. Novacek and Michael Irvin run option routes. If only one man takes Irvin, he runs a crossing route. If he is doubled, he hooks between the defenders. "The Redskins do a really nice job of running it with Gary Clark," Turner said.

Irvin hooked and made a diving catch right at the first-down marker. "I turned to Tony Wise," said special teams coach Joe

Avezzano, "and I said, 'This is what pro football is all about.' The cold. The noise. You could see the players' breath. All we needed was the voice of John Facenda."

Three plays later: third and 2 at the Denver 3. Turner called "draw right." In the huddle and on the sideline, several players said, "Draw right?"

Turner said, "I'm not much of a 'tendencies' guy. I mostly go on feel. I figured if they covered the three receivers, we'd make the first down. If they blitzed, it would be hit or miss."

They blitzed. "They were in a crazy defense," said tackle Mark Tuinei. "We were supposed to block different people than we actually blocked. But it worked."

The story of the season: somehow it worked.

On instinct, Emmitt Smith ran "draw right" more to the left. He found his own hole. He scored standing up. In 11 plays the Cowboys had covered 77 yards. Aikman had done what he does best: perform slow torture. He hadn't pulled an Elway—hadn't run three laps around pass rushers and launched a touchdown pass that traveled 78 yards in the air. He had completed 7 of 8 passes for 78 yards, eating up six minutes and eighteen seconds. This drive was made of execution and accuracy and patience. This time, the last-play magic was provided by Smith, with Aikman in a supporting-actor role.

When Turner's call took the pressure directly off him, Aikman had the presence to tell his receivers in the huddle he was going to point to them as if he were going to pass. He would signal to Irvin as if he had the "hot" route against a blitz. "Then," Aikman told them, "we'll run the draw."

Cowboys, 31–27.

Wannstedt, whose defense had given up 354 yards, shook Turner's hand and said, "Thank you."

Later, after a few sips of reflection on the plane ride home, Turner said, "You know, I really don't think that drive was that big a deal to Troy. But I think it was to the team."

Hurricane Jimmy

THERE ARE MANY JIMMY JOHNSONS AND THEY ALL COMMAND your attention. There is good-time Jimmy, life of the party (as long as it's his). There is bachelor Jimmy, a happy recluse watching football and blood-splattered action flicks. There is noble Jimmy, who loves his sons, gives to the needy, and appreciates intellectual, artistic, and spiritual endeavors. There is Jimmy the CEO, who has a degree in industrial psychology, dresses immaculately in starched white shirts and power ties and says he could run the world's biggest corporation at least as successfully as he runs his football team. There is Jimmy the football coach, who can take or leave all of the above and says he's happiest wearing hooded sweatshirts, studying game tapes, and talking the f-ing language that f-ing coaches f-ing talk. That Jimmy sometimes leads to the out-of-control Jimmy, who after big losses tumbles down his personal black hole of rage and doubt.

Beware that Jimmy. He bites.

Beware: Jimmy is to be called only Jimmy. A graduate assistant on his Miami staff made the mistake of calling him Jim. "The guy didn't last long," says Tony Wise. "Jim Johnson" is too ordinary. "Jimmy Johnson" has a ring to it. Jimmy is a forty-nine-year-old Jimmy.

But really, the dominant Jimmy is Jimmy the benevolent dictator. James William Johnson wants to rule the world—the football world, the only one that matters to him. Really, all he wants to do in life is win football games, yet his motives are different from most coaches'. Winning to Johnson isn't so much an ideal as an existence. It's not really important to him that he devise the strategy that gives his team the edge and him the personal satisfaction of knowing he outthought a rival. He mostly leaves that to his coordinators. He doesn't call plays; he calls for fake punts and onside kicks.

Washington coach Joe Gibbs, who stepped down after the '92 season, took humble pleasure in creating, teaching, and calling plays that sometimes allowed inferior talent to prevail. Not Johnson. Johnson boasted about many things, but he never said, "How'd you like that corner blitz I came up with?" Johnson frequently credited assistants for that sort of thing. But he wanted the world to know that the Cowboys ultimately won because of Jimmy Johnson.

Johnson isn't one to sit around with ex-players and reminisce about what, together, they accomplished. If for a while you help him win, your reward is the spoils of victory. But when you can no longer help him, he will go on winning without you and, as he says, "I never look back." That's his motto: Don't look back. Make decisions based only on winning, not conscience, and plunge forward. Don't get so close to someone that you lose control and lose sight of your goal. Get too close and your goals might be sacrificed by the paralyzing emotions of love and the price you might pay for it— hurt. You must keep looking forward, to the next game. You must win.

Win and you rule.

Johnson and Troy Aikman, who were on a collision course, approach life and winning from opposite directions.

Johnson knows that if you win football games in this society, even the president will look up to you. Before 1992, Johnson said the "greatest moment in my life was when the most powerful man in the world, the president of the United States, shook my hand and said, 'You're the best.' " This was when Miami won the national championship.

Win, and people love and admire you. Win, and media people everywhere want to know what you think. Win, and you'll always have friends when you need them. Win, and you get ringside seats at heavyweight championship fights. Win, and actors and singers and business giants want to meet you. Win, and you can basically tell the world to go to hell, if you feel like it, and the world will say, "That's just Jimmy."

Jimmy lives for world-recognized personal achievement—his world being the NFL. And as the Cowboys prepared for their second game with the Redskins, this one at Washington's RFK Stadium, Johnson set his heart on (1) beating the Redskins for the third time in four games at RFK, thereby dominating probably the most famous NFL rivalry; (2) clinching the NFC East by beating the defending Super Bowl champs in the nation's capital; and (3) improving his own NFL career record to .500.

"Clinching and reaching .500 at RFK," said PR director Rich Dalrymple, "would really mean a lot to Jimmy."

★ ★ ★

For the first time all season, the mood at Valley Ranch shifted dramatically from tense to tranquil. Johnson's Cowboys think they can beat the Redskins, and their confidence calmed the coaching staff. "It's amazing," Dave Wannstedt said. "Our guys just think they can win. It's not overconfidence. It's not something we talk about. It's just a feeling that we match up well with them. We've always been able to take away what they do best—hit the deep pass. And we've usually been able to stop the run against them. Our guys love to play at RFK. The fans are close and loud and it really gets our guys going."

Even the pessimistic realist, Norv Turner, gave his team a fifty-fifty shot: "I really think the Redskins came in here the first game thinking they were going to kick our ass. They were cocky, almost arrogant. This time will be very different. Now they'll be saying, 'We cannot be humiliated by these guys again.' So it will really be tough. But I think we can do some things."

Turner liked his big wide receivers against the smallish Redskin corners. He liked his interior blockers against the Redskins' interior linemen. He liked what Emmitt Smith had done his last four games against the Redskins—132, 112, 132, and 140 yards. "No magic to it," Turner said with a shrug. "We block these guys and we play great defense against them."

Michael Irvin's confidence spilled into rare cockiness. For all his trash-talking image, Irvin carefully sidesteps controversy during the week. "I've been around Jimmy too long," Irvin says. "I know what not to say." Yet on Thursday before the Washington game, Irvin made a point of telling reporters from Washington he was going after the arm that All-Pro cornerback Darrell Green had broken earlier in the season. "It's not healed," Irvin said. "I'm a lot bigger than he is and I'm going to block him and block him and block him. Bam, bam, bam on that arm."

Privately Nate Newton explained, "Mike thinks he can really get inside Darrell's head. He told me, 'I'm going to send him a little message, really distract him.' "

Speaking of rare confidence, Jerry Jones stunned *Washington Post* reporter Leonard Shapiro during Jones's media luncheon. The Redskins, who had been favored by 2 points over Dallas in Dallas, now were favored by 3 at RFK. The Cowboys had won the first game, 23–10. They had won the year before at RFK, 24–21. The Redskins had just won their last two games to improve to 8-5. The Cowboys had just won three straight to hit 11-2.

Jones said the Cowboys should be favored this time. "I don't agree with [the point spread]," Jones said. "We've played very well up there."

"Can you believe an NFL owner saying that?" said Shapiro, a veteran Redskin and NFL observer. "I think it's great." Chuckling, Shapiro hurried off to write another story about the incredibly confident Cowboys.

Equally incredible was what happened Sunday morning at the team hotel in Washington. Supreme Court justice Clarence Thomas spoke at the team chapel service. That wasn't so incredible; Thomas said he was honored that the Dallas Cowboys wanted him. Thomas says the only periodical he didn't cancel after being appointed to the Supreme Court was *Dallas Cowboys Weekly.*

But what happened afterward amazed and amused several players and officials.

Team chaplain John Weber says, "Jerry Jones opened with prayer. His first line was, 'Thank you, Lord, for this time of year when you sent your son to us,' which was very good. Clarence's basic message was, 'When you're down and at your weakest, God is at his strongest.' He was very impressive and effective.

"He stayed for the pregame meal and he and Charles Haley really hit it off. They live near each other in Virginia, and after a while, they were slapping each other on the back. Clarence actually gave Charles his home number. I couldn't believe it."

★ ★ ★

RFK stadium, which has the feel of an old, oversize minor-league baseball park, sometimes feels as if it might collapse during Redskin-Cowboy games. When the Redskins are rolling, fans begin to stomp or bounce and the stands actually begin to roll as if in an earthquake. Entire rows move up and down in rhythmic waves. Watch too long from the opposite side of the stadium and you'll get dizzy.

Sometimes, the noise itself seems to be rocking the place on its rickety foundation. But as darkness descended soon after the four P.M. kickoff, RFK sounded more like the Library of Congress. In breezy 43-degree weather, the Cowboys shut down the Redskins and shut up the crowd just as they said they would. They led 17–7 by halftime—and the Redskins' touchdown came only when they resorted to trickery, a 41-yard scoring pass from running back Earnest Byner to tight end Terry Orr. Quarterback Mark Rypien's first half was a smashed thumbnail of his inexplicably awful season—5 of 17 for 51 yards and an interception.

Up in the visiting owner's box, Larry Lacewell told Jerry Jones, "You are watching a Super Bowl contender." Later, Lacewell said, "I know Jimmy was thinking the same thing."

The Redskins drove for a field goal with 4:59 left in the third quarter to cut the lead to 17–10. Near the end of the quarter, the Cowboys faced fourth and 6 at their 49. Vintage Jimmy: Johnson called for a fake punt. Fullback Daryl Johnston took a short snap 13 yards to the Redskin 38.

"Jimmy was really proud of that," said one Cowboy coach who

asked not to be quoted by name. "On national TV—Madden and Summerall—Jimmy had shocked the world. That's why what happened after that drove him even crazier."

The Cowboys moved quickly to third and goal at the 2. Score a touchdown and they would lead 24–10 with 12:25 remaining. "You never know," Norv Turner said. "But that could have done it. People said, 'Why not play safe for the field goal and take a ten-point lead?' But that hasn't been our style all year."

Encouraged by Johnson, Turner called a pass that had produced touchdowns against the Eagles and Cardinals. The ball was on the right hash mark. Kelvin Martin lined up right, but went in motion to the left, giving the Cowboys "trips left"—three receivers on the left side. Washington blitzed a linebacker, who was blocked. Usually in Washington's scheme, a blitzing linebacker means man-to-man coverage. But not this time.

Turner berated himself later, saying, "On the right hash, I shouldn't have put Troy in a position to have to look over his shoulder pad to the left. That's harder than you think for a quarterback. He glanced [to find Martin] and didn't see [linebacker Andre] Collins."

Collins was not playing one man. He was roaming. Aikman hit him right in the hands, a yard deep in the end zone. Fifty-nine yards later, Jay Novacek caught Collins at the Cowboy 42. RFK rocked. When least expected, Aikman had thrown the nitrolike momentum to Washington.

Dallas would not get it back.

Dallas would blow itself up.

A Redskin field goal made it 17–13, Dallas. On third and 8 Aikman hit Irvin, who covered 20 yards before Darrell Green caught him and punched the ball out of Irvin's grip. The Redskins recovered. But on fourth and goal from the Cowboy 2, Rypien missed Gary Clark.

Cowboys, first and 10 from their two. Daryl Johnston bulled for 3 yards, creating a little elbow room. Turner called a pass. Green broke quickly and correctly on Irvin's route and was in position to make an interception. On replays Aikman's arm appeared to be starting forward when he thought better and tried to pull back. Redskin defensive tackle Jason Buck exploded through center Mark Stepnoski and hit Aikman's arm.

The ball—and all hell—came loose.

Incomplete pass? Fumble? The refs saw a fumble. No whistles were blown. In the end zone Emmitt Smith scooped up the ball and fled left. As he was tackled in the end zone, he attempted to underhand the ball forward with his left hand to tight end Alfredo Roberts and avoid the safety. But replays showed—and NFL officials confirmed—that Smith's knee was down before he unloaded.

Safety? No, no whistle. Another loose ball in the end zone. Mad pileup. Redskin safety Danny Copeland leaned in and yanked the ball from between the legs of Cowboy tackle Erik Williams. Copeland actually ran the wrong way, back out to around the 50-yard line, where he waved the ball and celebrated. Only then did refs attempting to sort through the pile realize Copeland had the ball. If he had it, they deduced, he had to have acquired it with his feet in the end zone.

Touchdown, Washington. Redskins, 20–17.

That's how it ended.

But for the Cowboys the night had just begun.

One thing Jimmy Johnson hasn't been accused of being is a gracious loser. This time his postgame press conference lasted about ninety seconds before he walked off. This was not unusual behavior for Johnson after losses.

He dressed quickly and headed for the team bus. There he is always given a tape of the game, taken straight off the network feed so he can hear what the announcers had to say. Johnson watches the game on a small-screen tape player. Usually, halfway through the flight home, Johnson has finished watching the game as the TV audience saw it.

But this time Johnson almost had time to finish before the plane took off from Washington's National Airport. This time Dallas–Fort Worth Airport was closed, because of thunderstorms. And pilots and flight attendants on the Cowboy charter had their own thunderstorm to navigate. Johnson lost control.

The crew people were not strangers to Johnson. He knew most of them from many past team flights. But he told the pilots to "get this fuckin' plane off the ground." He was told they had orders from air-traffic control in Dallas to remain on the ground in Washington.

"I don't care," Johnson said. "Just get us the hell out of Washington. Just fly somewhere." He was serious, said incredulous flight attendants. They tried to calm and console him. He cursed at them, saying, "Leave me the fuck alone."

He began to hit the Heineken. "He wouldn't even ask for another one," one flight attendant said. "As soon as one was gone, he'd just grunt and shake his glass of ice at us and we'd get him another one."

Flight attendants and first-class passengers said Johnson downed at least ten beers in the next two hours. He later refused his dinner, which wasn't unusual. But Johnson ordered flight attendants to quit serving dinner to anybody, as if the entire plane deserved to go hungry after what had happened. Johnson was eventually talked out of that.

The plane was thirty or forty minutes late leaving Washington. By then Johnson was into the fourth quarter of his game tape. Again he watched the Cowboys give it away with three fourth-quarter turnovers. His face grew red—beaten red. He stepped over Wannstedt, in the aisle seat next to him, and walked to the coach-section entrance. Turner was standing there chatting.

"Sit down," Johnson told Turner, and pointed to Turner's seat, 4A, directly behind Johnson's. For a second Turner thought Johnson was kidding. He smiled. Johnson did not. Turner quickly sat.

Johnson moved down the coach aisle to the row in which Cowboy radio analyst Dale Hansen was playing the usual card game with broadcasters from the Spanish-speaking radio network. Johnson just stood there, smoldering silently. Hansen and the others shot nervous glances at him but kept playing.

Johnson, eyes darting, mind apparently racing, turned his attention to the back half of the cabin, where the players sat or, in a few cases, stood. Johnson, who always takes off his suit coat during flights, was still wearing it. He stood in the middle of the aisle watching the players' section for probably five minutes that seemed as long as the entire fourth quarter. Perhaps he was calculating the odds: What if he blew up at a player in full view of thirty or so members of the media? Johnson furiously smacked his lips, a sure sign of agitation.

Nate Newton had been warning players that trainer Kevin

O'Neill said Johnson might make an example of any player who got loud. But the back section was relatively subdued. About fifteen rows from where Johnson stood, Aikman, punter Mike Saxon, and several other players were playing cards. Aikman watched Johnson watching his card game and said quietly, "Uh-oh. We better stop." Saxon said, "I tried to slide back into my seat and wound up looking like a girl with her legs over the end of the couch."

Johnson pounced. However, he did not pounce on Aikman. Or Irvin. Or Emmitt Smith. Or even Saxon.

He jumped backup center Frank Cornish, who was standing beside his seat. He cursed Cornish and told him to get back in his seat. Cornish, regarded as one of the nicest guys on the team, thought Johnson was kidding. Johnson often kids around with players. But now Johnson said, "You think it's fuckin' funny, Frank? It's not funny."

Johnson also lashed out at backup running back Tommie Agee and rookie Robert Jones, ordering them to sit down. Johnson spoke to them as if he had never met them and had no respect for them. "It was scary," said one player. "He was just so hateful."

Finally Johnson wheeled and went back to his seat.

A flight attendant said Cornish was so upset he asked her to go tell Johnson he was sorry and that it was a misunderstanding. Cornish, she said, had been standing because he was waiting to use the rest room, which was occupied. She said something to Johnson, who immediately walked back to Cornish's seat, snapped at him again, and returned to first class.

No, this wasn't Mike Ditka, screaming and breaking things. But in a way this was worse. The damage was potentially deeper. The team's fearless leader was biting the hands that fed his obsession. The players were seeing a side of Johnson they hadn't seen. It was as if Jimmy were pulling a meanspirited Haley. Was this how he really felt about them?

Privately, many players called Johnson's actions "ugly" and uncalled-for. Johnson had implied—and would continue to indicate to the media over the next two days—that the team wasn't taking the loss nearly as hard as he was. This especially infuriated Aikman.

"A lot of players were extremely upset," Aikman said after the season. "I was fortunate in that I had seen that side of him before.

The guys who were here in '89 saw it after the Denver game in the preseason. We were two and oh and they beat us in overtime. Jimmy just blew up at us [on the plane after the game] and said it didn't hurt us enough to lose. . . . But [after the Washington episode] there was just so much discussion and bitterness by so many guys. Here we'd done everything we could for this guy. We'd played our guts out, and it was only our third loss. It was like he sold us out."

The next day, a veteran who asked not to be identified said, "A lot of guys were saying, 'Kiss my ass, Jimmy.' We knew we blew it. We were frustrated, too. But we still have a two-game lead [in the division]. And we actually played pretty well, except for the turnovers. I mean, this was the Jimmy Johnson a lot of the younger guys are in awe of. I don't know if Troy and some of his buddies always buy what Jimmy says, but a lot of guys do. This time, Jimmy went too far."

A friend of Aikman's says, "Troy really thought what Johnson did was chickenshit. Frank Cornish? Tommie Agee? Come on. Guys like Troy and Daryl Johnston and Mark Stepnoski were just sitting there shaking their heads at Johnson. Does he seriously think losing hurt him any worse than it did those guys?"

As soon as Johnson was again back in his seat, here came Jerry Jones, heading back toward the players. Jones was smiling. Immediately after the game Jones's emotions had mirrored those of victorious coach Joe Gibbs. In the Cowboy locker room Jones said, "Wasn't that a hell of a football game? Great setting, two teams giving it everything they had."

In the Redskin quarters, Gibbs said, "That stadium and that game will be one of the great memories in sports for me. There were two teams that played their guts out."

Now Jones circulated among the players, talking about what a hell of a game it had been and about how "we're okay. Let's just bounce right back and take care of Atlanta." Was Jones shrewdly playing the good cop to Johnson's bad?

No, he was just being Jerry. He didn't even know what Johnson had done until he heard about it the following day. Unwittingly, though, he had provided a cheerleading counterbalance—a critical role he often played for Johnson's psyche.

But one member of the traveling party did attempt a peacemaking mission into the players' section. After Jones returned to his seat, Dave Wannstedt walked back to talk to the players. Seeing Wannstedt, several players said something like, "Man, we're glad you came back here. Jimmy's gone nuts."

Wannstedt just kept telling players not to worry. Jimmy's Jimmy. He'll be okay. Everything will be okay.

Later, Wannstedt said, "To tell you the truth, I felt sorry for Jimmy."

★ ★ ★

The following morning Johnson made several calls to members of the charter flight's crew. Said one, "He didn't apologize. He just tried to explain that's just the way he is." At least it was taken as an apologetic gesture.

Johnson gave basically the same "I'm the way I am" speech to the players that afternoon. By then, it seemed, most players were just hoping he would drop it and bounce back to being the old Jimmy. "Everybody was still upset," Aikman said. "Privately, I kept telling guys, 'Look, we understand how he is. We don't agree. But if we'll put this behind us and take care of business in Atlanta on Monday night, the Washington loss will mean nothing.' I hate to say a loss would mean nothing, but that was the truth."

Johnson wasn't putting it behind him. Later that afternoon a morose Johnson wore a black sweater and black slacks for his usual Monday media briefing. At one point, he said, "This was for me, personally, as big as a play-off game."

The "personally" didn't sit well with lots of players.

On Tuesday, Johnson plunged even deeper into mourning and self-analysis.

Each Tuesday at eleven-thirty A.M. in Valley Ranch's theaterlike meeting room, Johnson fields questions from seventy or eighty newspaper, TV, and radio reporters. Johnson, always in CEO coat and tie, speaks from behind a podium on a small stage. But this time Johnson had more on his mind than next Monday's Falcons game. Johnson needed to talk about Jimmy.

Randy Galloway of *The Dallas Morning News* asked Johnson, "Are you ready to move on to Atlanta or are you faking it?"

And for about ten riveting minutes Johnson delivered a to-win-or-not-to-win soliloquy.

He began, "I've moved on to Atlanta." Then: "Anybody who has been around me for very long knows I have a difficult time losing something I had my heart set on. Not that I have a difficult time losing at everything . . . I play golf and lose on a regular basis and it doesn't bother me a bit. I pay my little Nassau and go on.

"Some people approach everything with a forty-hour workweek: 'Give me my paycheck and I'll do my job.' I don't approach coaching the Cowboys that way. . . . If it ever comes to the point I can accept losing, then I shouldn't be coaching the Cowboys. But when you give your heart and soul for something and you don't get it, it hurts. Believe me. It" [pause] "hurts."

Tears came to Johnson's eyes.

". . . Sometimes people who have not been around me might not understand certain things. I'm not saying I'm right. I'm just saying that's the way it is. . . . If people can go on about their business and lose something they wanted very badly, and not let it affect them, hey, more power to them. But it affects me. When you thought you had it . . ."

Johnson rubbed his thumb and fingers together, as if he could still feel a victory at RFK.

". . . I don't think I hurt more than a particular player. We all hurt the same. We just deal with it in different ways. But I don't really have a whole lot of respect for someone who puts a token effort into something that is very important to them. But some people are in the habit of doing that. They never really hurt, but they're truly never really happy, because they've never, ever totally committed themselves to something because they're afraid they're not going to achieve their goal. I'm not afraid to lose. If I was afraid to lose, I wouldn't take the chances I take.

". . . I don't think any loss has ever pained me as much as losing the national championship in 1986 [to Penn State in the Fiesta Bowl] because I truly felt like we had the best college football team that had ever played the game. And we came up short. Now, we won the national championship the next year, we were undefeated, but it really wasn't one of the best teams that ever played the game. That's when it hurts."

Don't give Johnson an undefeated team that overachieves. Give him a team that dominates Penn State in a national-championship matchup and is regarded as the greatest team ever.

"I don't want players on our team that it doesn't hurt 'em to lose. . . . Because if they don't get that sick feeling, then the next time, so what? And then the next time, and the next time and then after a period of time you'll put a token effort into it. And you'll become just like a lot of other folks. And I don't want to be like a lot of folks."

On lashing out at players, Johnson said, "I don't care who's standing next to me. It could be one of my sons that I love with all my heart. Brent and Chad understand that I'm liable to snap at them, but they deal with it because they know how I am."

When psychologist Don Beck read the text of Johnson's remarks, he said, "Here is a man who believes in controlling and manipulating everything, who was trying to control and manipulate himself. He was trying to put a cap on the furnace. This is the only way he knew to deal with himself."

★ ★ ★

Jerry Jones was concerned with Johnson's dark mood only because of the team Christmas party that night. He was afraid Johnson's required presence might "turn it into some kind of wake." Jones had memos put in players' lockers encouraging their presence, but only about half the team showed up. One player said, "God, the last thing I want to do right now is be around Jimmy."

Johnson and Aikman wound up talking for quite a while at the party. "We talked briefly about the Washington game," Aikman said. "It mainly was me asking him how he was feeling and me telling him, 'Look, I'm just trying to get these guys over this.' Then for the next thirty minutes he talked about tropical fish."

The next day, said Aikman, "I spoke out more than I usually would [to the media]." Aikman told reporters, "The longer we sit here crying about Washington, the harder it's going to be getting ready for Atlanta. I see his [Johnson's] pain. I see my pain. I see everybody's pain. It's not fun losing. Fortunately, we're eleven and three. I'm not going to let this loss distract from what we can accomplish."

The *Fort Worth Star-Telegram* quoted players as saying practice was "like a morgue."

Aikman said, "That whole week was pretty awful. But I know I have never put in more time preparing for a game or felt more pressure on my shoulders for any game in my life. I was really scared of their defense. I knew if we had breakdowns or didn't pick up their blitzes, it would be a dogfight. In fact I was so uptight that I blew up that Friday night. I usually have some people over on Friday night, and I kicked a guy out. I had people highly upset with me. I had to call people the next day and say, 'I don't know *what* I'm doing. I'm losing it.' "

What Aikman was doing was exactly what Johnson had wanted him to do since drafting him—only, Aikman was doing it in spite of Johnson, not because of him. Aikman was heaping pressure on himself, just the way Johnson often did. He was preparing to put the team on his shoulders and carry it all the way to Atlanta and back, if necessary. Aikman had finally put himself in a put-up-or-shut-up position. He had spoken out against Johnson to reporters. He had told teammates they were going to beat the Falcons no matter how their coach acted. Aikman had loaded himself up, and unfortunately, he had unloaded on an unsuspecting buddy. But he could tell him, with all sincerity, that he knew just how that buddy felt.

By Saturday, Tony Wise had seen no improvement in Johnson's mood, and he was no happier about it than the players. "Look, I've been with him for nineteen years, and if he wants to go into his shell, fine. I'm going to go ahead and do my job to get us as ready as I can get us. That's what I told Norv. We've got to take up the slack by doing as much as we can."

The 6-8 Falcons, said Wise, "are classic NFL—a very talented team that just hasn't played well. Deion Sanders. Andre Rison. Michael Haynes. They could just explode on you."

Wannstedt figured the Atlanta coaches were experiencing the "candy-store effect. It's like, 'Where do you start?' They figure Larry Brown can't cover anybody. But neither can Ike [Holt], and Kevin [Smith] is a rookie. Sometimes we laugh about it and say maybe it works to our advantage because they get too greedy. But Atlanta has four receivers who could start for most teams, including [receiver/cornerback] Deion. The key to this game will be if our offense can control the ball and keep their offense off the field.

"You just know [Coach Jerry] Glanville will try something crazy on 'Monday Night Football.' I figure he'll let Deion throw it off a reverse."

Johnson does not care for Glanville. For Johnson, losing to Washington at RFK could be approached in ignominy only by losing to Glanville's team on the Monday-night stage. A few weeks earlier I had written in a column that Johnson was 0-2 vs. Glanville. He was actually 1-1. Johnson had PR director Dalrymple call me to point out the mistake. "If it had been anyone other than Glanville . . . ," Dalrymple said, chuckling. Assistants said Johnson considers Glanville "blatantly arrogant and an egomaniac."

A new face appeared on the team flight bound for Atlanta. Rhonda Rookmaaker, Johnson's girlfriend, was making her first trip of the season. Flight attendants speculated that Johnson wanted her next to him on the way back, to help keep him in line. She did take Wannstedt's seat on the return flight. But on the way, she sat in row eight of coach.

Several players commented that Rookmaaker isn't as flashy as they figured Johnson's lady would be. A hairdresser by trade, she had light, short hair not nearly as striking as Johnson's. The joke, of course, was that Rookmaaker knew the way to Johnson's heart was through his hair. But Wise says, "Jimmy's hair was just the way it is now long before he met her. I don't think he needed any help with it."

Johnson knew Rookmaaker in Miami; she moved to Valley Ranch, where she lives near Johnson. Those who have observed them together say what Johnson likes about Rookmaaker is her flashy personality. She matches wits with him and makes him laugh. She drinks beer and watches football with him. Above all, she knows football comes first. One night, she and Johnson bumped into a couple of writers and Johnson began talking football with them. He said, "Don't mind her. We're talking football." She patiently made herself inconspicuous.

A woman who knows Rookmaaker describes her relationship with Johnson as being almost like the "other woman." That's because, says the woman, "Jimmy lives for football. But she still gets to be recognized as 'Jimmy Johnson's girlfriend,' and though he doesn't believe in giving gifts on Christmas, he surprises her with gifts lots of other times. She's a big girl, very tough, hard. She was married before. But she really gets along great with Jimmy's sons. She has her own house and her own job."

Lesley Visser, in a feature story on Johnson for CBS, mentioned he had put up his first Christmas tree in years. But Johnson told Dallas reporters that Rookmaaker put it up at his house for a Christmas party she threw for the coaches' wives. Visser, who met Rookmaaker, later said, "I really liked her. She's fiesty. You know, I'm going through some problems with friends [who have relationship complications], and the thing I respect about Jimmy is that at least his cards are on the table. At least there isn't a hidden agenda. She knew exactly what she was getting into."

Johnson didn't want Rookmaaker to be interviewed for this book. She was quoted in the *Sports Illustrated* and *Dallas Morning News* stories that came out as the season began, and he said, "She was uncomfortable with it. I probably overstepped my bounds [in asking her to be interviewed]."

When Johnson was asked about his relationship with Rookmaaker, he shrugged and said, "It keeps me from running around. I don't need to be doing that." Johnson has told people around him that if Rookmaaker ever wanted too much from him, he would end the relationship and "would not look back."

★ ★ ★

Another road game, another event. In the new Georgia Dome the Cowboys played before another echo-chamber sellout. "Three straight road sellouts," said Norv Turner, "is something befitting the Redskins or 49ers or Buffalo—a Super Bowl team. This team is just so young, and every week it's a make-or-break game that's sold out. Everything's just getting accelerated, but you wonder if one of these weeks all this will just overwhelm this team."

Not this week.

As Turner watched Aikman warm up, he couldn't help noticing that every throw was a stinging spiral right in somebody's hands. "He was so zeroed in it was scary," Turner said.

Aikman said, "Philadelphia had won the day before [beating Washington to stay alive in the division race]. Atlanta was a game that if we don't win, our season ends. Everybody was still pissed. Everything would have come completely apart. I wasn't even as close to uptight for the Super Bowl as I was for Atlanta."

If only Aikman could get this uptight weekly.

Atlanta did lead, 7–3. But that was quickly forgotten. Atlanta did throw for 372 yards, as Wannstedt feared. But that didn't matter, either. In the first half Aikman took over the game. Aikman hit 15 of 17—including 13 straight—for 196 yards and 2 touchdowns. That was Aikman's smoking response to the Washington loss and to Johnson.

As Wannstedt hoped, Dallas had the ball for twenty first-half minutes to Atlanta's ten. Dallas led at halftime, 20–10. In the second half Emmitt Smith put on a 132-yard show, including spectacular now-you-have-him, now-you-don't TD runs of 29 and 29, and the Cowboys took it out on the Falcons, 41–17.

Said Aikman, "It got to where I felt like I couldn't miss. At one point I came off Mike [Irvin, the primary receiver] and hit Alvin Harper on a fade route for a touchdown. Nine out of ten times I would have just hit Mike."

Aikman, Smith, and Irvin had entered a highlight zone. Aikman: 18 of 21 for 239 yards and 3 TDs. Smith: 174 yards on 24 carries. Irvin: 6 catches for 89 yards, mostly on his buddy Deion. On a rainy night in Georgia, lightning had struck the Cowboy offense, melding the quarterback, backs, receivers, and line into a dominant unit. "Tonight," said Nate Newton, "we took it up to another level. Everybody was cookin' at once."

Yes, the Falcons were ranked twenty-seventh in pass defense and some of their tacklers appeared to lose interest in the fourth quarter. But the point was, the Cowboy offense's confidence had risen near an unstoppable level. "No turnovers," Newton said. "When we don't turn it over and we execute like that, look out, NFL." Again, the Cowboys had played keepaway, holding the ball 33:05 to Atlanta's 26:55. Though the Cowboy offense wasn't yet considered as explosive as San Francisco's, which led the league in yards and points, the Cowboys would finish No. 1 in an underpublicized category: time of possession. The Cowboys averaged 33:57 per game to the opponents' 26:03. Sometimes Dallas's No. 1 defense actually was a No. 1 offense. Opponents couldn't open Wannstedt's candy store if they didn't have the ball.

In the locker room, Turner spoke in awe of Aikman's command. "Troy was so efficient, so exact. He's as accurate a passer as I've ever seen, and he was especially accurate tonight."

Turner also bristled with pride over the team's—and specifically the quarterback's—reaction to Johnson's post-Washington storm. It appeared that for perhaps the first time, Aikman had yanked the team leadership away from a reeling Johnson. Aikman and several other key players had basically said, "We'll get ourselves ready this time. We'll show him that winning is fairly important to us, too."

Pointedly Turner said, "Our guys were really focused on winning tonight. You could really feel it before the game. Washington hurt these guys as much as it hurt anyone. Their way of responding was to go out and have a hell of a game. Another team might have let it linger."

So given Johnson's obsession with control, the questions arose: Did he script his blowup on the plane home from Washington? Was it calculated to detonate the Cowboys in Atlanta? Was "out-of-control" Jimmy really very in control?

"No," Aikman says emphatically.

"No way," says Jerry Jones. After observing Johnson for the week, Jones thought Johnson had gone a little crazy only because he blamed himself for the Washington loss. An interesting theory, but no assistant coach or player mentioned that possibility. Jones made it clear he was speculating. But he said, "Maybe Jimmy was looking at the big picture of the interception Troy threw down there on the goal line [at RFK]. Yes, we had been going for it all day. But—and I'm hindsighting here—if you play safe and kick the field goal there, you win. Maybe that wasn't pointed out strongly enough to Jimmy [by his assistants]. So I think Jimmy's behavior all week was just Jimmy, stewing in his own stew, being hard on himself."

But Jones insisted Johnson didn't script this incident or the "Irvin Misses Plane" headlines before the Detroit game. Jones said, "To say he's so artful and skillful that he's planning all this—I don't think so. But what could be happening is that he's like an actor—he's becoming his part. He's believing his own scenarios. It's like an actor plays Davy Crockett with every fiber of his being until he believes he is Davy Crockett."

Two weeks later, in an interview for this book, Johnson seemed to say his post-Washington behavior wasn't planned, but was instinctively the perfect reaction. Still testy, Johnson said, "A lot of people think that everything I do is totally planned out. Most things are calculated. But I can't always operate that way. I have to react sometimes. They [the players] know I'm an emotional guy.

"Some players thought what I did [after Washington] was a bigger deal than it was because they were whipped down and wanted me to stroke 'em and I didn't stroke 'em."

It worked, he was told. He shrugged as if he had known it would.

"They were going to kick the shit out of Atlanta," he said. "They were bound and determined. We were a hell of a lot better off than if I'd said"—Johnson speaks as if to a child—"'Everything's okay. It's just fine.'"

★ ★ ★

So, late in the Atlanta game and immediately after it, was Johnson still spewing tough love?

Up in the visiting owner's box, shortly into the third quarter of the Atlanta game, Jones popped the cork on a bottle of champagne. "Daddy," chided his daughter, Charlotte, "it's too early."

The Cowboys had just increased their lead to 34–10. Jones had seen enough. He was ready to celebrate clinching the franchise's first NFC East title since 1985. In fact, Jones had made sure that blue T-shirts saying NFC EAST CHAMPIONS were waiting in each player's locker.

Shortly into the fourth quarter, the Cowboys scored again to lead 41–10. Deion Sanders fielded the kickoff, started to kneel in the end zone as if to down the ball for a touchback, then took off past Cowboy tacklers who had slowed in anticipation of a play-ending whistle. He made it to the Atlanta 28 before he was tackled. Johnson threw a fit.

Many times through the season Johnson protested a referee's decision. He probably works the zebras as effectively as any coach, even carrying a card with their pictures so he can call them by name. But this time Johnson set a personal record for agitation, screaming at the refs, exaggeratedly blowing an imaginary whistle, throwing up his arms and gyrating until his hair came unsprayed and actually fell in his eyes.

Five minutes later Atlanta cut the lead to 41–17 with 8:15 remaining. In a season first, Johnson called the team together and chewed it out on the sideline. Afterward, Johnson continued to rant and rage in the locker room before the media was allowed to enter. Perhaps the T-shirts irked him. Perhaps it was the contingent of friends and relatives of Jones who were allowed into the locker room, which was a human zoo. Perhaps it was some other unknown "uncontrollable." Johnson's interview session lasted about five minutes. He began by saying of the 24-point victory, "I thought it was sloppy there at times."

Aikman said later, "Obviously, I was excited by my performance. More than anything it had helped us put Washington behind us. But no one was real excited after the game. He didn't even congratulate us [for winning the East]. Guys were upset again. This would go on for a while."

As Johnson walked onto the team plane, flight attendants were stunned to see his mood was at least as foul as it was after the Washington loss. One said, "He was red-faced like he was about to blow. I asked Dave Wannstedt what was going on—I mean, they had won, forty-one to seventeen, and Dave said, 'I don't know what's going on. He blew up in the locker room. He may blow up again. He's like a time bomb.' "

Johnson appeared to calm down later in the flight, perhaps because Rhonda was sitting beside him. He even walked back and kidded with a group of leery players, saying, "I'm doing better this time, aren't I?" Several were brave enough to say he didn't seem to be doing so well on the sideline at the end of the game.

"Well," Johnson said, "you guys were getting sloppy."

Watching from the entrance to first class, Tony Wise shook his head, pointed to his seat in the row behind Johnson's, and said, "Can you imagine having to sit in that seat if we had lost? Merry Christmas."

Christmas was four days away. Wise hadn't yet seen the worst of his close friend Jimmy.

On the Edge

PUBLICLY, JIMMY JOHNSON MADE SURE EVERYONE KNEW HE hadn't softened. Bah, humbug: Scrooge lived. He hadn't been visited by any terrifying ghost of his dead partner. No, Johnson's partner was very much alive and often making Johnson's current life hell. Johnson didn't believe in ghosts or in Christmas, and that week he proudly told reporters he again would not celebrate it.

Johnson said, "This is a short week [because of the Monday-night game] and we do have Christmas coming up [on Friday]. This is not normally one of the times I pull back, but because of overwhelming suggestions from coaches and players, we will shorten the work schedule for players on Christmas Eve and Christmas. But we will have the same amount of practice time."

Okay, you Cratchits, fewer meetings on Thursday and Friday. But mind you, practice won't be a second shorter just because of some holiday.

Of course, Johnson knew this would trigger a fresh batch of letters, some arsenic-laced, from his favorite blue-haired ladies who worship Tom Landry. Coach Landry's favorite day was always Christmas; some considered it his birthday. But Johnson doesn't believe in forced gift-giving and phony family fellowship, and Jones was trying to be open-minded.

Jones said, "Now, I think Jimmy is missing something. But logically, what he is saying makes sense. He just doesn't want his two sons to feel obligated to buy him something just because it's December twenty-fifth. Jimmy's a giving person—just not on holidays. I know we've had years in our family where we've said, 'This year, let's just not exchange gifts.' Of course, inevitably somebody gets you something anyway. I definitely know the feeling of being pressured to buy for people.

"So it would be a mistake to say there is a contrast here in the way ol' Jimmy and ol' Jerry handle Christmas. This isn't Tom Landry, Jr., and the devil."

No danger there. To many people, Jones will never have to worry about being considered a Landry Jr.

"I mean, if I came off that way," said Jones, "people who know me would say, 'Boy, did he snow you.' The point is, Jimmy is not an atheist. In fact, he could argue he attends more chapel than I do, because he's always there on Sunday before the games. I've tried to go a lot more this year because I really think it's important. In fact, I've been thinking more and more lately how important that is [as Cowboy owner]. I was raised Methodist. I didn't go Wednesday nights, but I went Sunday morning and Sunday night. Gene was very strong in making our family a strong churchgoing family."

Jones himself hasn't attended services regularly since his childhood, though people around him say he tithes generously to his old church in Little Rock. In Dallas, Jones said he was considering joining Highland Park Methodist, not far from the home he and Gene were buying. Tom Landry belongs to Highland Park Methodist.

Jones said, "Gene's father was a layman in the church, and he had great influence on me. But I guess I didn't become a layman because I didn't ever want anyone saying, 'A layman wouldn't do that.'"

Jones grinned at himself.

"But believe me, I'm God-fearing enough to know that the Man Upstairs uses the Dallas Cowboys as one of his tools. I don't want to be sanctimonious about this. I don't expect to get to heaven and be awarded a Heisman Trophy. But I don't want to be put on waivers, either."

Another grin.

"I would like to think I have kept priorities in my life. It's not my place to tell Jimmy what to do with his, though the one thing I've told him is that I don't want him to become callous. This is nothing new for me. I've been around a lot of people who have made a lot of money or thought they had a lot of money and pushed away from their family or divorced and remarried. But you even look at Coach Landry—and I don't know him at all—but through some tough times he had his Christian work to fall back on. The one thing I would not want to see is for Jimmy to wind up in a mental institution.

"I also don't want to see some of Jimmy's stances become the image of the Dallas Cowboys. Right now he's doing this." Jones struck a stiff-arm pose against the outside world. "He doesn't want to be seen as celebrating holidays or being community-minded or a Christian man or whatever. But seriously, right now, given our success and what we could accomplish in the next month, do you think anybody really cares whether Jimmy Johnson has a Christmas tree or not? So you let it play on out, you hope you win the Super Bowl, then when you're on top and you have everyone's attention, you balance it out."

Meaning, you strongly urge your coach to do some charity work. Jones says that at least twice a week he donates his time to appear or speak at a community function. Johnson despises functions.

Johnson's response: "I am going to do something charity-wise, but I don't want *him* to know about it. And believe me, I will not be out talking to civic groups."

As the regular season ended, Johnson quietly had a Cowboy staffer setting up the Jimmy Johnson Foundation for Children's Charities, with the key fund-raisers a spring gala and golf tournament featuring college and pro coaches from around the country. The staffer, who asked not to be quoted by name or "Jerry would fire me in a second," said, "The difference between Jimmy and Jerry is that Jimmy's word is gold. If he says he'll do something, bank on it. With Jerry, you never know. Jerry's like a televangelist. You wonder what he's really saying behind closed doors."

Johnson's supporters at Valley Ranch say he's a closet Santa

Claus, while Jones is the real Scrooge. Jones's supporters say just the opposite.

Most holdover staffers from the Landry regime have developed an affinity for Johnson. One is Barbara Goodman, an efficient, dedicated, cheerful saint of a secretary who served Landry for several years. Given Landry's controversial dismissal, it was surprising Goodman continued to work for Johnson. But, says another secretary down the hall, "Barbara loves working for Jimmy. He shares things with her. She loves the way he treats his assistants with respect, how he'd go to hell and back for them. Coach Landry wasn't like that. I passed Coach Landry in the hall many, many times and he never said hi. Jimmy always says hi. Coach Landry almost wasn't real. He wasn't touchable. Jimmy has a very warm side."

Yet staffers Jones brought with him from Arkansas say most people have no idea how kind and philanthropic he is. He just doesn't tell the media about it, they say, but other staffers wonder why "generous" Jerry hasn't given them a raise in four years.

Back and forth it goes, as the JJs turn.

A few days before Christmas, near the end of a lengthy interview with Jones, the subject of Johnson's highly publicized private life came up.

"That's an interesting dichotomy," Jones commented with a wry smile. "If you think about it, you read and hear very little about my home life."

Amazingly true.

"You don't know that my TV has been sitting on an ironing board."

Because? Jones vaguely explained he and Gene have moved four times in the same high rise. That's as far as Jones would go.

Jones said, "If Jimmy's TV were on an ironing board, that would be front-page news. I'm exaggerating, but you see my point."

He probably was right.

For the record, just before Christmas Johnson gave gifts to Rhonda and his assistants, but made it clear they were not Christmas gifts.

★ ★ ★

Running-back coach Joe Brodsky taped a newspaper story about retiring Bear middle linebacker Mike Singletary to Emmitt Smith's locker. "Read this, Emmitt," Brodsky wrote in the margin. At age fifty-eight, Brodsky was the oldest Cowboy assistant by almost five years. For years Brodsky coached great high-school teams in Miami. He coached running backs for eleven years at the University of Miami. He has been around long enough to know Smith is a once-in-a-lifetime player.

Like the other Cowboy coaches, Brodsky kept trying to get Smith to realize he could be even better. The newspaper story was about Singletary's singular dedication—about paying some prices the frugal Smith found a little too high. Not that he ran too hard after hours or openly defied coaches; no, Smith's character ran deep. "Everybody really likes him," said Jim Jeffcoat, "because he's not a selfish person and doesn't take himself too seriously." No shoe company had chosen to turn Smith into an interplanetary superhero through a TV ad campaign. Outside Dallas, Smith was still pretty much a Smith to many fans. In the locker room, his ego caused no problems.

Norv Turner said, "He's a joy to be around day to day because he's so unaffected by all this."

Smith said he always got plenty of sleep. He always showed up on time. He listened to everything the coaches said—but some of it he discarded. He paced himself in practice. He didn't believe in expending too much energy in the weight room. He sometimes let his mind rest when coaches wanted him to be studying.

Nate Newton said, "Emmitt is a franchise. But"—Newton struggled with the words—"he's just not getting the most out of his ability. No, I can't say that, can I? Every time I think that —boom—he goes fifty yards."

That week Emmitt Smith was named to the Pro Bowl for the third time in three pro seasons. He was named a starter for the second straight year. Tight end Jay Novacek was the only other Cowboy starter. Troy Aikman, Michael Irvin, Mark Stepnoski, and yes, Newton made it as offensive reserves. "Imagine me in a grass skirt, baby," Newton said, looking forward to Pro Bowl week in Hawaii.

But on defense no Cowboy made the Pro Bowl. That quietly pleased Dave Wannstedt, who grinned and said, "I'll get some mileage out of that." Wannstedt didn't have an Emmitt on defense, a superstar who could dominate on rare talent alone. Even Charles Haley studied hard, practiced hard, conditioned hard.

Smith spent off days maximizing his earning power. He had turned himself into a Pro Bowl entrepreneur, starting Emmitt Inc., a marketing and promotions company, with the people he trusts, his family. His family runs Emmitt Smith Inc.'s 1st and 10 Trading Cards and Collectibles in Pensacola, Florida, their hometown. Smith often spent his hours away from football signing cards by the thousand to be sold by Emmitt Inc. One day he joked, "List me as 'questionable' with writer's cramp."

While Troy Aikman and Michael Irvin are happiest when they're practicing and playing football, Smith treats it as strictly business. "God blessed me with a talent," he says. "So I'm using it." Football is a duty, not a joy. "I do not like to hurt, and I hurt more and more. But that's how I earn my living, selling my body."

Coaches didn't enjoy reading quotes like these from Smith in the *Fort Worth Star-Telegram:* "[Being a running back] is like being in a car wreck once a week. Not a real bad, scarring, flesh-wounding car wreck, but a car wreck that jars the body quite a bit. . . . Your body just numbs up after a while. Your body can only take so much. Finally, it just goes numb and you don't feel a lot of stuff. Unless it's really serious, the body gets used to it. . . . But you can tell when the cold front is coming in. Your whole body is going to ache, spine on down.

"If I could play baseball as well as I do football, if I could play as good as Cal Ripken, Jr., or Cecil Fielder or Barry Bonds, or if I could get in the majors and work at being the best, I probably would. You have a hundred percent medical [coverage, unlike the NFL]. . . . You've got guys playing baseball in their forties. They will walk away from the game and still have a consistent walk. You've got guys that play football [whose] legs never heal back properly."

Smith had started every game since the second one of his rookie year. He hadn't missed a pro game because of injury. Yet Smith constantly reminded reporters—and himself—that his next carry could easily be his last.

Coaches and teammates could never quite figure out No. 22. "I call him Quiet Storm," Newton said. "You know, if he was a flashy motherfucker, nobody would like him. But he's arrogant in his own way. I try to get inside his head about what he sees when he runs, so I'll better understand how to block for him. He says, 'Don't expect a *damn* thing.' He sees what he sees. He just hates it when you stop in the hole. He says, 'Don't sit still. Keep movin'.' "

Newton didn't play that Sunday against the Bears at Texas Stadium. The game mattered only for momentum, so Johnson told Newton to rest his knee. But Smith did pretty well without his Pro Bowl guard. The Cowboys knew before the three P.M. kickoff that Smith needed 109 yards to win the NFL rushing title over Pittsburgh's Barry Foster, whose noon game was over. In the third quarter Smith broke a play called Bend Right for a 31-yard touchdown. That gave him 131 yards for the day—gave the Cowboys a 10–0 lead that soon spun into 27–0—and gave Emmitt Smith his second straight NFL rushing title with 1,713 yards.

Yet he didn't dunk the ball over the crossbar or spike it to China or heave it to his mother in the twenty-second row. He walked the ball through high fives and hugs back to the bench, where he stored it safely in a trunk for his collection. Who knows? Maybe he'll auction it off someday.

At that point Johnson also stored Smith safely on the bench, where he took off his shoulder pads, put on a Cowboy ballcap, and basked. What a day it was for Cowboy fans. Another rushing title and the NFL's No. 1 defense.

After holding the top position for nine straight weeks, Wannstedt's wonders secured the regular-season title by holding the Bears to 92 total yards. Once again the Cowboy defense had dodged a starting quarterback's bullets; rookie Will Furrer started (and finished) his first pro game. Still, the Cowboy defense was only the NFL's third since 1980 to hold opponents to fewer than 4,000 yards. The other two were the 1984 Bears and 1991 Saints, who dominated Pro Bowl selections. The '92 Cowboys, who allowed 3,933 yards, beat the second-place Saints by 142 yards. The Cowboys were also No. 1 against the run and No. 1 in fewest first downs and third-down conversions allowed. A year earlier the Cowboy defense had ranked seventeenth overall.

What a day this was, considering this team had been 1-15 just four years earlier. This team was winning its franchise-record thirteenth game. Interesting note: While Johnson doesn't believe in luck, Jerry Jones's lucky number is thirteen. He was born on October 13, 1942. He believes in omens. "This is an omen," he said with a wink.

As the third quarter ended, Jones made his triumphant entrance onto the floor of Texas Stadium. Many in the crowd of 63,101 gave him a standing cheer as he shook both fists. "After all we'd been through in four years," said Jones, "that moment meant a lot. I really believe we should all enjoy it. Setting the pace is what this franchise has always been about."

The Cowboy bandwagon was picking up momentum. Fans still skeptical of Jones and/or Johnson and/or just how good this team really was, were shrugging and joining the hoedown. Dallas, a city once known for its skyscrapers of mirrored windows, was falling for a team that did windows. This team was more huggable than the cold blue Cowboy juggernauts of the past. From the stands it just appeared to be having so much fun.

Some insiders initially thought it was Jerry Jones's halftime extravaganza that set off Jimmy Johnson. At halftime of the Bear game Troy Aikman was presented the Bob Lilly Award for sportsmanship, leadership, dedication, and achievement, as voted by fans. Aikman spoke to the crowd for three or four minutes. By the time he jogged up the tunnel to the locker room, it was almost time for the team to jog back down to the field.

The Bears reappeared before the Cowboys did and found the field still covered with ten Oldsmobiles. This was the culmination of a season-long promotional contest. Bear kickers began to punt and practice kickoffs over the Oldsmobiles.

"None of that bothered me," said Johnson.

But the two developments that bothered the hell out of Johnson, as noted in the first chapter of this book, were the prince and the young back who turned back into a frog.

Prince Bandar bin Sultan, the Saudi Arabian ambassador to the United States and Cowboy fanatic, accompanied Jones onto the field as the third quarter ended. Maybe Bandar wouldn't have been quite so conspicuous if it hadn't been for his six bodyguards. Bandar waved to and congratulated a few players he knows.

The Cowboys led Will Furrer, 27–0.

On the second play of the fourth quarter, second-year running back Curvin Richards fumbled. Two plays later Cowboy linebacker Godfrey Myles intercepted Furrer. But Cowboy quarterback Steve Beuerlein, who had relieved Aikman, threw an interception that set up a quick Bear TD. Five plays later Richards fumbled again, this one returned by Chris Zorich 42 yards for a TD. Cowboys 27, Bears 14, with 9:19 remaining.

That's when Johnson angrily called for the first team to get ready.

This surprised Tony Wise, who is on the sideline during games and helps coordinate offensive substitutions. Wise said, "Jimmy set the tone early in the week by saying he would evaluate at halftime [whether some backups would be allowed to play]. Lots of guys thought they were going to get a chance because Jimmy planted the seed. So I've got Frank Cornish at my elbow through the second half saying, 'Can I go in?' It was like a high-school game.

"Then Jimmy says, 'First team get ready.' So Emmitt throws his pads back on and Troy starts warming up. I usually try to stay as far away from Jimmy as I can, but I had to start asking him who he wanted in and out. As the offense started onto the field, you had to start singling guys out: 'You go in, you don't. You go in, you don't.' "

Norv Turner strongly suggested from the press box that Aikman and Smith not be sent back into the game. Johnson backed off, though he wanted some first-teamers back on the field.

The game ended Dallas 27, Chicago 14.

But for the 13-3 Cowboys, the postgame locker room was a subdued confusion of mixed emotions. Johnson chewed out the team for sloppy play. Then Johnson walked prematurely out of his press conference across the hall and left a trail of smoke as he walked back through the locker room to the coaches' dressing quarters.

Several players asked reporters, "Did we win or lose?" Later Aikman said, "What really concerned me is that he didn't congratulate us at all. That was really hard on a lot of guys. There was a lot of bitterness."

Johnson's irrational behavior hit Wise as hard as anyone. He was the last assistant to finish dressing. His face was as red as Johnson's had been. Wise also was close to irrational.

"It was never like this at Miami," Wise said. "This is crazy. That [coaching] job back at Ithaca is looking better and better. Whether anybody around here believes it or not, we beat a pretty good football team today."

Wise would soon be helping coach it.

"I mean, if you want to get upset about something, let Philly win at New Orleans [in one NFC wild-card play-off game] and let Washington win [at Minnesota in the other]. Let the guys in green come back here again. Then some people around here are really going to get hives."

★ ★ ★

As Wise spoke, Jimmy Johnson was already in Jerry Jones's suite. He was furious about the grand entrance by the Jones-Bandar entourage with a quarter to play, but later Johnson indicated his anger had been building all season—that he felt he constantly had to overcome Jones's intrusions. If Johnson controlled every inch of his world, the team would not have played an extra exhibition game in Tokyo; Michael Irvin, Jay Novacek, and Mark Stepnoski would have been signed early in training camp; Johnson would have a "football man" serving as his pro personnel director. If Johnson had total control, he would have an unlimited budget and an owner who left him alone; he would not have a Jerry Jones who brings princes to the bench area during games.

Johnson said he told Jones exactly why he had gone too far with Bandar. Jones said that, as usual, he just rode out Johnson's storm, assuring Johnson that the last thing he wants to do is interfere with his coaching. Fortunately, Johnson didn't see Jones's no-big-deal reaction the next day or he might have quit, as assistants feared he would the night before.

"Just part of the Jimmy package," Jones said. Typical. Predictable.

Many University of Arkansas boosters had wondered in 1983 why athletic director Frank Broyles didn't go for Johnson when Ken Hatfield was hired to replace Lou Holtz. Johnson was coming off an 8-4 season at Oklahoma State, including a Bluebonnet Bowl win. A source at Arkansas says Broyles knew about "the Jimmy package," too, and warned Jones he would have some problems if he hired Johnson to coach the Cowboys. Broyles had coached Johnson and Jones on the '64 Razorback team that went 11-0 and won the national championship. The source says, "People thought Broyles went for Hatfield because of Jimmy's reputation for running around and raising hell. But the truth was that Frank knew how Jimmy can be charming one day and impossible the next."

Jones said he knew exactly how to handle Johnson. Yet something Jones said indicated he didn't grasp the depth of bitterness Johnson had created in the locker room. Jones said, "If Jimmy did a Ditka and alienated much of the team, that would be another matter. But we're not talking about Ditka here. I certainly respect Ditka. But we're talking more intellect here. More people skills. More ability to reason. I know Jimmy is stretching himself to his limits, but he can handle it physically. I've known him for a long time and I believe he can handle it and come out of it. Hey, those first two years when I was so stretched and frayed, friends of mine told me, 'Jerry, you're not yourself.' Jimmy's going through a little of that right now. But from what I see, I'm eighty percent sure Jimmy will be fine through the rest of the season."

Aikman and other team leaders weren't nearly so sure.

But the night of the Bear game, says Jones, he finally soothed Johnson, even convincing him to sleep on his decision to cut Curvin Richards. "Jimmy told me from the start, 'Don't let me make a player move when I'm emotional.' I kid him about the night after a New York Jets game three years ago [the Cowboys lost 24–9] when he just didn't think he could win with a guy named Emmitt Smith."

Jones said Johnson was ready to trade Smith on the flight home.

"So I said, 'Let's see how you feel about Curvin tomorrow.' "

The next morning Jones, son Stephen, and Mike McCoy met with Johnson. McCoy says, "The question we asked him was, 'Would you trust Curvin enough to ever play him again?' 'No,' he said. So you cut him and save his salary. That makes sense. The coaches were already raving about how well Derrick Gainer was doing in practice, and Jimmy always had been a little skeptical about Curvin's attitude. Did it make Jimmy feel a little better to cut Richards? Probably. But it was still a sound move."

Of course, cutting Richards only served to convince lots of players that Johnson was certifiable.

During his Monday press briefing, a calmer Johnson tried to explain through the media to his players that "as much as I want to praise 'em, I still understand their success in '92 will be measured in the next three or four weeks."

Wise words. A 13–4 team would go down in Cowboy history as the one that set a franchise record for victories and lost at home in the first round of the play-offs.

Johnson ended that briefing with a cryptic reference. Asked why he again was so upset in his postgame press conference, he said, "I had two things on my mind and I corrected both of them."

One obviously was Richards. The other?

"That's something that only I know."

Well, Johnson and one other person for whom he intended the message.

★ ★ ★

On Thursday of that bye week Johnson agreed to do an interview in his office. Johnson's office isn't quite as long as Jones's, and Johnson doesn't do interviews on a couch. He sits behind his desk. Johnson's office is no Jimmy shrine: no trophy case or wall of pictures. It's tasteful but spare, and intensely neat.

At first Johnson's mood seemed only slightly improved. His digs at Jones continued.

He said he had spent about four hours questioning Bill Parcells about how he prepared his two New York Giant Super Bowl winners for the play-offs. Johnson had known Parcells since Parcells's days as a college assistant coach. Johnson said, "Bill was concerned we're going the wrong directions scouting-wise [cutting staff], and he's probably right. But that's not my department. That costs money. He was kind of taken aback we don't even send scouts to games [of the next week's opponent]."

For the first time all season Johnson had arranged to send scouts to the two wild-card games that would determine the Cowboys' opponent. But his shoestring scouting budget could cost the Cowboys in another area, Johnson warned. For the first time since Bill Bates was lost on October 11, a key player had suffered a season-ending injury. Tight end Alfredo Roberts had torn up his knee against the Bears. Roberts wasn't a starter, but he was often used as a blocker and occasionally as a surprise receiver.

"It will hurt losing Alfredo more than anybody will understand," Johnson said. "And not having a pro personnel guy really hurt [as Johnson looked to replace Roberts]. I had thirty-five names. Derek Tennell had played [for Cleveland and Denver]. I watched some tapes of him. Now we got what we got." In other words, they now had Tennell, like it or not.

Johnson talked more about his deteriorating relationship with Jones. He again vowed if it got any worse, he'd be gone: "I don't know if I'll be here five or six more years or five or six more days."

And what if he found the grass wasn't greener anywhere else in the NFL?

Heating, Johnson said, "The grass is greener wherever I'm standing. Anyone who knows me knows that."

But a few minutes later, near the end of the interview, Johnson's mood surprisingly brightened when he was asked about his relationship with Aikman and his team's mood entering the play-offs.

On Aikman: "Our respect for each other has grown tremendously this year. At least, I sense respect."

On his team: "They're as confident and as hungry to play as I could ever hope for. They're primed and ready to go."

Huh? Was Johnson talking about the same quarterback and team who were whispering about him? Whatever, this was an early hint of things to come.

★ ★ ★

Philadelphia (by 36–20) and Washington (24–7) had come from behind to win convincingly, sending Philly back to Dallas and Washington to San Francisco. Meanwhile, in the AFC, Buffalo rallied historically from 32 points down to shock and eliminate Houston. Cowboy coaches sometimes said that Houston, their pre-season sparring partner, was the most talented team they saw all season. Later, Norv Turner and Dave Wannstedt would mention that the Cowboys probably caught a break in the AFC bracket when Buffalo caught and edged Houston, 41–38.

But here came the guys in green again, ready to cause hives in Dallas.

In Monday's tone-setter meeting the Cowboys were surprised, if not shocked, to see good-time Jimmy smiling back at them from the podium. Said Mike Saxon, "His theme for the week was, 'It's the play-offs. Just relax and have fun.' Guys are like, 'Huh?' But you can feel a big drop in tension around here."

However, for the moment there was no drop in tension between Johnson and Jones. That was because of an article quoting only Jones that appeared atop page four of *The Dallas Morning News* sports section the next morning, January 5. The writer was Sam Blair, whose only direct involvement with the Cowboys is a weekly collaboration with Jones on his *Morning News* column.

The article said, "Cowboys owner Jerry Jones acknowledges he has received feedback from fans critical of coach Jimmy Johnson's behavior off the field this season, with some fans wondering if

Johnson's overall intensity could drive him toward a breakdown.

"Jones said he will talk with Johnson about his concerns after the season and that he still supports [Johnson] completely."

Johnson was waiting at Jones's office that morning when Jones arrived. Several observers said Johnson was steaming.

Jones later explained, "Sam had a little thing going for the way Jimmy had treated one of his brethren. I didn't know about it, but there was something about Tim Cowlishaw [who covers the Cowboys for the *Morning News*] going to Jimmy's house."

Cowlishaw says he and Johnson had kidded about how close they live to each other. So one evening the previous spring when Cowlishaw needed a quick response from Johnson for a story he was writing for the next day's paper, Cowlishaw rang the coach's doorbell. Rhonda Rookmaaker answered, says Cowlishaw, and went to get Johnson, who appeared wearing only gym shorts.

Cowlishaw says the one-way conversation lasted just long enough for Johnson to say, "This is my private residence. You made a mistake."

The next day, says Cowlishaw, Johnson told him, "I laid down those ground rules. You knew I'd react that way."

"But I don't have your home phone number," Cowlishaw said.

"That's why you don't," said Johnson, who doesn't want to be bothered even by phone when he's in his private residence.

Cowlishaw chuckles when telling the story. He and Johnson appear to get along fine. But Jones says Blair was not amused. Blair is a veteran reporter and columnist who wrote extensively about Landry's Cowboys.

Jones: "Sam said, 'Jerry, Tim didn't go over there just to see Jimmy's pretty face. He has a job to do.' I understand that. We're all just trying to be part of this and do our jobs. I always said the person who is short with a waitress has never waited tables. The fact that somebody is waiting tables instead of out there jigglin' 'em tells you something. That person may wind up running a company someday.

"So Sam says, 'Jerry, I'm going to have to write something.' I was a little surprised by how it came out. But Jimmy and I did talk and we're fine. Jimmy's point was that this isn't something we need to do through the newspapers, and he's right. The one thing I should not have said was, 'We'll sit down.' To most people that means,

'Uh-oh, this could really be something.' But for Jimmy and I that probably means we'll probably talk about it for about two minutes."

Maybe so, though it's hard to believe Jones could tell Johnson in two minutes everything he thinks about Johnson's lifestyle and community involvement.

Jones says his wife read the article and said, "There you go again, defending your coach." Yes, no matter what happened, Jones remained Johnson's biggest booster. That week, perhaps, Jones's optimism helped save Johnson from himself. Jones was the only one at Valley Ranch saying he liked the energy being generated by Johnson's fury. "This," said Jones, "is the kind of tension that creates a Super Bowl team."

Psychologist Don Beck says, "With Jimmy's roller-coaster nature, it wouldn't have worked without Jones the positive cheerleader."

Jones said he reminded Johnson of what Johnson always told him: "Give me a chance to know a team as well as they know us and I'll win." Jones said, "We know Philadelphia. Plus, we're just a better team than Philadelphia. That's the only reason I'm scared to death: we should win. Now you worry about things you can't control. You flash on Troy's interception at Washington. No, Troy, no! This time you can't just let it all hang out the way we did at Washington. Patient, patient, patient. No turnovers, and we will win."

★ ★ ★

Here came the big bad wolves again, but this time Valley Ranch was made of brick. The Eagles were huffing and puffing in the newspapers, but Nate Newton said, "We don't pay no attention to their bullshit no more."

Eagle linebacker Byron Evans was quoted as saying, "Nobody put it to 'em like we did and they know it."

Eagle safety Andre Waters said, "We have the advantage mentally and they know it." Waters said he was pushing to return from a broken leg just so he could "get even" with Emmitt Smith. When Waters's leg was broken, Smith told reporters, "What goes around comes around"—a statement other Cowboys had quietly applauded.

The Cowboys were no longer afraid of the Eagles. No one

seemed concerned even about Aikman, who faced the double whammy of (1) his first-ever play-off start against (2) his old tormentors.

Johnson bristled when asked during his press conference if he worried about Aikman being intimidated by the Eagles. "Not one iota. To say Troy Aikman might be intimidated by anybody is saying you don't know Troy Aikman. . . . The more I'm around Troy the more I'm amazed at his ability to keep things on an even keel and stay focused."

Johnson told the *Fort Worth Star-Telegram*, "A quarterback who stays in control is an asset for me because I can be, well, emotional et cetera."

Yes, Johnson's mood was swinging dramatically toward warm and contrite. Was this Johnson's way of apologizing, especially to Aikman? It certainly looked that way. Was he again trying to publicly stroke a quarterback who had responded before to Johnson's stroking? Maybe.

By Friday, following the week's final practice, Johnson was, according to nationally respected *Philadelphia Daily News* columnist Ray Didinger, "as confident as any coach I've ever seen before a big game."

So, basically, was Dave Wannstedt. His game-planning had been disrupted by reporters' questions about being a rumored candidate for four head-coaching vacancies: Giants, Bears, Broncos, and Patriots. But he said, "I'll be okay because I know [the Eagles]. The key is to stop the run. Herschel—we'll shut his ass down. The key is stopping Heath Sherman [who had 105 yards rushing in the wild-card win at New Orleans]. Last thing I told our guys today: 'Stop the fuckin' run or we'll lose.' But I really feel good about this one."

In offensive meetings, though, hives were breaking out. Tony Wise said, "It annoys me the way the Eagles approach these games with us like they're on a mission. For them to be 'out for Dallas,' that's comical with all the talent they have. Here we're the youngest team in the league and just a year ago we had a 'questionable' offensive line. And now they're transporting Jerome Brown's locker on the road for inspiration. What a bunch of underachievers."

Stubbornly realistic, Norv Turner said, "Tell me this: What happens if they play their best game and we play ours? What if their five guys [stars on defense] play way up here? Erik Williams wins NFC offensive player of the week [when Dallas beat Philly on November 1] and now what's Reggie White going to do to him? I know I'm the only one back here [in the offices] who thinks that way, and maybe it will be my downfall. But if people will just be patient with this group, it will win a Super Bowl in a couple of years."

★ ★ ★

It was 38 degrees and drizzling as the teams warmed up for Sunday's eleven-thirty A.M. kickoff. But on the Cowboy end of the field, it was tropical. Jimmy Johnson's dimples were out and his thumb was up.

Mike McCoy said, "I was down on the field before the game and I caught Jimmy's eye and he gave me the thumbs-up. Jimmy Johnson, giving the thumbs-up before a game? I said, 'This one is ours.'"

Johnson slapped palms with Stephen Jones, who said, "I've never seen him that way before a game."

The Eagles scored first on a 32-yard field goal. But Aikman drove the Cowboys 46 yards in 10 plays for a touchdown, which came on a 1-yard pass to . . . Derek Tennell? How 'bout that crack Cowboy scouting department? What's more, the play was the same one Turner had called to disastrously open the first game at Philadelphia—the bootleg. Turner said, "I told Jimmy earlier in the week that if we got in close, I was going to call the boot. He looked at me like, 'I don't know.'"

The teams arm-wrestled through the second quarter, Turner playing it patiently. But he got the matchup he wanted, 6-4 Alvin Harper on 5-7 rookie corner Mark McMillian on a route called Nine Pump. The 41-yard completion set up the 14–3 TD. Cowboy Darren Woodson forced a fumble on the kickoff, and the Cowboys added a quick field goal before halftime.

Dallas, 17–3.

The Cowboys received to start the second half, and Turner went back to two routes that hadn't clicked in the first half. Boom: 23 yards to Michael Irvin. Boom: 20 yards to Jay Novacek. Then Turner guessed right with a draw to Emmitt Smith, who split an Eagle blitz for 23 yards and the 24–3 TD.

It was 27–3 after three quarters. The Eagles scored with fifty seconds left in the game on a Randall Cunningham scramble-and-fling TD pass of 18 yards. That cut the final margin to 34–10.

The Dallas Cowboys had dominated the Philadelphia Eagles, no ifs, ands, or unkicked butts. Numbers of this kind were beginning to look familiar: Dallas led in yardage, 346–178. Emmitt Smith had 114 yards on 25 carries; Herschel Walker was held to 29 on 6, Heath Sherman to 12 on 6. Dallas was 7 of 12 on third-down conversions; Philly 1 of 11. Dallas had just one turnover. Dallas controlled the clock, 35:17 to 24:43.

A relieved Turner smiled sheepishly and said, "Hey, I've been wrong before."

Said ex-Cowboy and current Eagle guard Brian Baldinger, "Dallas just beat our butts, no questions asked. We got beat by a superior team. Dallas simply outplayed us on both sides of the ball. I don't think there's a man in here who won't tell you the same thing."

Nate Newton's told-you-so: "The media and fans said, 'Uh-oh, here comes Philly.' We just said, 'Let's get ready.' This isn't a team that talks trash. It just plays—plays sound and hard for sixty minutes."

Whatever its coach's moods.

So who was that guy impersonating Jimmy Johnson in the interview room? This guy was almost giddy. This guy began by congratulating everyone in the organization for all their hard work "from Jerry Jones on down." Time-out: Johnson made a point of crediting Jones?

Several players said Johnson "basically apologized" to them in his postgame address. "Yeah," said Tony Wise, "he was all apologetic for being such a fuckin' grump."

Johnson even told the media he broke one of his rules "by looking ahead" and arranging to have one of his practice fields soaked. The day before, Johnson had watched the 49ers finally mud-wrestle the Redskins into submission, 20–13, at Candlestick Park. So, anticipating a win over the Eagles and a trip to Mudville, Johnson made some phone calls to set up a simulated Candlestick at Valley Ranch.

Johnson was that cocky, that happy. He told his press conference, "There's been some concern in the past that I haven't been up here as long as you'd like. I'll stay here as long as you want today." As reporters ran out of questions, Johnson concluded, "It's a big win for us. We've got bigger wins coming."

Dallas's Team

FOR THE 1992 COWBOYS, THE CATCH TO PLAYING THE 49ERS IN the NFC Championship Game at Candlestick Park was The Catch. "I see it 10 times a day," Emmitt Smith said with irritation. "I can't turn on the TV without seeing it. If it wasn't for the media, no one on this team would give The Catch a second thought."

Smith was twelve when it happened. On the evening of January 10, 1982, 49er Dwight Clark rose out of the mud into the fog and came down in the back right corner of Candlestick's end zone with a 6-yard pass from Joe Montana. Montana and Clark had killed the wicked witch: San Francisco 28, America's Team 27. The Bay Area's joyous shock registered 5.1 on the Richter scale. Coach Bill Walsh's kids had beaten Coach Tom Landry's supermen. San Francisco fans remained in a delirious fog as the 49ers went on to win their first of four Super Bowls in four appearances.

The Cowboys did make it back to the NFC title game the following strike-shortened season, but lost badly in Washington, 31–17. They played only two more play-off games in Landry's reign, losing to the Rams in '83 (24–17) and '85 (20–0). What if Clark hadn't held on to a pass that—according to many ex-Cowboys—Montana privately admitted he was trying to throw away? What if the Cowboys had gone on to beat the Bengals in that January 1982 Super Bowl? Would the Cowboys still have crumbled toward 1-15?

Now the '92 Cowboys had an opportunity made for sports editors across the country: to reverse history, to avenge The Catch, to do to the 49ers what they had done to Tom Landry's Cowboys. Start the presses: this called for pipe-smoking essays and Toynbee-like reconstruction of the '82 game and its aftermath. By week's end, distant relatives of ex-Cowboys who were on injured reserve in '81–82 were being quoted on how The Catch changed their lives and their children's. At least, that's how it seemed to the '92 Cowboys.

They perhaps read quotes such as these from Dennis Thurman, currently the defensive backfield coach at Southern Cal. As a Cowboy cornerback, Thurman had an out-of-body experience as he and his teammates attempted to stop San Francisco's 13-play, 89-yard drive that '82 night: "It was like everything was happening in slow motion and I had just stepped back and started watching it unfold before me. It was eerie. I never doubted somebody was going to make a play. We didn't take San Francisco nearly as seriously as we did the Redskins or Eagles. It was like, 'Hey, we are Dallas.' Nobody drives on us in the last two minutes and makes plays like San Francisco was making. That's what *we* did. It wasn't just Clark's catch. They made plays all through that drive. In terms of consistent execution, I've never seen one better."

Thurman said he hadn't seen a ball-control offense execute as crisply and flawlessly until he started watching the '92 Cowboys.

Thurman added, "If the Cowboys win Sunday, and I think they have a legitimate shot, it will be very interesting to see if this sends the 49ers in a downward spiral like the old Cowboys went through, while it propels the Cowboys into the team of the nineties. The similarities are amazing. Bill Walsh was a college coach (Stanford) who took over a terrible team. The Niners were the youngest team in '81; the Cowboys are now. The 49ers had three rookies on defense; so do the Cowboys. Troy Aikman is where Montana was—a young quarterback yet to prove himself. After replacing Montana, Steve Young is where Danny White was after replacing

Roger [Staubach]. Can Young get the monkey off his back and win the big one?"

Eerily insightful questions.

The '92 Cowboys' answer: Who cares? "Hey," said Aikman, grinning, "I was about fifteen then and I don't think I even cared about Super Bowls."

Nate Newton was not grinning when he said, "Fuck The Catch. We have enough to worry about with Jerry Rice and Steve Young. Guys like Kenny Gant, they don't know or want to know about The Catch."

That just about summed up the mood of a team that did a great job of staying in the now. "This team," said Newton, "doesn't worry about last week or next week. It's all about this week."

Jimmy Johnson wouldn't play along, either. The only history Johnson cares about is his career record. He told his weekly press conference, "I don't buy one game sending a team one way or the other. . . . What happens between January and July will determine what happens next year."

Johnson's theme to his team: forget about some game in 1982. Don't worry about how muddy the field might be Sunday. Focus on exactly what it will take to beat the 49ers.

No distractions.

★ ★ ★

Jerry Jones had warned Johnson about the pep rally. "I told Jimmy the week before the Eagle game that we really wanted to do something special if we won. He said, 'Is this necessary?' I said, 'Yes. I want to do something that's never been done before in NFL history.' I knew Jimmy wasn't happy about it. But this wasn't a Jimmy thing. Any coach would have felt the same way. He just didn't want anything to break the concentration, and that's understandable."

At first, several on Jones's staff were skeptical. A Thursday-night pep rally at Texas Stadium for a pro football team? Wouldn't it be a little embarrassing if only 10,000 or 12,000 showed up in a 65,000-seat stadium? Grinning, Mike McCoy said, "Of course, Jerry thought we'd get 168,000."

At first Jones wanted to call it The Mother of All Pep Rallies. But his staff convinced him that sounded like the Cowboys were about to bomb Baghdad. When no one could come up with anything better, the January 14 pep rally simply became known as The Pep Rally.

Or, to coaches, as "the fuckin' pep rally."

Tony Wise said, "Jimmy did give us the option to go. But I don't think they [Jones and Co.] have any idea what's going on here. Do they think we'll just automatically go fourteen and three every year? It doesn't happen just by magic. We have a lot of work to do preparing for a team we haven't seen in quite a while [since November 11, 1990]."

No assistant coach attended the pep rally. Though Jones considered it mandatory for the players, about fifteen came up with excuses—some of which might even have been valid. Johnson basically was under orders to show up and make some brief remarks to the crowd.

Privately Johnson wasn't as bothered by the interruption as by Jones's motives for staging the thing. "He just wants to sell more pennants," Johnson told assistants.

Jones said, "Jimmy told me some of the players were saying this was just another way for me to make more money, and maybe Jimmy was thinking the same thing. But I disagree with Jimmy on that. Listen, in this litigious age we live in, there are a lot easier, safer ways to make twenty thousand or thirty thousand dollars than to invite sixty-five thousand people to your house. One or two incidents, and lawsuits, could cancel everything you made. And by the way, we discounted everything in the Pro Shop [where Cowboy merchandise is sold], we gave away fifty thousand towels and pennants, and as it turned out, we made almost nothing on concessions."

Parking and admission were free. But so was publicity.

Jones, driving his staff to the edge, quickly spread the word to every media outlet in Dallas–Fort Worth that this was going to be a mother of a pep rally. It was almost as if every TV and radio station made this their event and decided to broadcast live that night from Texas Stadium. Every media outlet wanted to plug directly into the new blue magic, to feed feel-good feelings directly to listeners and viewers, and here Jones was asking them to be part of this historic happening. He was also asking them to ask anybody and everybody to come to Texas Stadium for a Cowboy love-in. Under Tex Schramm, the old Cowboys had basically been a private party at Landry's cathedral. A weeknight pep rally at Texas Stadium would have been inconceivable during the previous regime.

But again Jones's instincts were right: people were ready for this.

It had been a long time since Dallas had a team that hadn't embarrassed the city. After coming within a game of the NBA Finals in 1988, the Dallas Mavericks had turned themselves into the league's joke. As the Cowboys prepared for San Francisco, Mav fans prepared themselves for a run at the NBA's all-time worst record, 9-73 by the 1972–73 Philadelphia 76ers. For Texas Ranger fans, next year was forever going to be the year. No Ranger team had participated in a September pennant race in the twenty-one seasons the franchise had been in Texas.

But a Cowboy team that looked to be a year or two away had suddenly arrived, pulling up in a convertible and asking Dallas to come along for the ride. This team didn't want to be America's Team, just Dallas's. These guys—and their owner—didn't really care if you were rich or poor, old or young. Hop on the bandwagon, you all.

Suddenly, many Dallasites had a reason to shake hands, slap backs, propose toasts, feel great about themselves again. Dallas is a proud but insecure city whose national image has too often been associated with an assassination. Dallas isn't on an ocean or a major waterway. It isn't tropical. No purple mountains' majesty. No natural beauty to speak of. No colorful history. Part of Dallas fancies itself a second Hollywood, a "third coast," but few people outside the city see Dallas that way.

Dallas is foremost a nice, clean, upbeat place to live. Dallas, which calls itself the "can do" city, isn't littered with much apathy or cynicism. Dallas brims with the positive energy of lots of people from lots of places trying to make more money and friends. But without quite as many entertainment options as other major cities offer, Dallasites passionately follow sports. Dallas takes its sports as seriously as it takes itself. A winning team generates positive national recognition for Dallas. A winner unifies the city—or so say some Dallas leaders.

That week, several newspapers quoted novelist Marshall Terry, who heads Southern Methodist University's creative writing department. Terry said, "The psychological effect has been incredible and, of course, irrational. The Cowboys are winning and all of a sudden Dallas is a better place to live and the races get along better. That's what people tell themselves, anyway."

Or maybe that's what they were being told. Every radio and TV station and printed publication was telling people they were going crazy over the Cowboys. Jones was telling Dallas that an event was taking place on Thursday night that simply could not be missed. Everyone would be there. It would make history. It would be special.

And it was.

Ticket director Joel Finglass watched from the press box as the gates opened about five P.M. By then his better judgment had been worn away by Jones's relentless optimism. Almost apologetically, he said, "I actually think we could get forty thousand tonight. I'm not trying to kiss up to Jerry, but the key is that the owner sets the tone for a franchise. Jerry encourages people to come out and be rowdy. The old regime didn't want that. But we've gone from thirty-five thousand to about fifty thousand season tickets, and about five thousand didn't renew [after Jones bought the team]. So we have twenty thousand new people, and the average age [of those] is about thirty. It's a whole new feel."

Jones had recently announced a plan to add 70 luxury suites at Texas Stadium, which already led the league with 296 suites. But Finglass didn't anticipate this would be a big night for suite patrons. "With free admission," Finglass said, "we should get a lot of folks who are just crazy about the Cowboys and crazy about Jerry and just want to see what Texas Stadium is like."

About five thousand seats just below the press box had been blocked off for a fireworks display, so the actual stadium capacity that night was closer to sixty thousand. By the time the Cowboy Cheerleaders performed, just after seven, Texas Stadium actually appeared to be full.

Later, stadium officials admitted the night turned into a fire marshal's nightmare—people sitting in every aisle and, in many cases, two to a seat. The actual turnstile count, they said, was 69,609, meaning nearly ten thousand people didn't have seats. The reason Jones made very little off concessions was that very few people could get from their seats to the concession stands.

Police officers trying to direct traffic conservatively estimated that another twenty-five thousand were trying to get into the stadium and couldn't. Stadium lots were full. Texas Stadium, surrounded by freeways, isn't convenient to spillover lots or neighborhood parking, so after seven, traffic backed up for several miles in all directions with nowhere to go but home.

Inside, fans were acting as if Lin Elliott had just kicked a 54-yard field goal to win the Super Bowl. Texas Stadium has been louder only for rock concerts. Season highlights were shown on the Diamond Vision screen, each one setting off another warm roar. Jones said, "It was as if they were seeing the plays for the first time."

Who were these fans? Many were teenagers of all races—and perhaps many of those were there because it was free and they wanted to be part of what the radio was saying would be the biggest Thursday-night party in Dallas history. Jones said he was pleased to see so many people "from lesser economic backgrounds." McCoy later said, "We probably had about twelve season-ticket holders out there."

The ex-stars who first addressed the throng appeared genuinely startled and moved by its size and intensity. From the stage Roger Staubach told the crowd, "I think if we'd had a pep rally like this, we would have beat the Steelers." Tony Dorsett followed him to the microphone and said, "I think Roger's right. If we'd had this kind of send-off, I don't think we would ever have lost [Super Bowl XIII]. I don't think there's anything like this in the NFL, and I don't think there ever will be."

The one man in the stadium who didn't appear too excited was Jimmy Johnson. As he walked onto the field he reluctantly agreed to do a quick interview on the live set of KDFW-TV Channel 4. Johnson looked as if he had just been forced to kiss Jones on the lips.

Channel 4 anchorwoman Clarice Tinsley asked, "Have you thought much about what this pep rally would be like tonight?"

Johnson: "No, I haven't."

"Well, it's certainly pretty crazy. Did you think you'd get this kind of support?"

"I really haven't given it a lot of thought. We've been practicing."

"Coach, are you able to enjoy something like this?"

"This is enjoyment for the fans."

"And what about you?"

"I've got work to do."

(Aside from Larry Lacewell: "You have to understand coaches. Sometimes a thing like this increases the pressure they feel. You get there and see all the expectations on everyone's faces and you think, 'Shit.' ")

One by one as the players were introduced, they came jogging in street clothes or sweats out of the locker-room tunnel and onto the field. Many of them were prepared to be as bothered by the obligation as their coach. But standing together along the back of the stage, the NFL's youngest team appeared to get swept up in the emotion. Players raised their arms to the biggest Texas Stadium crowd they'd ever experienced.

Michael Irvin told the crowd, "We have more people here than most teams have at football games. That's why most teams are home and we're going to San Francisco."

Troy Aikman told the crowd, "I don't have but one thing to say: I'll see ya in Pasadena!"

But probably the most emotion-packed line was delivered by, of all killjoys, the Cowboy coach. Voice rising, Johnson told fans he would ask them just what he had asked the players in a meeting. "Are you satisfied?" Johnson yelled. "And I say it again: Are you satisfied?"

On the surface, of course, he was asking if just getting to the NFC Championship Game was enough. But Johnson is just calculating enough to be asking a deeper question: "Are you satisfied enough with the joy I'm giving you to accept me for what I am?"

Jones says that by the end of the program, Johnson made a point of telling him he liked it. "By the next morning," Jones said, "he really liked it."

No way, said assistants.

But the players said they loved it. Said Mike Saxon, "Everybody was talking about how neat it was. It really gave everybody a boost. The guys who didn't go really missed something. I know it's something I'll never forget."

Jones said, "These things just don't work as well after you win a Super Bowl. The emotion has been spent. It's better when you're anticipating. It exceeded even my expectations. It was something that will become larger than life because nothing like it has ever been done in the NFL and it won't be duplicated. What I told everybody [on his staff] the next morning was, 'Let's learn to trust our instincts.' That's how the Dallas Cowboys got to be the Dallas Cowboys—people dared to be great. Chances were taken."

The point, said Jones, was that the pep rally would have been immeasurably valuable even if it had cost him money. "This all contributed to the equity we're building in the Dallas Cowboys. I saw a lot of young people out there. So many of them around thirty tell me they have such fond memories of sitting in front of the TV with their dads getting all worked up watching the Cowboys. Now these thirty-year-olds have their own knotheads watching them get all worked up. A new generation is taking hold. So we built a lot of equity Thursday night. Hey, Reggie White will read about sixty-nine thousand at Texas Stadium for a pep rally. The 49ers will read about it. Maybe they'll all want to play for the Cowboys and be part of this."

Larry Brown often looked as if he needed pepping up. Brown, a second-year cornerback, sat in his locker-room cubicle and talked about how, this time, he would be run off the field and out of the league by Jerry Rice. "That's what everybody thinks, right?" Brown said with sarcasm. "Every week I'm supposed to get burned by another great receiver. Gary Clark. Fred Barnett. Andre Rison.

"And you know what? I had one bad game [against Phoenix]. Troy and Emmitt have bad games. I had one in sixteen. Since I've been a starter, we're twenty-six and four. Everybody says, 'Well, Dallas gives its corners a lot of help,' but that just isn't true. Our safeties think 'run' first. I promise you, we're in 'man' [man-to-man coverage] ninety percent of the time. Maybe more."

Secondary coach Dave Campo confirmed this, saying, "We do have them in 'man' most of the time, within a zone concept." Campo said of Brown, "Larry Brown is a pretty good NFL player, and that's pretty good. He doesn't have the hands to make a lot of interceptions. But really, you see more blue-collar players in the NFL than you think."

Dave Wannstedt on Brown: "Overachiever. Not great speed. Not great anything, except intelligence. A smart guy."

A cog. Not great, not awful. Functional.

The guy Campo and Wannstedt were beginning to rave about was safety Thomas Everett. Everett, they said, had solidified the secondary, lifting it to a play-off level. Campo said, "This man is a professional in every sense of the word. He gives you every ounce he has, on and off the field. He's a role model for the young guys. What he gives you probably won't show up on the stats. He probably won't win defensive player of the week. He may not be able to leap quite high enough [at 5-9] to make a play, but he will be in position, and if he gets his hands on a ball, he will catch it."

Wannstedt on Everett: "He's made a dramatic impact. His strong suit is playing the run, but he plays the pass pretty well, too. He has given us the confidence this week to go ahead and go after these guys. We are going to try to force some turnovers."

Where would the Cowboys have been if the Everett trade hadn't been made? Still, Everett wouldn't be covering Rice; Brown would. Michael Irvin calls Rice "Jesus in cleats." God bless Larry Brown? Everett occasionally would help out on Rice. But the coaches didn't seem all that concerned about "overachiever" Brown staying with the premier receiver in football.

Maybe Brown is better than the coaches give him credit for being. "All he does is run about four point four and vertical jump out of the gym," Nate Newton says. Somehow, week after week, Brown kept making great receivers basically disappear. Brown's problem was that he never did anything noticeably great. He had only one regular-season interception, though he did lead the team with 11 passes "defensed," or broken up.

No one—coaches, media, fans—was ever quite sure what to make of Brown. He wasn't drafted until the twelfth round because, said Wannstedt, "we really couldn't get anybody at TCU to say much good about him." Brown is from an upper-middle-class background in the Fox Hills section of Los Angeles. At L.A. Southwest Community College, Brown studied theater arts. He wants to be an actor. At times, coaches thought he already was a pretty good one. During his rookie training camp, he went home to L.A. for a week because, he said, his mother was very ill. Coaches heard reports to the contrary.

Whatever, Larry Brown returned to win a starting job in the season's fourth game. "I guarantee you," Brown said, "if I had been drafted high, I would have been defensive rookie of the year and made the Pro Bowl." Brown continued to stew over his lack of recognition from media and coaches. Coaches continued to indicate they were just getting by with Brown at corner.

Now he had Rice, the league's most explosive player, the main reason the 49ers finished No. 1 in offense. Jesus.

★ ★ ★

Omen No. 1: Jimmy Johnson felt good enough that week that he bought a new Corvette. Usually, Johnson prefers black cars. Black is his favorite color. But this time he chose green. In honor of his third win in four games over the Eagles? Or was he just feeling a little brighter? Johnson also prefers sports cars, but not for their speed, for their seats. He wants only two, if that. "I do not like family-type cars," he says.

Omen No. 2: San Francisco quarterback Steve Young, NFL MVP, was on the cover of that week's *Sports Illustrated*. Cover-jinxed? Troy Aikman hoped not. Aikman was rooting for Young to have a great game—and for Dallas to win. Aikman and Young had hit it off at the previous Pro Bowl when they had gone to lunch "because we were the only two guys without dates." Aikman says the two have become "very, very close." Aikman says the San Francisco week was tough on him because "I knew Steve was under an awful lot of pressure with Joe Montana ready to come back. As soon as we got out there, I checked out the newspapers and the first headline I saw was, 'If 49ers Lose, It's Young's Fault.' I was feeling an emotion I'd never felt in sports. I did not want to see Steve have a bad game."

That's another key difference between Aikman and Johnson.

Omen No. 3: The Super Bowl trophy, which is displayed from week to week in cities all over the country, had been scheduled in advance to be at the Tiffany's in Dallas that weekend.

Omen No. 4: At 10:29 A.M. the Friday night the Cowboys arrived in San Francisco, an earthquake registering 5.1 on the Richter scale briefly shook the Bay Area.

★ ★ ★

As the Cowboy plane taxied toward its hangar at San Francisco International Airport, Nate Newton started in on Charles Haley. Newton said, "Hey, this is where you started to evolve, homes.

This is where you were walkin' on your hands. This is where you were early Neanderthal."

Newton grinned. Haley tried not to. Haley, the ex-49er, was already wearing his game glower. Haley didn't need any motivational help.

Yes, he was going back to play on his field of dreams and nightmares. He talked to only one reporter that week, from *The New York Times*, and said, "I have a lot of anger in me that the only way to get out is to play them."

Jerry Jones said, "I want to see the headline 'Haley Wrecks 49ers.' I told him to envision that headline. Charles is very smart. He sees and thinks like a coach. He's not a nice, neat package, but neither am I."

★ ★ ★

Dave Wannstedt was trying to live two frantic lives. He was trying to prepare for his biggest test as a defensive coordinator, in San Francisco, while trying to decide whether to become head coach of the New York Giants. General manager George Young had contacted Wannstedt. Young said he respected Wannstedt's focus on the 49ers and said he would call again the first of next week.

Wannstedt couldn't quite seem to get comfortable with going to New York and retooling the Giants. They had some older players with whom Wannstedt didn't want to go to battle or do battle. He dreaded having to get rid of some big names and the big headlines that would cause in New York.

Wannstedt was more intrigued by the Chicago Bears' vacancy, but doubted the job would be offered to him. Bear president Mike McCaskey had briefly interviewed Wannstedt by phone and said he would call back Monday. Wannstedt told McCaskey he anticipated an offer on Monday from "another team." Obviously McCaskey knew the Giants were interested in Wannstedt; it was all over the papers. So Wannstedt hoped that would increase and speed McCaskey's interest in him.

"Who knows what will happen?" said Wannstedt, who appeared calmer about defensing the 49ers than deciding on the Giant or Bear job.

Because the 49ers script their first fifteen to twenty plays, Wannstedt had taken the time to scout himself, compiling his tendencies for the season and completely changing them. That way, he hoped, the 49ers would plan a play for a defense Wannstedt had usually called in that situation but would not this time.

The keys to stopping San Francisco, he told his defense, were sure tackling on a slick field and fierce tackling of 49er back Ricky Watters. "We will knock his ass off," said Wannstedt, who had coached against Watters when Miami played Notre Dame. "I promise you he will put [the ball] on the ground."

Had Wannstedt dreamed up a revolutionary new scheme to stop Rice? Maybe line up Haley on him, with cornerbacks on either side? "Nope," Wannstedt said. "We'll play him straight. Nothing new. We've stopped a lot of good receivers this year. I like our chances."

★ ★ ★

On Saturday morning Norv Turner sat on the couch of suite 3739 in the San Francisco Marriott. His wife was having room-service breakfast. Though he wouldn't quite let himself enjoy it, Turner was having the time of his life.

He had done pretty well for a kid from the East Bay who used to usher at Cal-Berkeley football games. He had returned home to match wits with the man who had recruited him out of Alhambra High to play quarterback at the University of Oregon. San Francisco coach George Seifert pretty much ran the 49er defense. Turner ran a Cowboy offense that had blended bits and pieces of the 49er offense created by ex-coach Bill Walsh.

"There are some similarities," Turner said. "The difference is, they've been running those same plays for ten years. If Troy had been in this system for four years with the same personnel, he'd be better than Steve Young. I'd like to be where the 49ers are [now] in two years."

For once Turner sounded more concerned about the Cowboy defense than the offense.

"The key to the game will be the first quarter. They can do so many things on offense that they can just come out and go *voom* and it's seven to nothing. *Voom* and it's ten to nothing. *Voom* and it's seventeen to nothing. We can't win a scoring battle with them. I mean, I love Mike [Irvin]. But right now these guys are another level. Rice is capable of just taking over a game, and remember,

[49er receiver John] Taylor was the Pro Bowl punt returner. That's how much ability he has."

The 49er defense? "It's the best run defense we've seen all year. Emmitt won't get the creases he's been getting. But one advantage we'll have is that people have underestimated us all year, and I think the 49ers will. They probably see us as big and physical but not as athletic as they are. I think we'll be able to do some things in the passing game."

One other thing: "If Montana were playing, I doubt we could win. But as great a year as Young has had, as dangerous a runner as he is, he has been turning it over. If he turns it over, we have a chance."

★ ★ ★

Had anyone seen Jerry Jones? In the hotel lobby his wife, Gene, sighed and said, "I have no idea where he is." Mike McCoy hadn't seen him. Neither had PR man Rich Dalrymple. "But sometimes," Dalrymple said, "I catch the scent of his cologne in the elevator and I know I'm getting close."

Several members of the traveling party said they had glimpsed Jones in Chinatown, blowing and going with maybe a hundred people following him. Yee-hah! The chicken-fried piper was turning San Francisco into one big pep rally.

A few minutes later, two security men hustled Jones through at least one hundred autograph seekers in the lobby and up to room 3542, a split-level suite with a spiral staircase, a wet bar, and enough complimentary fruits, cookies, and beverages to keep Nate Newton happy for four or five hours. Nothing but the best for the Dallas Cowboy owner.

Jones fixed himself—wisely—a caffeine-free soft drink and kicked back on the couch to do what he does best—talk. He said he was feeling great because he had actually slept "for two solid hours" the night before. How? "I took a little tranquilizer—just a little one—about three-thirty."

But he had bounced out of bed in plenty of time to accompany the team to Candlestick for its walk-through. Earlier that week about twenty-three thousand square feet of new sod had been laid to upgrade what had become a muddy mess. Too much rain on top of too much seepage from the nearby bay. The Cowboys weren't allowed to test the emergency turf; it remained covered with a tarp. But NFL officials allowed Jones a sneak preview.

"They gave me a pitchfork," Jones said, "and I stuck it in the new sod as deep as it would go—maybe two feet. I pushed and pulled as hard as I could and I couldn't move the pitchfork. Now, there will be some problems near the sideline. But the middle of the field is fine, and that's good news."

Discussions with the coaches had brought Jones to these conclusions: "Our defense is appreciably better than theirs. Their offense is not appreciably better than ours. And our special teams are significantly better than theirs."

Hence, edge to Dallas, a 4-point underdog.

Jones walked to the window and was actually quiet for a moment. At sunset, the thirty-fifth floor afforded a spectacular view through downtown buildings across the bay to Alcatraz. The sun had broken through the overcast, painting San Francisco in gold. "Just look at that view," Jones said. "You know, I think back to 1988 when I came out here and talked with the 49er people [to Walsh and executives about what goes into running an NFL team]. And to think that in just four years I'm standing here, looking at this view with a chance to go to the Super Bowl. It does not get any better than this."

★ ★ ★

Candlestick was no picture postcard for the 1:05 P.M. kickoff. More rain turned the crowd into a sea of yellow ponchos in a 50-degree chill. A sixteen-sided configuration of new vibrant green sod covered much of the field, but significant portions closer to the sidelines remained mostly mud.

To help combat 49er mystique, Jones asked Roger Staubach to wear his old No. 12 jersey and accompany the Cowboy captains to midfield for the coin flip. But Staubach insisted one of the captains call the toss. Charles Haley called tails. It was heads.

The 49ers went *voom*.

But the Cowboys were blessed the way Staubach's Cowboys sometimes were.

On the game's first play, Steve Young hit tight end Brent Jones for 14 yards. Rookie Cowboy cornerback Kevin Smith banged up his shoulder and dragged it to the sideline. Replacement Ike Holt made it onto the field just in time to tackle Ricky Watters after a 2-yard gain. Meanwhile, Wannstedt was told Smith was okay and would return immediately. Wannstedt called a blitz. Smith didn't quite make it back into the game. Young found Jerry Rice on Holt.

Holt can't run with Rice.

Rice blew by Holt on a post route. The blitz was blocked. Young hit Rice with a picture-postcard pass. Rice was gone 63 yards for a touchdown. Candlestick erupted. "You wonder," Norv Turner said later, "if we would have been able to recover from something like that."

The Cowboys didn't have to. San Francisco guard Guy McIntyre was called for holding Haley. A 63-yard touchdown pass became first and 20. It would be that kind of day.

Smith hustled back in for Holt. Young went right after Smith, John Taylor taking him deep. Smith, doing just what he was drafted to do, ran stride for stride with Taylor and broke up the pass. The 49ers were forced to punt.

Significantly, Turner let Aikman throw on his first two plays, and he hit Michael Irvin for 19 and Daryl Johnston for 10. For Aikman, who readily admits he gets butterflies before games, it's important to relax into an early rhythm. He had done that. But Emmitt Smith, who lost two yards on his first carry, had not.

Mike Saxon punted to Alan Grant, who was tagged by Dixon Edwards. Grant fumbled. Daryl Johnston recovered at the San Francisco 22. To win at Candlestick, the Cowboys needed help. They had their first of four turnovers.

Aikman threw another dart to Irvin, powering up a seam for 21 yards to the 1. But Smith was thrown for a yard loss, and two pass plays failed. On fourth and goal from the 2, Johnson took the 20-yard field goal.

Voom: 49ers, 48 yards in 8 plays, 7–3.

Two straight 49er sacks forced another Saxon punt, a poor one returned 15 yards to the Cowboy 47. On third and 10 from the Cowboy 33, Young took off on one of his halfback-style scrambles and was free for at least the first down, maybe more, when Jimmie Jones tripped him up from behind. Young gained only 4. Could the Cowboys have recovered from 14–3? Instead, Mike Cofer hooked a 47-yard field-goal attempt. Still 7–3, Niners.

On Emmitt Smith's next carry, one Cowboy coach could be

heard in the press box yelling, "Hit the hole, cocksucker!" Later, Turner admitted he was "teetering" on abandoning the running game. The Cowboys punted.

On the next play Watters broke free for 16 yards before Thomas Everett introduced himself thunderously. Watters fumbled. Perhaps Cowboy defenders were thinking, "Just like Dave said."

And the Cowboys ran probably the most important play of the day for Turner's psyche. On a toss sweep left, Emmitt Smith gained 4 yards. Smith might as well have gained 114, his eventual total. Turner regained enough confidence in the running game to come right back to Smith on a sweep right, which gained 14.

Soon, on third and goal from the San Francisco 7, Aikman found no one open and appeared to throw the ball away, preserving a field-goal attempt. But in a puzzling interpretation of the rules, an official called holding on 49er lineman Pierce Holt. Holt did more than hold Emmitt Smith; Holt tackled him. But the play had begun with Aikman faking a handoff to Smith. In a split second, how was Holt to decide Smith didn't have the ball and that he was a potential receiver?

That kind of year.

On first and goal from the 2, Smith bounced left and scored. Dallas, 10–7. The 49ers moved quickly for a field goal. Tie game. The Cowboys moved just as quickly into field-goal range, but Elliott missed to the right from 43 as the half ended.

Turner said, "We felt really good ten to ten at the half. We just went in and said, 'This is our game,' and asked everybody to leave everything on the field the second half—to play the half of their lives."

Turner was about to call the half of his life.

The Cowboys took the second-half kickoff 78 yards in 8 plays for the 17–10 touchdown. The key plays were an interception dropped by linebacker Bill Romanowski and a potential interception by cornerback Eric Davis that glanced off his hands and into those of Alvin Harper. Given the gray day, Davis's explanation sounded laughable: "The sun got in my eyes." Yet the sun had actually flashed through the clouds just long enough for that 38-yard completion. Then it was overcast again, and ten minutes later it was raining. Meant to be?

The 49ers flashed for a field goal from 42 yards. Dallas, 17–13.

And for the next nine minutes, Dallas held the ball. Nine long Pasadena-here-they-come minutes of Turner and Aikman, big brother and little brother, one as hot calling plays as the other was executing them. Nothing spectacular. Nothing worthy of Jerry Rice or Dwight Clark. Nothing complicated. Just basic plays, flawlessly executed at unpredictable times. Just 4 third-down conversions, the last a little pass to Emmitt Smith, who shot 16 yards for a touchdown. The drive covered 79 yards in 14 plays. Nine minutes, 24–13.

Nate Newton said, "The defense is mesmerized, not knowing if you're going to run, pass, play-action pass. They're going, 'Damn, this can't happen to us.' " Dennis Thurman knew the feeling on January 10, 1982.

"I guarantee you," Turner said, "those guys [on the 49er offense] were standing over there on the sideline frustrated as hell. It's like, 'Damn, when are we going to get the ball back?' " In a rare admission, Turner said, "I did make a few good calls. What happens sometimes is that you get on a roll and you just stay one play ahead. Every time they countered, we were one play ahead of 'em, and eight [No. 8, Aikman] was as good as you can be. That second half was as good as [we] can play."

San Francisco's frustration mounted as it quickly gave the ball back to Aikman/Turner. Young appeared not to see linebacker Ken Norton and threw an unsightly interception to him.

With 7:13 left in the game, the Cowboys faced fourth and 1 at the 49er 7. Johnson went for it. Smith didn't make it, stopped for no gain by former Cowboy Mike Walter. But, said Turner, "you've got to admire Jimmy for doing that. That was our style all season. Sometimes you can lose a game like that by playing not to lose."

Nine plays and 93 smoking yards later, the 49ers had cut the lead to 24–20.

And on first and 10 from the Cowboy 21, Turner did not play to lose. He called a pass—a fairly safe pass, 896 F Flat, but a pass just the same. "We could have thought about what happened to Troy at Washington and played safe," Turner said, "but we didn't." Aikman threw a strike to Harper on a quick slant. Until that moment the footing had been pitchfork good. But finally someone slipped— 49er cornerback Don Griffin. Seventy yards later the Cowboys were set up for the 30–20 touchdown with 3:48 remaining.

Cowboy safety James Washington ended San Francisco's hopes with an interception, the second thrown by Young. Wannstedt said, "It was the first time all year James really made a play. He read Young's eyes and broke on the ball and cut up inside Brent Jones."

Here's mud in your eye, Frisco. A Cowboy fan in the stands displayed a sign that said, "Catch This." The Cowboys wound up dominating the second-half clock, 18:49 to 11:11, even though the game's total yardage was almost even, Dallas 416 to San Francisco's 415. Rice had his usual 8 catches for 123 yards. Young was 25 of 35 for 313. But the 49ers just didn't have the ball enough, in part because they turned it over four times to the Cowboys' zero. Aikman's numbers (24 of 34 for 322 yards) were almost identical to Young's. But Aikman was about to be a Super Bowl quarterback.

As the Cowboy offense ran off the rest of the clock, tackle Erik Williams began to pump his arms and celebrate. But in the huddle Aikman jumped on Williams and told the offense, "Look, show some class. These guys dominated the eighties and they always won with class. Let's show them some respect and act like we've been here before."

Johnson's teams have always been known for gloating. As Johnson said, "I can gloat with the best of 'em." But with these orders to the huddle, Aikman showed this was no longer just Johnson's team. Aikman was now setting the tone, at least for the offense. Stay humble, snapped Aikman, who had often been a little too humble for Johnson's taste.

As the game ended, Aikman trotted to Young and hugged him. "I couldn't say anything," Aikman said. "I didn't know what to say."

★ ★ ★

Over on the Cowboy sideline, Larry Lacewell knew what to say to Johnson. As they hugged, Lacewell said in Johnson's ear, "You've come a long way from Wichita State."

The hug shared by Emmitt Smith and Michael Irvin must have lasted two minutes. Smith kept saying, "They said it couldn't be done, Michael. They said no leading rusher ever had made it to the Super Bowl. We're in the Super Bowl, Michael. We're in the Super Bowl."

Laughing, Irvin said, "I know, Emmitt. I know."

In the walk-in closet that is the visitors' locker room in Candlestick, Johnson could barely contain himself. His postgame remarks to the players began with the expected reminder that they still had one more game—that their work wouldn't be done for two more weeks. But then Johnson spilled over with joy. "All I've got to say is, 'How 'bout them Cowboys!' " The players cheered heartily, as if Johnson had finally proposed a toast to them and signaled the start of the year's first celebration.

"That night," says Aikman, "we were finally allowed to celebrate."

Johnson's new slogan—"How 'bout them Cowboys!"—wasn't an original concept. For years various bowl-bound groups of college fans have used it to refer to their teams. But Johnson made a point of opening his postgame press conference with "How 'bout them Cowboys!" and the media and fans soon picked up on it. Johnson was ready to tell the world that he had pushed "them Cowboys" to the edge and that they had responded. "Time and time again we demanded more and more, to the point where the players might not be able to give. But they responded in a positive way, and now we're one game away from where we want to be."

Then Johnson was overcome with emotion. He slowly uttered the words that struck closest to the heart of what had happened in the previous four weeks, if not four seasons. Johnson said, "Troy [pause] Troy has come a long, long way [pause] and now he's brought me with him."

★ ★ ★

Johnson again surprised wary flight attendants as he boarded the team charter. "He was very affectionate," said one. "He started hugging everybody and didn't stop the whole way home. He just couldn't stop grinning. He usually pounds [drinks] everything we have for him. But he really didn't drink that much. He even ate dinner. It was quite a contrast."

The entire flight was a stunning contrast to the return trips from Washington and Atlanta. The aisle was jammed with giant bodies. Players wandered up and down, climbing over and around each other from the open cockpit door to the rear rest rooms. Often players hugged and said, "We're in the Super Bowl." Some sounded as if they wanted to add, "Aren't we?" Members of the PR staff commented that many players just couldn't believe it had happened. A team that truly had taken it one game at a time was now having a difficult time realizing the next game was *the* game. For the first time all season, the most popular feature on the plane became the credit-card phones built into the backs of seats. Some didn't work; lines formed for those that did. Players wanted to call family or friends and say, "We did it, didn't we?"

Tony Wise still seemed dazed. "People are saying, 'This is a dream come true.' Dream? Hell, I never even dreamed of being in the Super Bowl. I have a hard time saying the words *Super . . . Bowl*. This is a fantasy. I told Joe Avvy [special teams coach Avezzano], 'It just won't sink in. Maybe we should all go out Tuesday or Wednesday night and just get shit-faced and eat everything in sight, just to make it official.' "

Jerry Jones called out to the players, "We're going to the Super Bowl!" Then he purposely misspelled it: "S-u-p-p-e-r." It was a reference to Jones's old "Jethro" image, an attempt to say, "We Clampetts did pretty good, didn't we?" Nobody seemed to get it.

Then Johnson took the plane's microphone, again congratulated the team, and introduced "the owner, general manager, and president of the Dallas Cowboys, Jerry Jones." Jones said, "It's great to be introduced by the boss."

Jones promised he would have replicas of the NFC Championship trophy made for each player. That received halfhearted applause. A few players rolled their eyes as if to say, "We'll believe it when we see it." Several still didn't trust Jones's generosity. For the next two weeks, several would quietly complain that Jones had given players the bare minimum of Super Bowl tickets.

As Jones finished his PA remarks, Newton and other players started a chant: "Goin' to the Bowl, you all, to the Bowl, you all, to the Bowl . . ."

Newton looked as if he could have flown back to Dallas on his own. "I am one big happy motherfucker!" he said, toasting the world with his beer. As the plane descended, flight attendants asked players to please sit down and buckle their seat belts. Everyone did but Newton. He was wearing his tape-player headphones and singing terribly off-key. As the plane bounced on the runway, Newton lost his balance and went tumbling back down the aisle, all 320 pounds of him. Several teammates shot out of their seats trying to break his fall. They all ended up in a giggling pileup as the plane taxied toward an unexpected sight.

Through the windows, players could see nothing but crazed Cowboy fans. Thousands of fans had taken over the small, private parking area that usually was so quiet and convenient. Now, around midnight, thousands of fans with painted faces and HOW 'BOUT THEM COWBOYS! signs stood between the players and their cars. Jones's dream of grass-roots Cowboymania had become a momentary nightmare.

Worse, without adequate security or traffic control, the two-lane leading into the parking area had been turned into a one-way street, incoming. Without many parking places, impatient fans just parked in the street and walked to the arrival area. It was one big happy mess.

Pilots radioed for police reinforcements. It took over an hour to get all the players and coaches free of the mob and the traffic jam. The only person who didn't seem to mind was Jones, who continued to circulate through pawing revelers with the championship trophy. Cowboy staffers worried because Jones had no police protection. "No," said Jones, "I was fine. I wanted as many people as possible to be able to touch that trophy."

Go With the *Flow*

Two nights after the San Francisco game, Tony Wise flipped on the TV.

Dave Wannstedt sometimes kidded that "I'll be watching 'Monday Night Football' and I'll call Tony and say, 'Did you see that play?' And he'll be watching 'Hogan's Heroes.' "

But now Wise was watching the sports report.

There on his screen was the new head coach of the Bears, Dave Wannstedt, answering questions at his kickoff press conference in Chicago. "There," said Wise, "was my best friend. It was really strange, watching him." For a moment, Wise forgot that Wannstedt was like a brother to him. He was watching this new head coach of the Bears, thinking, "Hey, he comes across as a big, tough guy who's in command."

Wise said, "He really has good presence, doesn't he? That's what they say about actors. It's about seventy-five percent presence. Dave has that."

Jimmy Johnson has that.

Another strange sight: Out in the middle of Sunday night's bumper-to-bumper bedlam on the backside of the airport stood Wannstedt's wife Jan, directing traffic. (She's called Jan by everyone but her husband, who calls her Janet.) "I'm just trying to get us out of here," she said, stopping one car while waving through another. She got her husband out of there, all right. Within hours, they were back at the airport, flying first class to Chicago. The traffic cop was about to become a first lady.

Monday morning, the phone rang at nine-thirty in Wannstedt's office. He answered it. It was Bear president Mike McCaskey. "He said he was prepared to offer me the job," said Wannstedt, who was pleasantly shocked. "Janet and I were on a plane by eleven. I had been on my knees praying, 'Please make this decision easy.' I said, 'Thank you, God.' "

Johnson helped Wannstedt negotiate a contract that would pay him about $550,000 a year—reportedly slightly more than Johnson was making at the time and nearly a $450,000 raise for Wannstedt. Johnson said he was all for Wannstedt becoming a head coach and wrapping it up immediately "so we can get all the distractions behind us and Dave can focus on getting ready for Buffalo." Buffalo had beaten the Dolphins in Miami, 29–10, for the AFC title.

Wannstedt jumped at the Chicago opportunity because "they've got a bunch of guys you could take out in the parking lot and they'd fight you until you killed 'em." So that night, he and Jan wound up in a Chicago hotel room watching the sports report. "They come on and say, 'We've got Mike Ditka live.' I said to Janet, 'Uh-oh, here it goes.' And Ditka said, 'If it's true the Bears have hired Dave Wannstedt, that would be a good choice.' I said, 'Thank you.' "

Wannstedt, however, did not say thanks to Jerry Jones. "The Giants come up, then the Bears, and he never says a word to me. That's incredible." Wannstedt shrugged. "Jimmy says he doesn't know if he'll be here much longer, anyway." That week, several south-Florida newspapers reported that Miami coach Don Shula was considering retirement as early as after the 1993 season.

But for Johnson and Wannstedt, the immediate problem became which assistants would stay or go to Chicago after the Super Bowl. It was assumed Wise would go with the one he calls Wann. As Johnson always said, "Dave and Tony are inseparable." Wannstedt also wanted to take nickel-defense coach Bob Slowik, who went to high school with Wannstedt in Pittsburgh. Johnson eventually allowed that.

But later that week Johnson walked into a coaches' meeting just in time to hear several assistants talking about who was and wasn't going to Chicago. Johnson threw a fit. According to a source, Johnson said, "Fuck all of you. Why don't you just all get the fuck to Chicago?"

That reaction was understandable, considering the Cowboys did have one more fairly important game.

But for Wannstedt and Wise, Johnson's anger cut deeper. Their friendships with their boss flew apart that week, leaving Wise especially disillusioned. For several days Johnson quit talking to the two guys he had called "two of my very few close friends." On the Sunday flight to Los Angeles for the Super Bowl, Wannstedt did not sit next to Johnson on an outbound leg for the first time all season. Rhonda Rookmaaker did. Also for the first time, Jan Wannstedt flew with the team. Johnson and Wannstedt had an excuse not to sit next to each other; "a very convenient excuse," said an insider. "They weren't speaking."

Wise was hesitant to talk about his wounded feelings. As close as he was to Wannstedt, Wise wasn't quite as anxious as people thought to follow him to Chicago. It wasn't that easy, after all the work and suffering, to walk away from a team that could dominate the 1990s. He enjoyed living in Dallas. He had a new girlfriend, a flight attendant on the team charters.

But he realized his "friendship" with Johnson was only a working relationship. As long as he contributed to Johnson's success— helped turn Johnson's offensive line into one of the best and occasionally made Johnson laugh—he was Johnson's "friend."

Asked how emotional it was to break up the old gang, Wise said, "Oh, for me it is. For Dave it is. But ... it's a one-way street."

Clearly upset, Wise groped for the right words. "He . . . he likes to be alone."

Johnson wants to be self-contained?

"Yeah, he thinks he can be self-contained. I don't think anybody can be. I mean, I have *friends*—people from back home who call and say, 'Tony, it doesn't matter if you're one and fifteen or thirteen and three. We're your friends.' "

So will Johnson miss Wannstedt and Wise as friends?

Wise thought for a moment. "I just don't want to comment on that."

Wannstedt shrugged off the same question. Wannstedt never seemed to have any illusions about his relationship with Johnson. They were good—no, great—for each other. Wannstedt was the emotional force behind a Super Bowl defense without a Pro Bowler, and he was an emotional backstop for Johnson. Johnson had given Wannstedt the opportunity to be a coordinator, had taught him everything he knew about defense, and had recommended him as a head coach.

"Jimmy's Jimmy," said Wannstedt. From all the time I spent observing these two, I'm left feeling Johnson will miss more about Wannstedt than Wannstedt will about Johnson.

★ ★ ★

Norv Turner was standing in a Valley Ranch hallway talking to an interviewer when Troy Aikman walked by. Aikman said, "I need to talk to you for a second."

Turner said, "You quittin'?"

Aikman grinned. The bond between these two was as obvious as the cord connecting Wannstedt and Wise.

But at the moment Aikman was more concerned about Turner quittin'. ESPN had reported that Turner was now a top candidate for the Giant job. Rumors circulated in Los Angeles that the Raider and Southern Cal jobs would open and that Turner would top both lists. More rumors flew that at least two other NFL teams were prepared to just about double Turner's entry-level salary and hire him as their offensive coordinator. Yes, after the Super Bowl, the Cowboys were in danger of losing both the coordinators so essential to what had been built so quickly.

"I heard the Giants probably will call," Turner said. "I could make three or four calls, but I won't. But I'd definitely have to take an opportunity like that. I'd just hate leaving Troy before we were finished."

Turner chuckled to, if not at, himself. "But while I'm sitting here thinking we're two years away from being as good as the 49ers, I guess they're out there thinking we already are as good as they are."

Turner was not chuckling about Jerry Jones. Like Wannstedt,

Turner was stung by how unimpressed Jones seemed to be about his contribution. "The other day he said to me, 'Well, you've got some talent to work with now.' I'm thinking, 'Yeah, the same guys who couldn't get a first down two years ago.' Hey, he is going to have to pay people around here if he wants to keep winning. And I don't mean just me. I just can't understand that attitude."

Even as the Super Bowl approached, a coaching staff now regarded as one of the NFL's best was teetering emotionally. It was unified only by what it saw on tape that week.

★ ★ ★

By about Friday the Cowboy coaches realized they had won the Super Bowl—barring total collapse. The harder they looked at Buffalo, the easier it was to see that the AFC's Bills simply weren't in the NFC's league. Yes, the Bills had won at San Francisco on September 13 and at New Orleans on December 20, but most Cowboy coaches simply didn't think Buffalo, at this point, could stop their offense or avoid turnovers against their defense. Yes, the Cowboys remained the NFL's youngest team at that point, averaging 26.6 years per man, while Buffalo had experienced two straight Super Bowls. But the Bills had lost two straight and Cowboy coaches couldn't logically see how their third time would be a charm.

Amazingly, after a long season of doubt and turmoil, several coaches thought the Cowboys should have been favored by more than the opening line of 7. Their Super Bowl had been won in San Francisco.

For Johnson this didn't lead to overconfidence. It drove him. Several times Johnson mentioned to the media, "This is the one football game people all over the world watch." Johnson didn't just want to win it, he wanted to dominate it.

This would be Jimmy Johnson's stage. He already was in rare form.

He gave a speech to his players that was equal parts Patton, Rockne, and Academy Award Jimmy. The more impressionable young players were ready to come out of their chairs and carry Johnson out to the practice field on their shoulders. Rookie kicker Lin Elliott said, "Jimmy started out by saying, 'Look, they've got some good players. We have to stop Thurman Thomas. We have to block Bruce Smith and Cornelius Bennett.' Then he said, 'But we beat Philadelphia and San Francisco, and this team isn't as good as Philadelphia or San Francisco. If we play like we've been playing, we will kick the shit out of Buffalo.' Guys were ready to play right then. It made me wish I were more than just a kicker."

Wannstedt was asked if he worried about his guys getting caught up in and overwhelmed by seven straight days of Super Bowl hype. This Super Bowl wasn't being played in Minneapolis or Detroit; Super Bowl XXVII would be staged near Hollywood, in Pasadena, and the NFL was asking the teams to arrive by Sunday, a day earlier than usual.

"Our guys, overwhelmed?" Wannstedt said, grinning. "Most of our guys got no idea what's going on. They don't know enough to be overwhelmed."

Was Wannstedt overwhelmed by Buffalo's no-huddle offense— the perfect antidote to Cowboy substitions? "Not really. We'll start in our '45' [with regular linebackers Robert Jones and Vinson Smith replaced by coverage linebacker Godfrey Myles and nickel backs Kenny Gant or Darren Woodson]. It takes 'em twenty seconds to run a play, so I think we'll still be able to substitute. I heard the Redskins were able to run all their stuff [in a 37–20 Super Bowl XXVI win over Buffalo]. We've renamed all our stuff—simplified it so guys running in [from the sideline] can hear and comprehend the call on the run. Simple names. 'Pittsburgh.' 'Buffalo.' 'Bread and Butter.' 'Jam.' I don't think we'll have any problem."

Even with Buffalo's four-receiver attack? "It's like Jim Kelly once told me: the key to stopping the run-and-shoot is stopping the run. Thurman Thomas is just like Emmitt: he can make something of nothing. We have to stop him. The most dangerous receiver is Andre Reed, and Washington knocked the shit out of him early and that was about it for him. We've got to do the same thing."

Were Wannstedt's guys ready to run through one last brick wall for him? Or were they deflated that he was leaving them? Didn't they feel betrayed that he had already accepted the job and had done a press conference in Chicago?

Just the opposite, said Wannstedt. "I told them, 'This will be our last week together. But coaches get jobs because players play hard. I just want to thank you for what you've done for me.' I mean, sometimes I sit back and wonder how we've done it. I've had to try all sorts of things. I've pulled Ditkas at halftime and broken things. Sometimes I've gone in and all but begged somebody to make a play. But the one thing about these guys is, they've always responded."

So he expected them to respond even more emotionally this one last time?

"With my modesty, I have a hard time saying that. But . . ." Wannstedt grinned again. "Kenny Norton already told me all the guys were talking about really laying it on the line one last time."

Even a lame-duck defensive coordinator had turned into an advantage.

Incredibly, for this game, even Turner was confident. For Turner this qualified as a Joe Namath–guaranteed victory. Aikman was surprised by Turner's serenity: "I thought, 'Uh-oh, Norv has two weeks to think about this one. He'll be going nuts.' Instead, I sensed great confidence from him. He made the whole week very enjoyable."

After studying the 49er game and hearing from coaching friends around the league, Turner was ready to admit he was wrong about his offense. He had underestimated it. "We're better than I thought. We could be very special. Emmitt is the best at his position. Jay [Novacek] is the best at his position. Jerry Rice is better than Michael, but the thing is, Michael thinks he's the best and the quarterback thinks he's the best and keeps throwing to him. Alvin [Harper] has made remarkable strides, starting with that catch against the Raiders. Now Alvin has confidence. Kelvin [Martin]—I was wrong about Kelvin. I'm learning, too. I've gotten better this year, too. Kelvin is a lot better than I thought. Our line is better than I first thought.

"I'm sure other teams look at us and say, 'Well, they don't give you a lot of formations and movement. What's the big deal?' They don't figure it out until they're on the plane home. Because of our line, we're a power rushing team that can throw, and that combination is very hard to defend. I heard Emmitt say on ESPN that what we do is very simple, nothing complex about it, but that we're very comfortable with it. I just sat back and applauded."

Turner had even been won over by Wannstedt's defense. "I just don't think people have figured it out yet. It's just different. They put a big guy over the tight end and they take away everyone's outside running game and make 'em run up inside, and it's tough in there. They give you the underneath [passing] stuff and make you drive the ball. Now Dave has started blitzing a lot more, which makes them even tougher on third down and helps them stop drives."

So what, Dallas by four touchdowns? Turner smiled a rare mid-game-plan smile. "I hate to say this—it isn't like me—but I feel better about this game plan than any all year. We can throw on both of their corners. Cornelius is playing out of position [at inside linebacker instead of outside]. The only thing I worry about is, can Bruce Smith just take over the game? We will give Tuey [Mark Tuinei] a lot of help [with Smith]. If he gets by Tuey, somebody will be right there to knock the shit out of him. I mean, he will get hit in the ribs [Smith had been slowed by sore ribs]. We have really stressed that Smith will get hit."

Turner, the staff outsider, was beginning to sound a little like Johnson and Wannstedt. Soon, Turner would be the new Wannstedt. Turner didn't hear from the Giants, who hired Dan Reeves. Soon, Johnson would make Turner his new assistant head coach.

★ ★ ★

That week, Emmitt Smith made the cover of *Sports Illustrated.* Jinxed? "Nope," Smith said. "We're in the off-week. Super Bowl ain't till next week." Blessed again.

★ ★ ★

It was Saturday the twenty-third, the day before the Cowboys were to depart for L.A., and Jerry Jones already looked as if he had been doing Hollywood for a month with Guns 'N' Roses. "I am exhausted," he said. "I couldn't sleep at all last night."

He had a bad cold. He faced another long day of media interviews. He had been doing up to ten a day, on the half hour, for five straight days. He figured he was just getting warmed up. In L.A., Jones planned to do something no NFL owner had done during Super Bowl Week: make himself available at every players-and-coaches media session. Usually, NFL owners are about as accessible to the media as Marlon Brando.

"But do you realize the possibilities here?" Jones said, sipping orange juice between autographs at a French bakery and café. "I've been to, gosh, fifteen Super Bowls and I've never focused on the magnitude of the media buildup. We've been told [by league officials] the majority of the stories done will be on the Dallas Cowboys, mainly because this is Buffalo's third straight year. We have the fresh new story to tell. Only in America can you get your tail kicked the way we did and in just forty-eight months be in the Super Bowl. We've all but made a mockery of the traditional management staff that needs an NFL 'guru.'

"You can say that I'm doing all these interviews for my ego, but the truth is, all these interviews are what makes all this go. It creates all the attention and the energy that make this happen. Jimmy needs me to keep doing what I'm doing. He understands that, or he better understand that.

"I hope everyone on this team understands that they've been prepared all year to handle the media attention they're about to receive. No team gets interviewed more than this one does, starting in Austin. Do you realize that more could be written and said about the Dallas Cowboys next week than has been in half their history?"

And Jones was off to find the team doctors. He had to get well in a hurry. He had to entertain about five hundred people, sponsors and friends, he was flying to L.A. from Dallas and one hundred and sixty more from Little Rock. In L.A. he would be hobnobbing with some of the world's wealthiest and most influential people. This, he said, was the biggest week of his life.

★ ★ ★

Late Sunday afternoon, as the team charter came to a stop at L.A. International Airport, Jones remembered he had some carry-on luggage that somebody would have to carry off. With so many newspaper and TV photographers aiming at the plane's exit, would it look right for the owner of the Dallas Cowboys to carry off such items as his daughter-in-law's baby stroller? Jones wondered out loud.

According to several witnesses, Johnson sarcastically said, "Oh, I'll carry it for you." Jones just grinned. Arrangements were made for porter assistance.

Soon after checking into the Loews Santa Monica Beach Hotel, Johnson and several players were due at a press conference on the premises. Jones arrived before Johnson, who was running a couple of minutes late, so Jones stepped to the microphone and began fielding questions. Johnson walked in and had to wait. He folded his arms and began to redden as Jones spoke for about fifteen unscheduled minutes. PR director Rich Dalrymple insisted Johnson was not irritated with Jones, but several members of the Dallas media thought otherwise.

It appeared the JJs were off to the PR races.

★ ★ ★

Media members from Dallas–Fort Worth who arrived ahead of the Cowboys figured Johnson would last no longer than one night at the Loews Santa Monica before moving the team to one of the retiree hotels just up palm-lined Ocean Boulevard. The Loews Santa Monica, a resort hotel on the beach side of Ocean Boulevard, isn't particularly conducive to preparing for a football game. Lots of movie stars stay at the Loews Santa Monica. Jane Fonda and Ted Turner keep bicycles there for weekend getaways. Seen in the lobby that first night were Gene Hackman, Tom Berenger, and Betty White. Seen in the lobby bar was an all-star team of models from a New York agency in for several days of sand-and-surf photo sessions.

The Bills had been assigned by the NFL to a downtown L.A. hotel about twenty miles east on the Santa Monica Freeway in the smog and congestion. The league had scheduled far in advance to house the NFC representative at the Loews. Several Cowboys laughed about how ticked off the Bills probably were.

Yet the seven-storey Loews didn't exactly qualify as a peaceful hideaway. The elegant, airy atrium lobby of muted pinks and greens was already buzzing with metallic blue. Hundreds of Cowboy fans had all but pitched tents by the elevators. Even as players stepped out of their rooms on the first couple of floors, they could be spotted by fans down in the lobby. Troy! Emmitt! Michael!

For Johnson, it seemed, this would be Hotel Hell.

But for the coach, one Loews feature offset all the distractions: the Loews afforded a CinemaScope view of the Pacific and its sunsets. As Johnson said in his *Dallas Morning News* column that ran the next day, "Our hotel . . . has a great view of the ocean. If there is anything that would make me feel a bit more relaxed, it might be our proximity to water. I've always felt comfortable around a large body of water. In Port Arthur it was the Gulf of Mexico and in Miami it was the Atlantic Ocean."

The view from his hotel room, said Johnson, would "add to the special feeling of the week."

Johnson also had begun reading a book given to him by psychologist Don Beck, *Flow: The Psychology of Optimal Experience* by Mihaly Csikszentmihalyi. Normally Johnson isn't much of a reader. But when asked at an early-week press conference if he had any scholarly tendencies like Buffalo coach Marv Levy, Johnson was quick to talk about *Flow*.

Beck says, "It's very basically the concept of 'flowing' through fear by ignoring it. It's the ability to concentrate only in your current time frame. I've never seen any other coach really be able to do that. Any time Jimmy has spent watching his fish has been a 'flow' experience. That's why the book hit him so hard. He's only in Flow 101. I gave him a book for graduates."

Johnson was also intrigued by *Flow*'s concept of learning to enjoy the pain required to reach a goal. "It's like the marathon swimmer [in the book]," Johnson said. "At the time, the pain is excruciating. But you look back and say, hey, that was a great feeling. It's not the end result that makes you happy."

So Johnson was trying to enjoy the inevitable pain of Super Bowl Week: The distractions. The potential incidents or injuries. The owner. Johnson was more relaxed and upbeat than he had been since, well, probably the staff's off-season trip to the Bahamas, several assistants said. That first night in L.A., Johnson took his girlfriend, Rhonda, out to dinner and gave his team the night off without curfew.

★ ★ ★

The next morning, Norv Turner rose as usual at five to study some Buffalo tape. Walking down the hall, he passed some players who were just returning from their night out. They hadn't broken any rules; there weren't any. Turner half-kidded, "Here I'm going to work and you guys are just coming in. I hope you're taking this thing as seriously as I am."

Troy Aikman was hoping the same thing: "I was pretty concerned. Half the team was up all night. That's why I thought that first practice was really important."

But, said Tony Wise, "that was the idea. Let 'em get sloshed the first night and get it all out of their system. Then we'd get down to work."

Ironically, though, fans across the country were soon given the impression the Bills were the team that wasn't taking the Super Bowl too seriously. That happened because several Cowboys told reporters from Dallas–Fort Worth they had seen Magic Johnson's bodyguard punch Bills linebacker Darryl Talley in the face at Roxbury, one of L.A.'s hottest hotspots. Mike Fisher of the *Fort Worth Star-Telegram* wrote the story, which said Talley and Bills quarterback Kelly engaged in a shouting and shoving match with Johnson and the bodyguard that ended with a one-punch fight. Fisher quoted a Cowboy as saying, "Even a professional linebacker doesn't want to mess with a professional bodyguard."

The altercation began, said the Cowboys, when Kelly began joking with Magic Johnson and the joke went too far. Johnson later told L.A. radio station KMPC that his bodyguard, Anthony, took Johnson home, then returned to Roxbury to settle things with Talley. Talley denied a punch was thrown, although at least four Cowboys said they saw it. Because the story was broken by a Fort Worth paper, Bills coach Levy insinuated that the Cowboys had concocted it and planted it to distract the Bills.

Naturally, reporters from across the country, hungry for a rare scrap of news during Super Bowl Week, ran with Anthony vs. Talley. The Roxbury altercation became the week's biggest "news" story. Yet it had broken because there were lots of Cowboys, as well as Bills, at the club. Nothing nationally was made of the fact that the Cowboys challenged the team Super Bowl Week record for Least Sleep, First Night.

★ ★ ★

Johnson warned his team the first practice in L.A., at UCLA's field, would be the most physical of the year. "That's fine with me," said Jim Jeffcoat. "I think that's been the secret to our success. We're very physical in practice and we're much more physical in games than other teams expect. For us, the physical intensity of games isn't much different than practice."

Quite possibly, that Monday's practice was rougher than the game the Cowboys were about to play. "It was incredible," said guard John Gesek. "I'm just relieved nobody got hurt. I got rolled-up-on. So did Nate." Gesek meant that teammates had fallen against or been blocked into Gesek's and Newton's legs from behind or from their blind side. That's how knees are wrecked. But Gesek and Newton survived. Jones had been using a new word for this sort of blessing: *serendipity*. Questioned about the word, Jones chuckled and said, "Look it up in the dictionary. It means luck."

That week's practices, said the coaches, just kept getting better. Wannstedt and Turner agreed it was easily the best week of practice all season.

The player dominating practices was Aikman, who was calmed by his old UCLA stomping grounds. Aikman said too many players were too tired or hung over for Monday's practice to be technically crisp and productive on offense. But after that, he agreed, "I'm not sure we missed a pass."

Receiver coach Hubbard Alexander said, "Troy has been unbelievable. I told Norv, 'I'm afraid to say anything because he's in such a zone.' I've never seen a quarterback in a zone like he's in. Every pass is dead on the money. He hit K Mart [Kelvin Martin] with an 18-yard comeback, and K Mart said, 'Nice handoff, Troy.' "

More and more of Aikman's teammates were saying he had arrived as the undoubted leader of the team. These were now Troy's 'Boys. The way Aikman had stood up to the pressure against Philadelphia and at San Francisco had made believers of every last skeptic. Aikman had taken over at Candlestick in more ways than one. He hadn't just let his spectacular performance speak for itself. He had been more outspoken in the huddle and locker room. Almost by the snap he was growing more comfortable with his leadership role. His body language was expanding into more shaken fists, more jumps for joy, more outward emotion.

Yes, he and his coach had come a long, long way.

Punter Mike Saxon said, "I think everyone senses that Troy is The Man now. Everyone will look to him Sunday to see what his mood is. If he's confident, we'll be confident. If he plays the way he has been, I guarantee you we will not lose."

Until the previous few weeks Saxon and other vets had gauged the team's chances by Johnson's moods. They still looked to the coach for overall direction and reassurance, but the team no longer relied solely on a coach who had shown he isn't always reliable. Now Johnson shared top billing with Aikman. Wasn't that the way it inevitably had to be if the Cowboys were going to win the way Johnson desired? A coach can take only so much credit because a coach can take a team only so far. Eventually a player has to carry a team physically and emotionally over the championship threshold. Sometimes that one transcendent player is a pass rusher or running back. Most of the time it's a quarterback.

That week Jerry Jones smiled and said, "Let's just say Troy has exceeded Jimmy's expectations this year. I think the key to our season has been what has happened at quarterback."

Newton provided a balanced view of Aikman's evolution—if not revolution—from the Washington loss on. Newton and some of the street-tough black players hadn't been quite as angered by the way Johnson had treated the team the last three weeks of the regular season. Newton took it hard, but not personally.

"Coach Johnson challenged us as a team," Newton said, "and we could have folded. But we answered the bell. But Troy, it really did something to him personally. He felt like the team was all on his shoulders and it gave him a new confidence. He talked more. He started feeling like the players around him were believing in him, and it really loosened him up as a player. I had a new respect for him. He was proving a lot of people wrong. The way I looked at it, he was finally playing the way they drafted him to play—like the first player picked. After all those busts, the Cowboys finally had hit on one.

"It all finally came together for Troy. He was in his second year with Norv Turner's offense and he had all his pieces around him. As great as Troy was the last part of the year, don't underestimate how important it was to have Emmitt. Put the ball in his hands and you've always got a chance. Michael Irvin, Jay Novacek, our offensive line—Troy wasn't doing it by himself. But the key difference was, he wasn't beating us anymore. That first Philly game was good for him because he tried to force some things and he got burned and he learned when to gamble and when not to. By the play-offs he had taken his game up another level and we just had too many horses for everybody. A lot of people thought we didn't have a chance against San Francisco. Jerry Rice this, John Taylor that. But we always had one more horse than everybody. Troy suddenly went from having a good year to having a great one."

In L.A., Aikman was gaining more confidence by the day as he read the newspapers. From former Cowboy safety Cliff Harris in *The Dallas Morning News:* "There are two priorities to winning [a Super Bowl] . . . defense is a given. The other is the quarterback. Does your guy believe he can win the Super Bowl? That seems like a simple question, but I'm telling you, there are quarterbacks out there who can't handle it at the top level. To me, Jim Kelly is one of those guys. So is Elway and Marino. I'd have loved to have played in a Super Bowl against any of 'em.

"[Aikman] is one of those guys I didn't like to face. My job as a free safety was to look in the eyes of that quarterback before every snap. What I wanted to see was emotion. I didn't care if it was confidence he was showing as long as I could read his eyes. . . . Sooner or later you would see it all, frustration, pain, whatever. . . . I used that to my advantage.

"Aikman, however, is an ice man. He never tips you off. If he's going bad, if he's frustrated, you will never see it in his eyes. Those kind worried me. Roger was like that and so was Bradshaw. So cool. You couldn't mess with their psyche. Boy, do I like Aikman a lot. Not a hot dog. Not a glory hound. Just an old-fashioned football player. He'll be fine."

Aikman's friend and ex-teammate Babe Laufenberg told the *L.A. Times:* "The Super Bowl was created for Joe Theismann. But they could shut down the Rose Bowl and move this game to Henryetta tomorrow and Troy would walk the whole way just to play football. That's why this team is going to be good for years to come. You won't be reading the Troy Aikman book if he wins the Super Bowl."

★ ★ ★

Perhaps the only Cowboy who wasn't floating confidently toward Sunday's game was Saxon, who grew up not far from the Rose Bowl. From Arcadia High School, Saxon went on to punt at Pasadena City College and San Diego State. Saxon, a six-foot-three blond, was as "California" as the Loews Santa Monica—"flow" incarnate—at least on the surface.

Saxon had slumped through the second half of the season. His 33.5-yard average net was the lowest of his eight-year career. He just wasn't striking the ball solidly, and he and kicking coach Steve Hoffman were studying tape to locate the flaw. They talked about a higher release point—about letting the ball drop from his right hand instead of forcing it down toward his foot.

But a week after the Super Bowl, Saxon said the flaw probably was psychological. He said it had been a long, hard season—"the tryingest times I've ever been through." Two grandparents on opposite sides of the family died during the season. Saxon's dog, a cocker spaniel named Delaney, was run over and killed. And Saxon had been seeing the team psychologist because of marital problems. He and his wife Sheri were headed toward a divorce.

"I'm usually so carefree," Saxon said. "But I had an awful lot on my mind."

Saxon was about to be the focal point of Dallas's one near-disastrous Super Bowl play.

★ ★ ★

Later, when asked what he remembered most about Super Bowl Week, Jerry Jones said, "The incredible scene at Dodger Stadium, such a beautiful stadium with such great tradition on such a gorgeous day. . . . Looking out there and seeing thousands of media people waiting in the bleachers while we took our team picture. . . . Seeing our players and coaches spread out all over the field and up in the stands, being interviewed by reporters from all over the world."

Welcome to the annual Media Day, which most reporters find excruciatingly forgettable. It's always on Tuesday. And yes, this one was held at a baseball stadium. Cowboys for the first hour; Bills for the second. The biggest names were spread out in the lower-deck stands on the third-base side: Johnson, Aikman, Irvin, Smith. Other players stood behind elevated podiums along the third-base line. Those least in demand wandered around the infield.

One of the biggest crowds gathered around the man in the stands behind home plate. Batter up: Jones surprised lots of reporters and columnists with his willingness to talk with them instead of down to them. Many, of course, were surprised an owner would make himself available at all.

Mike Lupica, the influential voice of the New York *Daily News* and ESPN's "The Sports Reporters," said of the entire week, "I found I really liked Jerry. I thought he was terrific."

Larry Lacewell on Jones: "What's incredible about Jerry Jones is that he's never anyplace that he doesn't act like he belongs. He acts like he belongs here [at the Super Bowl]. Hell, he thought he'd be here last year."

About twenty feet to Jones's left, another media swarm was jostling to hear what another man would not say. But Charles Haley did speak. Some staffers feared Haley might pull a Duane Thomas, turning into a silent Sphinx the way Thomas did during the media sessions before the Cowboys won Super Bowl VI. But Haley answered every question that didn't concern his personal life or his 49er past.

Haley even paid Johnson a stop-the-presses compliment: "He's a disciplinarian. There's no guessing game. You know where you stand with him, and I respect him."

Still, Haley made sure he didn't quite follow the NFL rules requiring players to make themselves available for the duration of interview sessions. With about thirty minutes left, Haley abruptly ended his interview. As he rose to leave, he said, "We did good today, men. Don't you just love America?"

Jones and Haley: only in America.

★ ★ ★

The Cowboys' Wednesday and Thursday media sessions were held at the Santa Monica Civic Center, about two blocks from the hotel. Johnson began both sessions by doing a mass interview from a podium in one room set up with a couple of hundred chairs. The players were spread out at tables and interview stands in a larger adjacent area.

Johnson was ready.

PR man Dalrymple said, "Before big games, Jimmy really takes it up another level with the media. We talked about it. He knows this is where images are made."

Johnson made a resounding impression. Several beat reporters, columnists, and network broadcasters said Johnson was as open and quotable as any Super Bowl coach they could remember. Johnson mesmerized them with his wit and outspoken insight.

Johnson had prepared himself to answer a question he's seldom asked in Dallas. At Valley Ranch he quickly made it clear in 1989 that he was not amused by questions about his hair.

On Media Day, Johnson was first asked about his hair by MTV's "Downtown" Julie Brown, a slinky Brit who has shown up during several Super Bowl Weeks to flirt on camera with players. But Johnson rendered Brown speechless by quickly giving her a big kiss on the cheek. How many Super Bowl coaches would kiss

Downtown Julie in full view of several dozen reporters? There's just one Johnson, man of many moods.

Johnson was officially asked about The Hair early in Wednesday's more formal interview at the Civic Center. Johnson said, "If I could do something different, I probably would. I have real fine, straight hair, and this is the way it falls. If I don't use a touch of spray, it falls in my eyes and I don't like that. It's one of those real simple things a lot of people make a big deal of."

Johnson readily admitted he used "a little" spray. "I'm not a closet sprayer," he said, and grinned.

Just before the play-offs began, Tony Wise offered an enlightening view of Johnson's appearance: "First you have to understand that he is a very meticulous dresser. He likes to be viewed as sharp. He likes to have the appearance that he has taken the time to be well-groomed, whether he's being interviewed or seen on the street. He'll laugh at other [coaches] he sees on TV. He'll say, 'God, he looks terrible.' When we were at Oklahoma State, we were classic coaches: sans-a-belt slacks, golf shirts, sport coats. But in Miami, Jimmy found himself constantly in the presence of bankers and other businesspeople in suits. He told me, 'Wait a second, I can't show up with an open collar.' That's when he made the change and started wearing suits to the office. At some points he was overdressed, but he said he never knew when he'd see somebody important.

"But with his hair, people think he stands in front of the mirror for hours. So all the jokes started. But I can promise you, he gets out of the shower and that's where it lays. It is not an ego thing. He wants it perfectly in place, but he doesn't have to do much to make it that way."

Several of Johnson's answers over the next two days caused double takes among his questioners. Images can also be remade during Super Bowl Week.

Image No. 1: Because Tom Landry won't acknowledge Ring of Honor invitations from Jones, Landry won't acknowledge Johnson.

Remake No. 1: Johnson volunteered that he and Landry have "visited" a couple of times at a charity golf tournament. "I said to Tom, 'You probably would advise me not to play young players.' He laughed and said, 'I'm not accustomed to playing a whole lot of rookies.' "

Image No. 2: The Cowboys have a first-class budget.

Remake No. 2: Johnson slipped in, "We don't have a pro personnel director or even a personnel director." The collective media
reaction was: Say what?

Image No. 3: He and Aikman haven't gotten along.

Remake No. 3: Johnson said, "You know, Troy and I were laughing the other day about how we came here thinking, 'Oh, my,
there are going to be so many distractions—three thousand press
credentials.' We agreed it's easier here [with the media] than at
Valley Ranch." And: "I can't imagine a coach and quarterback
having a better relationship than Troy and I have."

And No. 4, the most pervasive image: Johnson and Jones are
best buddies who planned as roommates at Arkansas to one day win
an NFL championship as coach and owner. That very morning,
former Kansas City Chief coach and current CBS radio analyst
Hank Stram was quoted in the *L.A. Times* as saying, "If anybody
has a chance to maintain a high level in the nineties, it's the Cowboys. The fact that Jimmy Johnson and Jerry Jones are old friends
is a tremendous advantage."

Remake No. 4: Carefully, Johnson told the truth about Jones. He
did not get angry and say, "I don't know where those ridiculous
stories started about our so-called friendship." He wasn't sarcastic.
He took no shots at Jones. Pleasantly he said, "We were roommates twenty nights or so on road games. My plans were to become
an industrial psychologist and make companies more productive,
and I think Jerry planned to make money. He was driving a
Cadillac; I was driving a Ford. I had no plans to go into coaching
at that point. We didn't talk about our futures. I don't think either
one of us thought we'd be getting together later in life."

Come again? This answer probably ruined or watered down
"buddies from Arkansas" stories requested by sports editors across
the country.

★ ★ ★

Johnson made a point of saying he did it.

No, said Jones, it was his idea to remove Lee Roy Jordan from
Friday's closed and heavily guarded practice at UCLA.

In 1989 Jones inducted Jordan into the Ring of Honor. Jordan
obviously belongs; as a middle linebacker from 1963 to 1976 he was
to the defense what Roger Staubach was to the offense. One reason

Jordan wasn't inducted much earlier was that he had publicly stood up to Tex Schramm during a contract disagreement.

Naturally, Jordan had become a supporter of the new regime. Jordan and a group of Jones's friends and sponsors were watching practice when either Johnson or Jones asked them to leave.

Johnson took credit in his postpractice interview, saying, "People want to be in the know, and they might see some play we're working on, then brag to someone. Then that guy will tell someone else, and before you know it, someone on the other team hears that and will know what we're doing."

Yet when asked about Johnson's decision to remove Jordan and the others, Jones said, "No, no, that was my idea. I knew we were getting down to some sensitive areas, and they were happy to go. They understood. They had gotten to see quite a bit."

Jones made it clear he was still in command and that there was no problem "whatsoever." Everything, said the owner, was going like clockwork. From practices to interviews to league meetings, Jones went in the back of his black limo, often flanked by reporters from *The Dallas Morning News* and *Fort Worth Star-Telegram* who were recording his every grin. For some editors, Jones still held a "Beverly Hillbilly" appeal, especially now that he was flashing in and out of Beverly Hills in a limo. Who knows? Maybe Jones would suddenly say, "Hey, turn here! Let's stop by and see if Elly Mae's sunbathing out by the cement pond."

The only small glitch in Jones's week had come Tuesday night, when he had been more than an hour late to his thirtieth wedding-anniversary party at Chenois Restaurant. He had gotten involved doing an interview with ESPN and lost track of time. Gene said she forgave him.

Only in Hollywood: The Cowboys were favored by six and a half to win the Super Bowl with James Washington starting at safety. Sometimes coaches had to pinch themselves. Earlier in the season, they had discussed closing their eyes and starting rookie Darren Woodson in place of Washington. They definitely planned to give Woodson every chance to beat out Washington next training camp. When Washington was signed off Plan B in 1990, he was considered little more than a stopgap.

But one day during Super Bowl Week, Washington walked up to Wannstedt and said, "I just want to thank you for all you've done for me."

Wannstedt was moved: "Listen, that really meant a lot to me."

No more than starting in a Super Bowl in the L.A. area meant to Washington, who was born in Watts six months after the 1965 riots. "I was raised in the aftermath," Washington said. No father. Pimps and drugs and every opportunity to go bad. Washington said he nearly did, before escaping to UCLA.

And now he was starting in a Super Bowl at the Rose Bowl. "A dream come true," said Washington, who happened to be in the right place, Dallas, at the right time.

★ ★ ★

Michael Irvin was obviously mad and hurt. Jealousy had blind-sided him. When he least expected, one of his teammates was asked to do the Arsenio Hall show. The Playmaker was *born* to do Arsenio.

Arsenio had asked Emmitt Smith.

Irvin had taught Smith everything he knew about how to dress and act cool. Now the teacher was going to have to watch the pupil get interviewed by Arsenio.

Irvin said, "I'm going back to the hotel and I'm going to take my phone off the hook and I'm going to sleep. If Arsenio tries to call, he won't be able to get me."

On the show, at least Smith gave his teacher a plug. In a better-be-careful tone, Arsenio mentioned that Buffalo was playing in its third straight Super Bowl. Smith's quick response: "They've been there twice. But what is their record?" As Arsenio gave Smith a *touché* nod, Smith said, "Michael Irvin taught me that."

★ ★ ★

For Aikman it had been a perfect week. Everyone who mattered in his life had come to L.A., and he had managed to find time for them. He had fulfilled all his media requests. He felt completely comfortable with the game plan and his ability to execute it against the Bills. He had even found time to go out with Janine Turner, no relation to Norv. Janine, from the Dallas suburb of Euless, stars on "Northern Exposure."

Super Bowl Week had swirled in slow motion around Aikman. In the five weeks since the Bear game and the end of the regular season, his feelings about his leadership role and his team had changed dramatically. For the first time he felt in total control of a team that had matured on fast forward through the play-offs. During the San Francisco game, Aikman had even come to trust the Cowboy defense: "They really made a believer out of me."

So on Saturday afternoon, as the team bus pulled away from the Loews Santa Monica, Aikman said he felt "totally serene. It was like I was in a perfect world. I was so at peace with everything. It was very strange."

To get away from fans, friends, and family, the Cowboys were moving to the Beverly Garland Hotel in North Hollywood. However, Aikman didn't anticipate sleeping. He had slept well the night before, about eight hours, and figured he would have to rely on that. He had read everything he could find about what other Super Bowl quarterbacks had done the night before the game. Bob Griese said he couldn't sleep and wound up in the hotel coffee shop at five A.M.

Aikman was prepared to have a very early breakfast. Kickoff wasn't until 3:18 P.M. L.A. time.

As usual the night before a game, Aikman went to visit the room of offensive linemen Gesek and Dale Hellestrae. Then he wandered back to his room and figured he'd better kill some more time by calling "this girl I know." When Aikman hung up, he was so calm he was giddy. So about midnight he called a buddy and they talked until around one. The buddy said, "Man, you better get some sleep."

Aikman doubted he could.

"But would you believe I had the best night's sleep I had before any game all year?"

The way things were going, how could you expect anything else?

Troy's Boys

JERRY JONES HAD TURNED INTO A REGULAR RIP VAN WINKLE, sleeping six whole hours the night before the Super Bowl. But now he was up, fired up, power-dressed for a day on national and international TV in a dark blue suit, white shirt, and a conservatively stylish tie of lighter blue designs. Now he was blowing through the early-morning lobby of the Loews Santa Monica, chest out, toes pointed out. Keeping up with Jones isn't easy; walking with him is more like a race.

Into the hotel restaurant he strode, past the hostess stand to a table that could have seated ten. At the moment Jones needed only a table for two, but he never knew who might want to join him. That's Jones: choosing the largest table in the place.

But the waiter didn't know Jerry Jones from John Paul Jones. It was almost time for the Sunday-brunch rush, and this table had been reserved. As politely as possible, the waiter said, "So there'll be, what, five others coming?"

"No," Jones said. "Just us."

"Then you'll need to see the hostess."

"No, we're sitting here. Get your captain."

Just then the restaurant's manager appeared. Jones said, "I'm Jerry Jones, owner of the Dallas Cowboys."

"Oh, Mr. Jones!" said the manager.

Within five minutes, Jones had all he wanted for breakfast: oatmeal and orange juice. Jones said, "I've been committed all week to trying to eat right, get my rest, and stay away from too much of that." He pointed at an unused champagne glass.

A spoonful of oatmeal didn't quite make it into Jones's mouth before dropping back into the bowl. "I'm so damn nervous I can barely eat," he said. "I just hope we don't fall on our ass in front of two hundred million people."

Jones wasn't nearly as confident as he had been before every other game. This time the coaches' cockiness hadn't rubbed off on him. He said, "The key is: Can their no-huddle take us out of what we do—running those linemen in and out and keeping those legs fresh? And of course, our quarterback must play the way he has been—that goes without saying."

Four bites of oatmeal and two sips of orange juice were all Jones could handle. It was time to fire up the limo and head for the new team hotel, for chapel and a last-minute chat with the coaches. "Here we go," said Jones.

But before he went, he made a point of apologizing to the waiter. Jones said, "Sorry I was so scratchy with you, as we say."

John Weber, the team chaplain, felt strongly about his Super Sunday message. He wasn't sure any of the players or coaches or management staff wanted to hear it—or would. A few hours before a game of this magnitude, participants hear without hearing and see without seeing. The brain clings only to the basic Xs and Os. Often the soul is shut down.

Still, Weber considered it important to deliver a warning. His basic message: "If you think this is the biggest, most important thing that will ever happen in your life, I pity you."

The scripture he chose was Proverbs 30: 8–9. It says, "Remove far from me falsehood and lying; give me neither poverty nor riches; feed me with the food that is needful for me, lest I be full, and deny thee, and say, 'Who is the Lord?' "

Layman's translation: Cut through seven days of Super Bowl

hype—of being treated like gods. Approach this as no more than the biggest, most important football game you have ever played. Don't let its glare blind you to the more important things in your life—family, friends, charitable work, role-model responsibilities. Don't let this game seduce you into believing you're so powerful you no longer need God. Expect too much from the Super Bowl, and it will come and go and leave you empty. "The Ultimate Game" didn't ultimately matter, was Weber's message.

Troy Aikman was about to experience that phenomenon in a way few athletes have or will.

They say it never rains in southern California, but for this occasion Hollywood turned on the overhead sprinklers. It rained hard on Saturday night, washing away the smog and setting the stage for one of those L.A. days that inspire the bumper sticker, "Ho hum, another day in paradise."

As the Cowboy buses climbed up the freeway into the mountains around Pasadena's Rose Bowl, the scenery was startlingly clear and beautiful, sort of a tropical Rockies. "Like we're in a movie," James Washington said. Not too hot or cold. Almost no wind. Nothing but 60-degree sun.

"It was a gorgeous day," Aikman said. "I was still feeling very relaxed. I think most guys were relaxed but very focused."

The locker room was a little quieter than usual, said several players. No music. All business. More deep breathing. Yet assistants said they could sense no alarming tension among players. "I kept looking all week for little signs," receiver coach Hubbard Alexander said. "Nothing. These guys just really didn't understand what they were involved in. We hoped they wouldn't until the party on Sunday night."

The only surprise came as the first wave of players trotted onto the field for warm-ups. From a distance, the field looked as vividly beautiful as the scenery.

But players immediately discovered the grass field was as wet as they had expected the Candlestick Park turf to be. Twice during warm-ups, Lin Elliott fell as if kicking on ice. Coaches were nervous enough about Elliott's nerves. This was downright scary.

Aikman had so much trouble getting traction with his plant foot that he decided to change to longer cleats. "But other than that," he said, "I was great. I was amazed because I kept waiting for the nerves to kick in. I felt like I was warming up before any other game. It just wouldn't hit me that this was the Super Bowl."

Aikman had warmed up before many games in the Rose Bowl, where UCLA plays its home games. Yet that wasn't completely comforting. The Rose Bowl also reminded him of the last line on his college transcript: Never Beat USC. In his two seasons as a Bruin, Aikman's UCLA couldn't beat the crosstown rival Trojans. "That's why the Super Bowl was probably even bigger for me," he said, "because I understood the stigma of not being able to win a big game at the Rose Bowl."

Still, serenity. "Troy was really zeroed in during warm-ups," Norv Turner said.

As the players spread out in rows to stretch, Johnson walked among them in his Jimmy Johnson model Cowboy jacket and white turtleneck. This was Charming Jimmy, clapping, joking, slapping shoulder pads with encouragement, radiating confidence. Johnson often leaned over to deliver some personal inspiration to a player. Johnson even hugged Steve Beuerlein, Kelvin Martin, and—yes—Charles Haley. Just six weeks earlier, assistants had privately promised that Haley would not be back next year. Now even Johnson was beginning to warm to No. 94.

After warm-ups, as the players trotted back toward the locker room, the Rose Bowl was nearly full. The announced attendance would be 98,374. Some paid the face-value $175 for a ticket; many paid much more. Scalpers in the Loews Santa Monica lobby said the best seats were going for $1,000. It's almost as if the more a Super Bowl fan pays, the more heightened his or her experience will be. The game's two-week buildup is so long and loud—two more weeks seem to pass in the two hours before kickoff—that the crowd's expectations rise to unreachable levels. As the player introductions finally near, it's as if 98,374 are about to witness Genghis Khan's Mongol Horde vs. Attila's Huns, with a special halftime performance by Bach and Mozart doing a duet of "Hooray for Hollywood." Yet the teams aren't really struck by this pent-up energy until it's unleashed during introductions.

In the locker room, Johnson's final emotional remarks to his team included a promise that "Buffalo *will* turn the ball over." A self-fulfilling prophecy? Partly, perhaps, but Johnson and his coaches did believe the Bills wouldn't quite be prepared for Dallas's defensive quickness and intensity.

At that moment, though, the Cowboys' biggest problem was that Aikman wasn't prepared for the quickness and intensity of the surreal world he was about to re-enter. As Aikman heard himself being introduced and felt himself jogging out onto the Rose Bowl floor, his heart began to pound. Suddenly Aikman's Super Bowl world went from slow motion to Tilt-a-Whirl. "All of a sudden I let myself get caught up in the excitement," Aikman said. "I was actually hyperventilating."

Suddenly the national anthem was being sung by Garth Brooks, five jet fighters were roaring low over the stadium, and the tension hit a crescendo as Lin Elliott's foot struck the football. Super Bowl XXVII finally, suddenly, actually, was happening. Happening very quickly. Advantage, Bills, who had been hit by this Super Bowl force field for two straight years. They didn't appear fazed by it. Football's youngest team, experiencing its first Armageddon, suddenly was feeling and acting its age.

For a while, 'Boys would be boys.

On Super Bowl XXVII's first play, Buffalo quarterback Jim Kelly calmly faded and found the matchup the Bills obviously were looking for—a nickel back or safety on slot receiver Andre Reed. For the first time all season Kenny Gant was starting, primarily to cover Reed, to get physical with him, rough him up early, knock him mentally out of the game. But you can't hit what you can't catch. Gant, whose strength isn't anticipating and mirroring a receiver's moves, couldn't stay with Reed from the first play on.

Kelly to Reed: 14 yards. Buffalo's plan: attack the Shark.

But on third and 1 at his 43, Kelly wasn't given time to find Reed or anyone else. The Cowboy rush quickly forced him to scramble. Safety Thomas Everett nailed Kelly for a 2-yard loss. Buffalo punted.

But Aikman quickly found himself in third and 9 at his 16. He launched a pass that finally landed about 40 yards away. The problem was, Michael Irvin was only about 10 yards away. Turner said, "Troy looked pretty jittery."

On fourth and 9 the Cowboys attempted to punt. For the first time all season rookie Robert Jones lined up as a punt-team blocker.

Because of Buffalo's four-receiver attack, Jones didn't start at middle linebacker. He had replaced Dixon Edwards on the punt team because Edwards had missed some assignments during practice and because a hamstring Edwards had pulled in San Francisco wasn't quite healed.

Jones missed this assignment.

Jones was supposed to at least slow the most dangerous man on the field, Buffalo's version of Bill Bates, Steve Tasker. Six times in his career Tasker had blocked punts. Tasker head-faked and cut inside Jones, who didn't touch him. For the first time in 53 games and 220 punts, Mike Saxon heard that sickening sound of the double hit: foot against ball, ball against flesh. *Thudpop.* Coaches had worried that as Saxon slumped over the season's second half, he was concentrating too hard on making solid contact and was getting punts away too slowly. Tasker's block was recovered at the Cowboy 16.

As Saxon trotted back to the sideline, Johnson jumped on him, saying, "You held on to it too long."

On third and 3 from the Cowboy 9, Haley tore through and sacked Kelly. But Robert Jones was penalized for defensive holding. It was starting to look like it would be a long day for people named Jones.

Two plays later, Thurman Thomas scored from 2 yards. Buffalo led, 7–0. As the Cowboy defensive line gathered around Coach Butch Davis on the sideline, voices rose and tempers flared. Haley stepped in and told everybody to calm down and shut up and "listen to Butch." Everybody listened to Butch.

Meanwhile, the Cowboy offense couldn't move. Aikman still looked jittery. Buffalo was playing a two-deep zone Turner hadn't anticipated. Saxon punted, this time successfully.

Irvin, who still didn't have a reception, stormed to the bench complaining to receiver coach Alexander. He wanted the ball, now. "They're giving me the inside release, Ax. They cannot stop me. We can go up and down the field on 'em. It's a fuckin' joke."

Buffalo, third and 16 at its 14. Kelly's pass missed James Lofton—but second-year Cowboy tackle Leon Lett couldn't contain himself and unloaded on Kelly well after he had thrown. Roughing the passer. Another immature mistake. Buffalo, first and 10. Kelly to Reed, 21 yards. Buffalo, first and 10 at the 50.

Tony Wise said, "Nobody wants to hear this. But at that point, everybody on that sideline was worried about the game turning into a blowout for them."

But rushed again, Kelly appeared to lose his footing and his grip as he released a pass in the general direction of Don Beebe. It fluttered off target. Like in a movie, James Washington intercepted. Blowout averted.

Aikman soon faced third and 16 at his 47. At that point he was 4 of 7 for 12 yards. "I kept telling myself to just calm down and everything would be okay," Aikman said. Finally he threw one of the passes few humans can—a 20-yard gunshot to Irvin. "That pass really loosened Troy up," Turner said.

Two plays later Turner tried a play—"scat right 370 F shoot pump"—he had modified for the Bills. Derrick Gainer, who's faster than Daryl Johnston, lined up at fullback and ran a "shoot" route into the flat and up the sideline. "The corner felt Derrick's speed," said Turner, "and it opened up a heckuva seam for Jay [Novacek]. The linebacker jumped Jay's out [went for his fake] and the safety playing deep middle had to worry about Kelvin and Michael underneath him."

Translation: Aikman laid a sweet spiral up for tight end Novacek, who cut upfield and caught up to it near the goal line for a 23-yard touchdown. The score was tied at 7.

But not for long. An illegal block on the kickoff return forced Buffalo to start at its 10. Haley had been saying on the sideline that Buffalo, going without a huddle, kept snapping the ball on the first sound Kelly made. He told coaches, "I might be offside if they change up, but I'm going to get to Kelly." This time Haley switched from right end to left and guessed right on the first-sound snap. All-Pro tackle Howard Ballard barely touched Haley before he creamed Kelly. The ball popped straight into the mitts of defensive end Jimmie Jones at the 2. Jones suddenly found himself in the end zone with the ball.

Quick as a flashbulb, it was 14–7, Cowboys.

But Kelly soon found Reed on Gant again, this time for 40 yards. Larry Brown could have given up; at first it didn't appear he could catch Reed. But Brown caught him at the Cowboy 4-yard line—a key tackle. It allowed the No. 1 defense to make a statement. First down: Buffalo's 232-pound Carwell Gardner pounded for 3 yards.

Second down: Thomas was stopped for no gain by linebacker Vinson Smith. Third down: as a guard pulled, linebacker Ken Norton bolted into the hole and came, as he said, "chin to chin" with running back Kenneth Davis just short of the goal line.

Dave Wannstedt said, "It's what we call BYOB—bring your own blocker. In that situation, the running back is his own blocker, and he shouldn't be stopped."

Norton stonewalled Davis for no gain. Big stop. Bigger statement: You ain't tough enough, Buffalo. The coaches loved Norton's explanation to the media: "It was all those squats I've done." All the weight lifting. As Johnson says, Super Bowls are won in the offseason.

On fourth and goal from the 1, Buffalo coach Marv Levy chose to go for the touchdown instead of taking the field goal. Kelly rolled right—into the path of defensive end Tony Tolbert—and lobbed up a jump ball toward 6-7 tight end Pete Metzelaars. But it fell short—and into the hands of 5-9 Thomas Everett, who intercepted. Wannstedt was credited by writers from Dallas to Chicago for hustling in a defense that confused Kelly. "That was a little mystifying," Wannstedt said, chuckling. He had actually called a standard defense with straight zone coverage, nothing fancy or deceptive—basic as you can get. "I wasn't sure whether they'd run or pass, so I wanted a defense that would work against either. Tolbert did a good job of getting upfield and . . ."

The Bills outsmarted themselves. Levy said, "We had called a play for their nickel defense."

Dave Wannstedt: defensive guru.

For Buffalo, four downs inside the Cowboy 5 had become pointless. The touchback interception even gave the Cowboys room to operate at their 20. They made two first downs before having to punt. Crisis averted.

Four plays later Norton flew over a blocker and crashed against Kelly's oft-injured knee, spraining it and ending Kelly's season. Kelly was replaced by Frank Reich—"a guy we thought was as good as Kelly," Wannstedt said. Reich had guided Buffalo's astounding comeback from 35–3 down against Houston a month earlier.

Reich's Bills cut the lead to 14–10.

But Turner and the Cowboy offense were settling into a comfort zone. "Only then," said Aikman, "was I really getting comfortable with the flow of the game. Some games start out one hundred miles per hour, then slow way down. By then it was like [their defensive] players were playing half-speed. Buffalo had cut it to four, but I was feeling like we were up thirty because I just didn't think they could stop our offense."

Turner dialed Emmitt Smith, who shot through a crease for 38 yards. Then Irvin threw a hard inside move on cornerback Nate Odomes, spinning Odomes around just in time to see Aikman's bullet stick in Irvin's hands for a 19-yard touchdown. Dallas, 21–10.

Turner said later that his old Oregon teammate and CBS analyst Dan Fouts called a few days after the Super Bowl and talked about how Aikman's delivery is "very hard to describe." It was getting quicker than the eye. Turner said, "Troy's motion is so tight and quick, yet he's so strong with the ball, his throws are so powerful. We worked a lot on starting his motion as his back foot hits the ground. With our shorter drops, that really makes everything fast. And Troy trusts Michael so much the ball is gone before Michael comes out of his break. It's very difficult to defend."

Chicago-bound Wise said, "I would truly hate to have to play the Dallas Cowboys. Troy Aikman is playing with a confidence very few players feel."

Buffalo tried again. But now Wannstedt was starting to send blitzers after Reich, speeding the tempo, attacking. "It was becoming a feeding frenzy," said Johnson, the term he used for what the Eagle defense once did to the Cowboys. Buffalo's Thomas, broadsided by Lett, fumbled.

Quickly Turner called a post-corner route to Irvin. Turner said, "Mike was supposed to take three steps to the post [before breaking toward the corner of the end zone], but he got excited and took just one big step. So Troy had to throw it much quicker than he was supposed to. He wasn't set. It was an unbelievable athletic play." Eighteen yards. Touchdown. Dallas, 28–10.

Aikman actually ran toward the end zone with his index finger in the air—a career first. Johnson, in a first for a Super Bowl coach, went running off the field as the first half ended pumping both fists in the air. Saxon quickly found himself sitting next to Aikman in the locker room. "I said, 'You had some butterflies, didn't you?' He said, 'Yeah, until midway through the second quarter, but I'm fine now.' It was a totally confident locker room."

The Cowboys' smoke-filled strobe-light show had almost rendered Michael Jackson's halftime performance anticlimactic. Almost. New Super Bowl record: Fewest Spectators Leaving Seats at Intermission.

"Thriller," the second half was not—unless you were a Cowboy or a Cowboy fanatic.

The Bills did cut the lead to 31–17, but it took a play that instant-replay officiating would clearly have reversed. Reich was two yards beyond the line of scrimmage when he released a 40-yard TD pass to Beebe. No matter; for the Cowboys, all heaven was breaking loose. Aikman lofted his best deep pass of the season, 45 yards to Alvin Harper, who dunked the ball over the goal-post crossbar. Everett made his second interception and returned it to the Buffalo 8 yard line. On third and goal from the 10, Emmitt Smith broke free over left guard for the 45–17 touchdown. Two plays later, Norton scooped up a fumble and ran it in for a touchdown from 9 yards.

Dallas, 52–17. Said Buffalo's Lofton, "The only thing that could stop the Cowboys is an earthquake in Santa Monica tonight."

The Super Bowl had unfolded just as the season had: early doubt and dissension. Refocused faith. Dramatic transformation. Dominance that surprised even the Cowboys and their coaches. No one expected to beat Buffalo 59–17. That's what the final score would have been if not for a bizarre scene in the nighttime mountain chill. Lett, the 300-pounder, ran deerlike 64 yards with a fumble for an apparent touchdown. But from Lett's blind side, just before he crossed the goal line, Beebe came flying and slapped the ball from the one outstretched celebratory hand in which Lett loosely held it. Lett, who first had impressed a Cowboy scout by going end-to-end for a basketball dunk, had blown a dunk on international TV. He'll probably be kidded about it for the rest of his life.

But who thought defensive players Jimmie Jones, Norton, and (almost) Lett would score Super Bowl touchdowns? Who thought Larry "Look Ma, No Hands" Brown would intercept a pass? Not even Johnson thought Buffalo would commit 9 turnovers.

But no Cowboy was surprised when Haley and Nate Newton

dumped an entire Gatorade cooler on Johnson's hair and it basically didn't move. Emmitt Smith couldn't stand it. Sometimes Smith gets something in his head and he will not be denied. He would not be denied the satisfaction of—just once—seeing Johnson's hair completely messed up. Especially that chrome front bumper.

Smith stepped in and messed up the front of Johnson's hair as if he were scrubbing it. Then Haley reached in and worked over the top and back of The Hair. Finally, it was okay for everyone on the team to applaud and laugh. Even Johnson laughed. Yes, this team had come a long way from Washington.

Moments later in the locker room, before the media descended and Johnson took off into "How 'bout them Cowboys!" ecstasy, he made a point of telling his players to understand that "the love and support you have for each other . . . got you here."

Their love and support for each other, through a stormy December, had gotten Johnson that far, too. Do as he says, not always as he does.

★ ★ ★

There, for the nation to see on NBC, was Jerry Jones hugging Jimmy Johnson. There on a makeshift stage in a locker room overrun with a hundred Prince Bandars, NBC's Bob Costas asked Jones what had been the key move in turning around the Cowboys. "Hiring Jimmy Johnson," Jones said quickly.

But when photographers asked the Buddies from Arkansas to hold the Super Bowl trophy, Jones soon pulled it from Johnson's grasp and thrust it aloft in his right hand. Johnson's smile changed slightly from ecstasy to amusement. But nothing was going to ruin the feeling he was feeling.

Watching the scene, an NFL official said, "Now every owner in the league wants to be Jerry Jones."

★ ★ ★

As the game had ended, Larry Lacewell had hugged Johnson and said in his ear, "You always said you were the greatest." Now, standing on the edge of the locker-room celebration, Lacewell said, "Listen, a lot of [coaches] don't know they don't know. Jimmy knew he knew. I know this is going to sound like I'm caught up in all this and going a little too far. But next to Coach Bryant, Jimmy Johnson is the best I've ever been around. I don't think he planned what he did on the plane coming home from Washington, but it was the right thing to do. It certainly got everybody's attention. It focused this football team. That was *the* moment—the turning point. It could have backfired. But it didn't."

Lacewell has coached national champs and bowl winners at every college level. He shook his head and said, "I just hope everybody here savors this, because it will never be quite the same again."

★ ★ ★

Upstairs in an interview area, Wannstedt stood at a podium surrounded by maybe fifty reporters. Maybe half of those were from the Chicago area. Perhaps they anticipated red-rimmed eyes and bittersweet emotions from the soon-to-be Bear coach. Wannstedt was asked if he had shared any tears with Johnson after the game. Quickly, without emotion, Wannstedt said, "No, there's no sadness. I feel really good about my contribution to the Dallas Cowboys and what they've given to me."

★ ★ ★

Aikman had done what he agreed to do. For $60,000, or about what several Cowboy assistants made for the season, Aikman had agreed with the Disney people to look into their camera as he walked off the field and say, "I'm going to Disneyland!" Also: "I'm going to Disney World!" But each line took Aikman several takes. "It seemed like about thirty," he said. Aikman didn't appear too comfortable doing his first national commercial.

The problem was that Aikman felt as if he had spent the last three hours at Disneyland. His world was still spinning.

Yes, Emmitt Smith had made an MVP bid with 108 yards on 22 carries, 6 catches for 27 more, and several devastating blocks on blitzing Bills. Irvin had stated his case with 6 catches for 114 yards and 2 touchdowns. But Aikman had been voted Super Bowl MVP with these credentials: 22 of 30 for 273 yards and 4 TDs. If an MVP award were given for the entire season, including play-offs, Aikman would have beaten out his buddy Steve Young for that, too. For the three-game play-offs, Aikman was 61 of 89 for 795 yards and 8 touchdowns without an interception. In fact, he didn't throw an interception in his last 135 attempts of the season—not since the one to Andre Collins at Washington. Aikman's play-off rating of 116.7 broke Bart Starr's all-time record.

Not bad for a guy once considered a loser by some people.

Now Aikman, in the largest interview room just across from the locker room, told the media, "This game means everything to me. A tremendous weight has been lifted off my shoulders. No matter what happens the rest of my career, I can say I took a team to a Super Bowl and won it. There aren't too many who can say that.

"This is as great a feeling as I've ever had in my life."

PR staffers eventually helped Aikman ease away from wave after wave of interviewers. Obviously, the Super Bowl MVP had places to go, people to see, an ultimate achievement to celebrate. As Aikman finished dressing, his agent, Leigh Steinberg, told the last few reporters that the quarterback with the name from Central Casting was about to become the most marketable player in the National Football League. The "Aikmania" that was sweeping Dallas was about to sweep the country, said Steinberg.

★ ★ ★

While Jerry Jones helicoptered over the traffic back toward the team party at the Santa Monica Civic Center, Wannstedt was in no hurry. He caught the last team bus. On it were just the ex-defensive coordinator and four players.

One was Ken Norton, Jr., another UCLA ex who'd had a memorable Super Bowl—and season. For twenty-six years Norton had been known mostly as the son of former heavyweight champ Ken Norton. But now Kenny Norton had achieved his equivalent of beating Muhammad Ali. Weakside and nickel linebacker Norton, the Cowboys' leading regular-season tackler, had led the team in the Super Bowl with 8 unassisted tackles, not to mention the dead bolt he threw on Kenneth Davis, the injurious hit on Kelly, and the fumble he returned for a TD. If a Super Bowl defensive MVP were awarded, Norton would have received it.

On national TV, Bob Costas had asked Ken, Jr., about a story (in *The Dallas Morning News*) that quoted his father as saying Ken, Jr., wasn't speaking to Ken, Sr. The son wouldn't comment for the story or for Costas.

But now the pressure was off for Norton and Wannstedt. Now, with plenty of room, Wannstedt and Norton sat sideways across two seats each and lost themselves in sharing memories of the season and game. The traffic was still so backed up that it took an hour and a half to get back to the Loews Santa Monica.

"That was the most peaceful hour and a half I spent all season," Wannstedt said. "I mean, I did not want that bus ride to stop. I just wanted to stay on that bus all the way back to Dallas."

★ ★ ★

Despite the security at the Santa Monica Civic Center, many people who were not close to players had infiltrated the team party. They just wanted to get close. "A complete zoo," Aikman called it.

Yet the party animals were not Cowboys. "Really," said Mike Saxon, "the players were all pretty subdued, just savoring everything and trying to get a handle on what had happened. I think for most guys it was just one big blur. Everybody was just too drained to go crazy."

C&W star Tanya Tucker took the stage and sang a song to Jerry Jones, who stood beside her, blushing and loving it. Later, one of Hollywood's biggest Cowboy fans, actor Gary Busey, enlived the evening by playing the guitar and singing the way he did as Buddy Holly in *The Buddy Holly Story*.

But there were no reports of players dancing on tables.

Wise said, "I think a lot of guys were just wandering around saying, 'I can't believe it.' It was a classic case of us just putting one good game after another until everybody wakes up and says, 'Wait a second, we just won the Super Bowl.' "

Wise was blissfully wistful. He was about to return to Dallas to sell his house.

Johnson was uncontrollably happy. Johnson was kissing everything in sight. He was about to head to the Bahamas for a week of snorkeling.

"Jimmy was grinning literally ear to ear," said PR director Rich Dalrymple. "The two sides of the room were a real contrast. On one side you had Jimmy on an extreme high. On the other you had Dave and Tony saying, 'It's never going to be this way again.'

"Then you had Jerry—the things that were going through his mind you can't fathom. What he had pulled off was so absurd you can't even dream about it—buying a bad team for one hundred and fifty million dollars and continually putting the bad behind him. He's like a faith healer."

Very late that night, several people thought they saw Jimmy kiss Jerry on the cheek.

★ ★ ★

As the Super Bowl MVP returned to the Loews Santa Monica, he realized he really didn't have any plans. Aikman had read stories about what other Super Bowl quarterbacks had done to celebrate their victories and MVP trophies. Somehow, Aikman figured memories were about to be magically made for him.

First, he went to his room, 226, by himself. While waiting for something incredible to happen, he ordered some beer from room service. He began calling the many family members and friends who had been at the game. But he couldn't reach anyone. They were all out celebrating Troy's game. They all assumed the MVP would be too swamped to see them.

"All of a sudden I'm sitting there by myself and I'd never felt so lonely," Aikman said. "I thought to myself, 'Man, it's lonely at the top.' The one regret I have about my Super Bowl experience is that I really didn't do anything to celebrate that night."

There sat the star of the most watched TV show in history. According to the A. C. Nielsen Co., 133.4 million viewers had seen at least a portion of Super Bowl XXVII.

There sat Bachelor No. 1, the man of a million dreams and at least that many fantasies. Troy Aikman didn't have a date.

He finally called "this girl I know." She came to the hotel. They decided, what the heck, they might as well wander over to the team party to see if anything was going on. There, Aikman was immediately surrounded. "I think she felt alienated," he said. They soon returned to Aikman's room. It was late, after one A.M. But Aikman was scheduled to be interviewed on all three network-TV morning shows, beginning around four Pacific time.

"So she and I just sat and visited until I had to do my shows," Aikman said.

Believe it or not.

It wasn't until the following morning, when Aikman talked to his sister, that something happened he will never forget. She told him that the night before, his father had said, "I'm as proud as I've ever been in my life." Troy had worked his entire life for his dad to tell him something like that. At least his dad had told his sister and his mom.

"Knowing my dad, that was incredible for him to say that," Aikman said. "That was the best thing that happened."

And You Still Have Problems

THE DAY AFTER THE SUPER BOWL, TROY AIKMAN DIDN'T TURN down one interview request. "I probably did thirty or forty that day," he says. "The second I'd put the phone down it would ring again." Before dawn the NBC, CBS, and ABC national morning shows lined up their cameras in the hotel media lounge. Aikman did them one at a time. Then Aikman did two twenty-minute interviews with Dallas radio stations broadcasting live from the lobby. The sun still hadn't come up.

As I checked out of the hotel at five A.M., I ran into Aikman in the lobby. The morning before, on ESPN's "The Sports Reporters," I had basically apologized to Aikman for saying on the same show in 1990 that the Cowboys should have kept Steve Walsh and traded Aikman. "I was wrong, Troy," I said on the show, which aired at eight A.M. Super Bowl Sunday in the Los Angeles area. Aikman had seen it.

In the deserted lobby he told me, "What you said on 'The Sports Reporters' meant more to me than anything that happened yesterday." My reaction was somewhere between honored and stunned. I could say only, "Thank you." At the moment it was difficult to believe that something I said meant more to him than winning the Super Bowl and MVP award. Only when I talked with him several weeks later did I realize what he had gone through in the hours after the game and what questions he continued to ask himself through a day of endless interviews.

By eight-thirty A.M. Aikman was at the Super Bowl media headquarters hotel, the Century Plaza. There, during a ballroom press conference, he was officially awarded his Buick Park Avenue Ultra for winning the MVP. Then it was back to the Loews Santa Monica. Phone ringing. Radio voice after voice, asking what it felt like. "Always the same questions," Aikman said. Quick nap. Another quick shower. Another limo ride, this one to Burbank. Troy Aikman had arrived. This time he was interviewed by Jay Leno on the "Tonight" show.

There Aikman was, looking relaxed even in a suit and makeup, opening up a little, going Hollywood, matching wit with Leno. So, asked the host, would Aikman do some sort of country-and-western album the way Terry Bradshaw did after winning Super Bowl MVP? No, said Aikman, "I don't sing, and from what I hear, Terry doesn't either."

The line got a laugh. Aikman was doing something he had seldom been comfortable with—letting the public share in his dry wit.

He even played along with Leno's apologetic sex-symbol questions. Aikman told the story of the woman who had walked up to him in a restaurant and tried to kiss him. As Aikman turned away, she "wound up licking me all the way across my face. Needless to say I wasn't very hungry after that." And Leno said, "Most guys would be saying, 'Lick my face. Please lick my face.'"

Yes, Aikman was maximizing the opportunity, as Leigh Steinberg had hoped. He was *hot* and seizing the moment. But Aikman was also doing so many interviews because he just wants to be a nice guy, and, well, he needed to hear himself talk about what was happening. Unfortunately, he was also striking while the irony was hot.

For the next several days, said Aikman, it kept hitting him that "I have realized my dream. We did it. Now what?" He said, "You know, it's like everything else in life. You wanted something so bad for so long. Then you finally turn sixteen and start driving your own car. And you still have problems."

You're still not sure whether she likes you or your car and license.

Now, more than ever, Aikman had to wonder whether people cared about him or about his earning power or that he had been chosen one of *People* magazine's "50 Most Beautiful People of the World." Now, *Playboy* was asking him to be the subject of its showcase *Playboy* Interview. He said, "I'm trying to decide if that magazine's really me." (He eventually did the interview.)

For that matter, Aikman still couldn't be sure if Jimmy Johnson really had come to care about him or deeply believe in him. Had Johnson kept telling the media how great Aikman had become just to prop up the quarterback's confidence? Would Johnson now somehow take credit for being the psychologist who finally brought out the best in Aikman? Would manipulating Aikman's emotions be Johnson's goal for the '93 season?

Aikman remains wary of Jimmy. A close friend of Aikman's says, "Troy just coexists with Jimmy now. They have a workable relationship. But they're never going to be close."

Winning Super Bowl MVP was making Aikman's life even more complicated and, at times, confusing. Aikman was working harder than ever at being normal so his buddies wouldn't accuse him of getting the big head and turning into some rock star they no longer knew. Yet Aikman's attempt to keep things in perspective began to confuse his fans, who knew only that he had officially arrived as a god.

The next morning, Tuesday, he took off for Honolulu and Sunday's Pro Bowl. Once, Aikman had dreamed of being voted by his peers to be a Pro Bowl quarterback. But the year before, that dream had also come all too true. After a few days in paradise, it had sunk in that this ultimate honor required him and the other stars to risk injury in a meaningless exhibition game that was little more than one last opportunity for the owners to make more money. So this time, he told Ed Werder of *The Dallas Morning News*, "No player is excited about this thing, and if I could get out of playing, I would."

That offended some talk-show callers. They suspected Aikman

was whining again. Wouldn't lots of other quarterbacks gladly trade places with him? He was sounding spoiled and ungrateful.

But in Hawaii, Aikman set off a real volcanic eruption in Dallas late in Sunday's game. Aikman had booked a seat on the last flight to Dallas, at eight P.M., and he was barely going to make it. He was anxious to get home for several reasons, the most important of which was a Monday-morning board meeting of the Aikman Foundation. This was the charitable organization to which he dedicated, for a star athlete, extraordinary amounts of off-season time. Aikman was trying to show everyone he was still just as committed.

The game ran long. Aikman said the coaches, from the 49ers, told him after the first series of the second half that he was through for the game; Steve Young would play the rest of the way. So Aikman decided to trot to the locker room and make a run for the airport. Aikman didn't tell head coach George Seifert, who said after the game he had no idea what happened to Aikman.

Aikman made his flight, but he was fined $5,000 by the NFL for missing the rest of the Pro Bowl. Aikman was blasted by talk-show callers and scolded by columnists for acting as if he were too big for the Pro Bowl. Aikman again was left wondering, "What's it all mean?"

Aikman actually began to look forward to what he hates most about playing pro football: training camp. The paper-thin dorm walls, the tiny beds, the forgettable food, the endless drills in Austin's broiling heat—bring it on. Enough of the star stuff. Aikman was beginning to realize that the striving was better than the basking, the daydreams better than the dreams come true. He said, or maybe hoped, "Once we're on the field in Austin, nobody will even remember we won a Super Bowl."

A day after Aikman returned from the Pro Bowl, he wound up making a public apology to an estimated 400,000 people who had gathered downtown to celebrate the Cowboys' Super Bowl victory. But Aikman's mixed emotions were the first and most trivial on what turned into a bloody holiday.

★ ★ ★

The week after the Super Bowl seemed like the week before Christmas in Dallas–Fort Worth. People seemed warmer and friendlier. *Excuse me. Thank you. No, you go first.*

Have a nice daze.

"We" had done it. "Our" Cowboys were back on top where they belong. Dallas was Oz again. People floated through the day on Cloud IX. Radio stations were playing Thin Lizzy's "The Boys Are Back in Town" as if it were "White Christmas" on December 24. You couldn't change stations without hearing a clip of Johnson's immortal "How 'bout them Cowboys!"

How about a ticker-tape parade?

Great! When? Immediately! Wait, what about the six Cowboy Pro Bowlers who wouldn't be back until the following Monday? Okay, said Mayor Steve Bartlett: Super Bowl parade on Tuesday, February 9.

The parade quickly turned into a political football. City Council members argued that it would cost too much, that on a weekday it would encourage truancy, that on a business day it would create massive parking problems because downtown lots already are full, that on a Saturday more working people and their children could take part. Yet how would downtown workers toss the traditional ticker tape from their windows if offices were closed? Wouldn't the Super Bowl glow fade if the parade wasn't held until Saturday the thirteenth? Besides, many Cowboy players and coaches had made vacation plans or had appearance commitments on the weekend of the thirteenth.

Your dream comes true and you still have problems.

Councilman Paul Fielding said, "I hope the Second Coming doesn't choose this building [City Hall] to come to, because we would debate that, too. Nothing is going to bring more goodwill to this city than a ticker-tape parade for the Cowboys. We should just quit squabbling."

The Council finally agreed on Tuesday the ninth.

Police officials warned team officials that players riding in open convertibles, two per car, was not a good idea. Security would be much more effective around flatbed trucks, with larger groups of players elevated above the fans. How many fans would show up at noon on a Tuesday? Nobody could know for sure. But Jerry Jones's Thursday-night pep rally at Texas Stadium should have given everyone a big hint.

Police officials later admitted they underestimated the manpower the throng would require. How much trouble could people cause in broad daylight at a weekday Super Bowl celebration?

Sure, in cities "up North" like Detroit and Chicago, championship celebrations had given hoodlums an excuse to vent their frustrations by burning and looting. But this was Dallas.

If as estimated 400,000 people gathered along Commerce Street, 300,000 were kids. Truancy rates topped 50 percent in many area high schools. These young celebrants had defied teachers' warnings about cutting school for the parade. So they weren't about to heed the sawhorse barricades along Commerce or respect the many older fans who had staked out front-row Polaroid vantage points since dawn.

The convertibles hadn't moved very far down Commerce when they were lost in an unruly rush of humanity and inhumanity. Thousands pushed and shoved and climbed all over the cars, which could no longer move. Hats were swiped off players' heads. Emmitt Smith took off his jewelry, for fear it would be ripped off him. "I honestly feared for my life," he said.

So did third-string quarterback Jason Garrett, who rode with Aikman. From above it appeared Garrett and Aikman had been lost in a plague of giant locusts wearing Cowboy shirts and caps. Soon, it didn't help that overmatched policemen with nightsticks drawn couldn't really see. About twenty tons of ticker tape were dumped from office windows and the tops of buildings, reducing visibility to about two feet.

A classic Corvette convertible overheated and caught fire. Hundreds of celebrants attempted to overturn a police cruiser. TV anchors in holiday moods, commentating live from command posts, kept saying things like, "This isn't quite what everyone expected."

It took an hour longer than expected for the parade to inch the seven blocks down Commerce. As the players finally made it safely to a stage in front of City Hall, the throng pushed through restraining ropes and police, took over a section of folding chairs reserved for dignitaries and media, and threatened to rush the stage. The program was shortened considerably.

Yet Johnson the benevolent dictator seemed to swell with the power of the crowd. He plugged into it, controlled it, felt it momentarily in the palm of his hand. He told the crowd, "They say victory has a hundred fathers, while defeat is an orphan. We had a victory and all of you can share in it." Twice more he emotionally asked fans, "Are you satisfied?"

He closed with "one final comment." He gave them what they

wanted: one more "How 'bout them Cowboys!" set off one more roar.

The crowd pushed forward. Quickly, Jones was asked to pose holding the Super Bowl trophy with Johnson. And once more Jones snatched it out of Johnson's grip, turning and shaking it toward the players. Johnson kept smiling.

How 'bout them JJs.

As the players were whisked to safety, thousands of celebrants began to wander away from City Hall back through downtown streets toward bus stops or cars. Among them were several newspaper, radio, and TV reporters. Suddenly, gangs of black youths began attacking white and Hispanic bystanders. Much of this was captured by TV photographers for all Dallas to see. The most chilling scene: An unsuspecting high-school-age white female, a cheerleader type, was slugged in the face by a black male. Blood streaming from her nose and mouth, she teetered back to her feet and, looking disoriented, mumbled, "Somebody get me a [bleeping] ambulance."

A young black male leaned into a TV Minicam and said, "We're just taking back from the white man what he took from us. You know how he used to beat us up back in the day? It's our turn."

Another said, "L.A. had its riot. We didn't get ours here."

Yes, a Dallas still divided into north and south by the Trinity River still has a race problem. A Super Bowl championship didn't magically solve that. Emmitt Smith and Michael Irvin weren't such huge heroes to these black teenagers that they respected this Cowboy celebration. Perhaps these kids viewed Super Bowl XXVII far more realistically than many Dallasites. To them, perhaps, it was just a big game. A Dallas victory wouldn't change their lives any more than it would change Aikman's.

They had invaded the Cowboys' stage to say, "How 'bout us?"

Sure, America in general has race problems. But many Dallasites aren't comfortable acknowledging their city has one. Especially not on Cowboy Parade Day. For so many good Cowboy fans the day was ruined. Oh, the shame: video of the victory parade shown on national newscasts was marred by what appeared to be a downtown-Dallas riot.

Actually, Dallas got off lucky. Many innocent bystanders were cut and bruised. A black-owned liquor store was looted. Several blacks selling Cowboy souvenirs on streetside tables were overrun by gangs of blacks who stole all their merchandise. Some shots were fired by police and some by troublemakers. But incredibly, no one was hit. No one was killed.

It was that kind of year.

★ ★ ★

Two coaches who had planned to be on the City Hall stage were not. Two days before the parade, Dave Wannstedt and Tony Wise decided to go on to Chicago. They had celebrated enough. They didn't quite feel a part of the Cowboys anymore. They had a new team and college crop to evaluate.

But Wise said, "You know, I still can't get over the thing. I see Troy saying, 'I want to go to Disney World!' and I say, 'Damn, I was there.' I won't forget Nick Buoniconti [on HBO's 'Inside the NFL'] saying, 'Dallas is going to win the Super Bowl because it has the best offensive line in the NFL.' The only guy who can appreciate that is me."

Wise got tears in his eyes when he read quotes like this from a coach the old University of Miami gang idolized, Don Shula. Asked about the Cowboy Super Bowl roll, Shula told USA Today, "The second half of the 49er game, then carrying over into the Super Bowl—that's about as near-perfect a football as I've seen played. They made all the plays. They made the big plays."

Wise said, "Who would have ever thought back in August things like that would be said about us?"

Wannstedt wasn't so sentimental in his parting thought on the Cowboy defense. He said, "I just don't think [the Cowboys] will be able to duplicate what happened. We had no injuries. Our chemistry really clicked. Next year they will have three guys in the Pro Bowl. How selfish will guys be? How hard will they keep working to get better? We were able to do a great job of keeping the focus on the team. The Cowboys have a good, solid base. But what they're about to go through is a difficult process to fight."

Complacency. Jealousy. Inevitable injury.

Was Wannstedt trying to light one last weight-room fire under his guys? Or, between the lines, was he saying his coaching would be missed? How will it affect Johnson not to have Wannstedt around to motivate and mediate? Publicly, Johnson scoffed at the loss. Only once in his fifteen years as a head coach, he said, had his staff remained intact through an off-season. Johnson's shrug said, "I still managed to do pretty well, didn't I?"

Johnson said line coach Butch Davis "will do a great job" as defensive coordinator.

Yet the words of PR director Rich Dalrymple echo faintly. Several times during the '92 season, Dalrymple said, "I'd hate to be going through this without Dave."

★ ★ ★

Two months and two trips to Hawaii after the Super Bowl, Nate Newton's weight had risen to only 340—not bad considering he had done a commercial for a fast-food restaurant and been through a knee surgery that limited his exercise. "I'm fightin' it, homes," he said.

Newton, too, sounded happy/sad about what his former 1-15 team had accomplished. He said he liked the Cowboys' chances of repeating as champs. But with free agency finally turning pro football into baseball—"guys changin' teams like crazy"—Newton realized that Super Bowl XXVII might have ended an era.

"Maybe we won the last Super Bowl that really means something," he said. "Now teams are going out and just trying to buy Super Bowls. We built something from the ground up, piece by piece. Now it's like Al Davis says: no more traditions."

★ ★ ★

Twenty-seven reasons the Dallas Cowboys surprised the NFL— and perhaps themselves—by winning Super Bowl XXVII:

• Johnson never had to find out if rookie Lin Elliott could make a last-second, win-or-lose field goal.
• The worst injury suffered all season by Troy Aikman, who had missed games because of injury nearly every year he played football going back to high school, was a blood clot under a fingernail.
• Emmitt Smith, who carried or caught the ball 511 times in 16 regular-season and 3 play-off games, didn't suffer so much as a hangnail.
• Holdouts Michael Irvin and Jay Novacek did not get hurt in the season's first couple of games. All-Pro Redskin holdouts Darrell

Green and Jim Lachey did get hurt and missed games soon after they signed. Through the season, the Redskins were hit by perhaps their worst injury plague in history.

- Newton's arthritic knee somehow held up through the Super Bowl. Even off-season surgery won't help it much, say team doctors. His leadership would have been missed.
- Daryl Johnston and John Gesek, arguably the team's most effective blockers, amazed doctors by playing through various shoulder, elbow, and knee injuries that required off-season surgery.
- The Cowboys controlled the ball an average of just under 34 minutes to their opponents' just over 26 minutes in 19 games.
- Kelvin Martin made a highlight film of key catches and punt returns. Turner says, "The guy I have the greatest feeling for is K Mart. Every time we asked him to make a play he did."
- Turner—and not Gary Stevens, Ted Tollner, or Joe Pendry— coached the Cowboy offense. If those three candidates hadn't fallen through and Turner hadn't fallen into place, it's highly doubtful that Aikman would have made enough peace with Johnson or another system to have the season he did. As modest as Turner is, he says, "As much as I respect those guys [who weren't hired], I'm not sure it would have worked with them. I was the right guy for Troy. Jimmy really did a great job with him this year, but I definitely was the right guy at the right time."
- The Pittsburgh Steelers decided to hire Bill Cowher as head coach instead of Dave Wannstedt, who turned down the University of Pittsburgh job in December. Wannstedt would have taken Wise with him.
- The Eagles tragically lost spiritual leader and defensive-line anchor Jerome Brown. They lost starting defensive backs Ben Smith, Wes Hopkins, and Andre Waters to injuries. They lost All-Pro tight end Keith Jackson to Miami via free agency.
- Coming off an arm injury, Joe Montana did not play in the playoffs for the 49ers.
- In half their regular-season games, the Cowboys faced three rookie quarterbacks, three backups, and two second-year quarterbacks with very little game experience. Phoenix quarterback Chris Chandler was lost to injury after a quarter against the Cowboys, and Philadelphia quarterback Randall Cunningham was benched after a half.

- The Raiders, Detroit, Denver, and Atlanta—all projected play-off teams—turned out to be average at best. The Cowboys went from playing a preseason schedule that ranked a close second in NFL difficulty (based on the previous year's won-lost records) to the league's easiest (based on '92 won-lost records).
- Quarterback Steve Beuerlein, the six-game starter at the end of '91, never did anything but lead cheers for Aikman. "Very important," Turner says.
- A new breed of Cowboy fans gave the team a home-field advantage because of unheard-of noise at Texas Stadium.
- Jones ramrodded the Charles Haley trade, and Johnson won Haley's respect. At the postgame Super Bowl party, Johnson asked Haley, a restricted free agent, to re-sign with the Cowboys. He soon did, for an average of $1.8 million a year for three years.
- Opponents underestimated the cumulative impact of the Cowboy defensive line, which did not miss Danny Noonan and didn't need Chad Hennings.
- Cowboy coaches underestimated how good defenders Ken Norton, Vinson Smith, Larry Brown, and James Washington are. Said former Cowboy personnel man Bob Ackles, "I don't think Jimmy and some of the coaches realize how good some of those guys really are."
- Jones pursued the trade for safety Thomas Everett, who replaced Ray Horton, who did not cause problems.
- Rookie cornerback Kevin Smith was able to replace Ike Holt in Week 11 and survive the stretch run and play-offs without once getting burned for a critical completion.
- The Cowboys got by with rookie Robert Jones, who didn't quite live up to Wannstedt's billing, because middle linebacker is the least critical position in Wannstedt's scheme.
- Rookie Darren Woodson, a Cowboy because of a Draft Day gamble, turned into a steal by leading the team in special-teams tackles and upgrading the nickel defense dramatically.
- The Cowboys were not devastated by losing 31–7 at Philadelphia on October 5. "Obviously we [coaches] all had doubts then," Turner says. "But the key to the season was that the players never lost confidence. They said, 'We're better than that.' That's a tribute to them."
- The NFL's youngest team didn't know enough to panic. PR di-

rector Dalrymple says, "When you thought it was going to come apart, youth held it together. It was almost total naíveté or even ignorance. They just kept listening to the guy in front of them [Johnson]. Not all of them always bought what he was saying, but enough did." Newton agreed, saying, "All year everybody thought we were 'too young, too inexperienced' and nobody really took us seriously. But the only time I got nervous was when the play-offs started, because that was uncharted water. Then I looked around me at all these young boys who just didn't give a fuck. They just kept runnin' and hittin' and partyin' at nighttime. And I wasn't nervous any more."

• Johnson did not quit.
• Jones did not fire him.

★ ★ ★

About three weeks after the Super Bowl, Jones announced that he was giving Johnson a raise, from about $550,000 to more than $1 million annually. That, said NFL sources, makes Johnson one of the league's five highest paid coaches.

"I am ecstatic," said Johnson.

All the assistants were given raises—some token, but not Turner's. Jones called in Turner and told him how much he appreciated him. Turner says, "We had a good conversation. He was completely fair with me."

A team source says, "You just wish Jerry would do things like that without being backed into a corner first. That's the way he always is with players—he pays them as little as possible until he has to pay them or lose them."

That's Jerral Wayne Jones, who can't forget that a rent-a-car agent once cut his credit card in two. He had won a Super Bowl with the NFL's nineteenth-highest player payroll. He then enraged many employees by refusing to give all staffers the traditional cash bonuses awarded by other franchises after winning Super Bowls. Soon after the raises for the assistants were announced, ticket prices were raised an average of $6.42 across the board to an average of $34.18, with a high of $45 for suite patrons.

Yet Jones said in 1992 that he would sign all his holdouts before the season opener, and he did. He said he would acquire a pass rusher and a safety, and he did. He said he would win with a budget, and he did.

When players and assistants thought Johnson had flown apart emotionally—when some in the organization believed Johnson was in need of counseling—Jones was the most optimistic that Johnson would pull himself together. And he did. Jones said Johnson would create positive we'll-show-Jimmy tension among the players. And Johnson did, by instinct or accident or a little of both.

Perhaps unwittingly, Jones created I'll-show-Jerry tension for Johnson.

Yet Jones's ego didn't require that he constantly put Johnson in his place and risk killing Johnson's spirit. Oh, Jones stood up to Johnson. He left no doubt who's boss. He refused to let Johnson take over the franchise. But Jones took more than his share of guff off his hotheaded coach. He put up with the many maddening Jimmys. At critical times he was unbelievably patient and supportive.

No, he didn't give Johnson a bottomless budget or complete control of trading or drafting. But Jones let Jimmy be Jimmy. He gave Johnson more room to flex and flaunt his talent than a lot of owners probably would have, because Johnson had something Jones wanted: the ability to coach a Super Bowl winner.

Yet Jones has something Johnson needs: the yin to his yang, the antidote to his poisonous moods, the illogical positive to Johnson's high-IQ skepticism. Johnson would never, ever admit this, but GM Jones complemented the coach with sound trading, negotiating, and move-making instincts. Will Johnson ever be able to give Jones a little football credit and appreciate and enjoy their coach-GM relationship? Probably not. But will Johnson ever get mad enough to quit?

Who knows? Assistants and insiders still doubt the JJs will last much longer than another season—unless they manage to win a second straight Super Bowl. Yet where would Johnson find a better situation? His will to win is matched only by Jones's. The one quality they share is creating a force field that inspires and ignites everyone around them. Johnson does it with the players and coaches, Jones with the front office and fans. Lacewell says, "I've never seen two people like these two who almost *will* victory."

Dalrymple, who adroitly juggled the JJs, says, "I sometimes wish they could accept how really good they are for each other. These are two uniquely talented people. Jimmy has the balls to make tough decisions, and Jerry has the balls to back him. Jimmy knows how to win football games; Jerry knows how to close deals."

They make a great team, the Buddies from Arkansas.

That was Johnson's mood the day his raise was announced. He was asked by Randy Galloway of *The Dallas Morning News* about the persistent rumor at Valley Ranch of a rift between the JJs. Johnson said, "The people who think there's going to be a huge blowup between us, no, it won't happen. Jerry and I, in my opinion, have the best relationship you could ever have for being in such high-profile positions, and for two such very proud people. . . . Not everything is hunky-dory. But everything considered, it's the best working relationship I've ever seen."

Will Johnson remember those words late in the '93 season when Prince Bandar gives him a high five as he enters the Texas Stadium locker room after a loss? Or was that Johnson's half-million-dollar raise talking? One indication that little will change between the JJs came just before Johnson's first-annual gala and golf tournament, when he quickly made it clear to an organizer that he did not want Jerry Jones prominently involved.

★ ★ ★

On Thursday night, March 4, the Dallas Cowboys dominated ESPN's first-annual ESPY awards, a black-tie gala in New York. The Cowboys were chosen as the outstanding team of the year in all sports. Emmitt Smith was the performer of the year in pro football. And Jimmy Johnson was coach/manager of the year in all sports.

After Dustin Hoffman had delivered a tribute to the late Arthur Ashe, and Jim Valvano, battling cancer, had spoken, Johnson accepted his award and told the audience, "Tomorrow, the president of the United States will shake our hand and say, 'Coach, congratulations, you had the best professional team in the country.' You know, those are special days. But when I hear Dustin Hoffman speak, when I hear the words of Arthur Ashe, when I hear Jim Valvano speak, it makes all of us realize the real special days are the special days with the people that we enjoy and care about, the people that we coach, the people that we work with. And all of us realize that we need to enjoy these people, because the day will come when they're no longer around. Thank you for this award."

The following day at a White House ceremony, the JJs flanked another guy with Arkansas roots who has done pretty well. President Clinton hugged them both.

Johnson told reporters, "Having the president, the most powerful man in the world, walk into the room, it makes chills go up and down your spine."

★ ★ ★

Troy Aikman's chills came the following two days back in his hometown of Henryetta, Oklahoma. This time he rode in a one-convertible parade down Main Street. People followed along in obedient awe. This was Troy Aikman Day. About three thousand people overflowed Henryetta High School Stadium for the program.

From Pasadena to the White House to Henryetta, Aikman was just trying to stay normal. Yet longtime friend and Henryetta High basketball coach William Skimbo told reporters, "Troy's like a rock star. People have put him on a pedestal and rightfully so. He's a good guy, a good player, and he's good for this community."

For more than two hours Aikman sat on a stage on the field while he was honored. He later said he was flattered but that he eventually grew very uncomfortable. "It was just too long," he said.

He was glad to get back to Valley Ranch on Monday. He wanted to hit the weights, play some racquetball, get back to doing the things twenty-six-year-old football players do in the off-season.

After his workout he bumped into Johnson. They chatted briefly. Aikman said he was on the way to do an interview for a book. Aikman said, "I guess it's fitting: all these media people are doing books and not one player is."

Aikman's between-the-lines point: in the end, the players won. Not the JJs. Not Turner or Wannstedt. Nobody but the players made the plays. And not even the Super Bowl MVP was collaborating on a book. "It's premature," Aikman said later. "I don't have a lot to tell yet."

But Johnson told Aikman that, well, uh, he was doing his own book. Before the season Johnson had said he wouldn't do a book until he retired. But now, he told Aikman, he wanted to set the record straight about some things that might come out. "I'm not doing it for the money," Johnson told Aikman.

Aikman grinned and said, "Then how about donating the money

to the Aikman Foundation?" No, said Johnson, he now has his own charity, the Jimmy Johnson Foundation.

★ ★ ★

During the 1992–93 Cowboy season, team play-by-play announcer Brad Sham came up with a pet theory, the "Joe Hardy theory." The more the team won, the more sense it made. "I mean, how else can you explain what's happening?" Sham half-kidded just before the Super Bowl. "You stand back and look at the players they're winning with, at all the incredible things that have happened, at the injuries that haven't happened, and you say, 'How else?' "

Johnson had sold his soul.

"And being the deal-maker Jimmy is," Sham said, "he didn't sell his soul for just one Super Bowl, but for a decade of dominance. For five or six or eight Super Bowls. He said, 'If I'm going to give up my family, if I'm going to lose my best friend [Wannstedt], if I'm going to live forever in hell, I want a decade.' "

But maybe the devil drove a harder bargain than Sham figured.

Maybe the devil said, "I'll give you a decade, Jimmy. But you and Jerry will be together forever."

Acknowledgments

THANKS TO THE FORESIGHT OF MY EDITOR, JEFF NEUMAN, THIS book was planned before the 1992 draft and season and well before many people involved with the Cowboys thought realistically about winning a Super Bowl. So what you have read was often raw, uncensored emotion born of pressure and doubt. I was able to share it with you mainly because assistant coaches Norv Turner, Dave Wannstedt, and Tony Wise shared it with me. They have allowed you a magnified look inside a pro football team because they allowed me so many hours of their time. In the heat of so many moments, they spoke their minds and hearts to me. They dropped their guards. They acted like human beings.

These are three of the better humans I've known, and I thank them for being themselves and for being so patient with me.

The same goes for Troy Aikman.

I also thank assistant coaches Joe Avezzano, Hubbard Alexander, and Dave Campo for teaching me so much about football and football players. These three deserved more space in this book; I had enough material to write two. If only more coaches were such a joy to work with.

Of course, large amounts of time and candor were provided by Jerry Jones and Jimmy Johnson, and I thank and respect them for that. But just as important, I thank their secretaries, respectively Marylyn Love and Barbara Goodman, who deserve almost as much Super Bowl credit as their bosses.

Thanks to PR director Rich Dalrymple for his insight and to his former assistant, Dave Pelletier, for his tireless assistance. Thanks to Larry Lacewell and Mike McCoy for so often making me laugh and think. Thanks to Stephen Jones for staying humble and making himself available.

But all the interviews I did wouldn't have mattered if it hadn't been for two people who had nothing to do with the '92 Cowboys. Without my friend and coworker Mike Fernandez, I might have quit researching or writing any one of about ninety-two times. Thank you, Mike, for the hours and hours of support. And without my friend and agent, Shari Wenk, I almost certainly would have given up very late one Saturday night. Thank you, Shari, for occasionally dealing with a third child.

Thanks to David Vaughn, general manager of *The Insider*, for allowing me the time to write this book. Thanks to Ron St. Angelo for his photography and to the Color Place.

And thanks especially to Jeff Neuman for again sharing his talent with me.